THE CYCLE OF KINDNESS

by Nathaniel Allenby

Copyright © 2024 Nathaniel Allenby

All rights reserved. No part of this publication may be reproduced, distributed, or transmitted in any form or by any means, including photocopying, recording, and other electronic or mechanical methods, without the prior written permission of the publisher, except as permitted by U.S. copyright law.

Front cover by Arthur Glenn Meier III
Edited by Mozelle Jordan
Book formatting by Clementine Kornder
For permissions requests, please contact:
Nathaniel Allenby
Allenbyarts@gmail.com
+1.619.419.6703
or
JOY PUBLICATIONS
Jeanette@JoyPublications.com
+1.707.572.9139

Printed in the United States of America
First Edition: 2024
Paperback ISBN: 978-1-61880-055-8
Ebook ISBN: 978-1-61880-056-5

DISCLAIMER: Events, locales, and conversations have been recreated using imperfect memories from fifteen years ago and journal entries. In order to respect the privacy of the people within this book and maintain their anonymity, the names, identifying characteristics, and details, such as physical properties, occupations, and places of residence, have been altered. Some events have been compressed, while the timeline is as accurate as possible. No charges have ever been pressed against the characters for any of the illegal-seeming activities.

An individual has not started living until he can rise above the narrow confines of his individualistic concerns to the broader concerns of all humanity.
—Martin Luther King, Jr.

One way or another, we all have to find what best fosters the flowering of our humanity in this contemporary life, and dedicate ourselves to that.
—Joseph Campbell

The sole meaning of life is to serve humanity.
—Leo Tolstoy

You must not lose faith in humanity. Humanity is an ocean; if a few drops of the ocean are dirty, the ocean does not become dirty.
—Mahatma Gandhi

To Dan, my best friend of twenty-four years, who recollects none of the adventures within.

Table of Contents

Prologue vii
Chapter 1: Doing the Impossible 1
Chapter 2: Genesis 7
Chapter 3: A Clean Slate 13
Chapter 4: On the Road at Last 23
Chapter 5: The Journey Is Greater than the Destination 35
Chapter 6: Willing Workers on Organic Farms (WWOOF) 53
Chapter 7: Becoming Brothers 67
Chapter 8: Berlin 83
Chapter 9: Mechanical and Energetic Breakdown 93
Chapter 10: Great Britain 103
Chapter 11: The Peak District 113
Chapter 12: Following My Heart onto My Own Path 123
Chapter 13: A Birthday Reunion 137
Chapter 14: The City of Love—Paris Je T'aime 147
Chapter 15: Preparing for Loneliness—Isolation Awaits 157
Chapter 16: A Lone Warrior Treks On 163
Chapter 17: The French Riviera 177
Chapter 18: Christmas and the Coldest Day of My Life 191
Chapter 19: New Year's Eve in Barcelona 203
Epilogue 225
Acknowledgments 233

Prologue

This is the incredible story of my life cycling 7,500 miles around Europe for ten months, essentially without money, not knowing anyone, and without speaking the local languages. It was the beginning of a greater voyage—a total life transformation. Between the years 2006–2011, I pedaled over 28,000 miles across ten countries and thirty states, without a home or a phone, accomplishing what many would deem impossible. It was never about the destination, but the journey.

Through this epic saga, I found a lost faith in the goodness of humanity, in the kindness of strangers, and in their generosity in times of need. From these experiences, I finally returned to my hometown with a completely reconstructed outlook on life and a desire to share everything I had learned. This adventure inspired me to create a profound and positive impact on the planet by being the change I wanted to see in the world. I have been striving toward a vision of mankind uniting as a species, no longer fighting amongst ourselves, instead living in harmony with our planet and each other ever since. Please help realize this dream with me.

Although many of these stories may seem too large for life, I aim to present the events that occurred with the utmost realism, rawness, and accuracy. Please, still understand that memory is only so good, especially fifteen years after the events. I strived to recollect these adventures to the best of my abilities. To help me achieve this, I referred to three online blogs and four paper journals that I carried with me at different times during the years while writing, with great nostalgia and profound emotions. From these stories, I want to encourage everyone to explore the world, travel in unusual ways, make decisions outside of your comfort zone, and live in a way that challenges and questions your beliefs; to find out what is true for you. Philosophers, poets, and dreamers have urged us to take the road less traveled, saying that an unexamined life is not worth living; I do the same.

Between a psychologically and physically tormenting older brother and a lack of protection from my father at home, combined with social ostracization and bullying at school, I lost faith in the goodness of humankind at a very early age. Despite the poor treatment I received as a child, these experiences have prepared me for a lifetime of introspective personal growth work and a willingness to embrace discomfort in order to break through into new ways of being. As I got older, I became determined to not allow others to define me, that the mean, degrading, and belittling comments I received were not true nor accurate reflections of my character, and that I would prove naysayers wrong. When I was fifteen, I met a friend who saved my life, helping me to live with purpose and meaning and restoring my trust in men, though we had hardly become men yet ourselves. He was fierce and impassioned, living boldly and with reckless abandon.

Through my journey, and later emotional intelligence training, I have gone through the process of liberating myself from being a victim, stepping into my power, and seeing the world through a new lens. After continually witnessing the kindness of strangers, it influenced me to be more giving, and the reciprocity I received in kind further reinforced this cycle.

I dedicate this book to Dan, who has since developed a memory condition and does not remember any of these stories. In our journey, I swore fealty to him, and I will hold myself to this unflinching loyalty for the rest of my life. To my dismay, he ceased all communication in 2022. I hope these stories someday restore his memory of our incredible adventures together.

Chapter 1
Doing the Impossible

I awoke before dawn on the day after Christmas, determined to use every moment of daylight for the arduous and dangerous trek that lay ahead. As I snuck out of my host's home, as silently as possible so as not to wake him, I whispered a prayer for myself and a blessing upon him, wishing for strength and perseverance and giving gratitude for not spending my first holiday season away from my family alone. For a moment, I thought of my best friend, Dan, who went home to be with his family, and wondered how he was doing and how much better I would feel if he was still by my side.

    I carried my bicycle from the small apartment with everything I owned strapped to it, a mere fifty pounds of possessions, yet still no small feat to carry down six flights of stairs. I wiped the sweat dripping from my brow as I set my faithful metal steed on the ground floor and steadied myself for what was to come. My first indicator of the hardships I was about to face was the icy chill of the metal handle on the exterior door as I uneasily pulled it open, a blast of freezing air hitting me in the face, charging into the room to equalize the temperatures. Out of shock, I inhaled, which caused my lungs to gasp and shrink, as if I had just been sucker-punched in the gut. I released several profanities under my breath as I stepped into the pre-sunrise morning, seeing a stark and eerie sight of not a single soul out except myself. I mounted my bicycle, Pearl, and talked sweetly to her, trying to settle myself and coax a small iota of courage to brave the ride ahead. I had previously inspected my potential route on a map and identified the quickest way to the bike path heading east; it being along a decent sized river, the Canal du Midi, that would lead me all the way back to temperate climate along the Mediterranean, where I was just a week before. I knew that the body of water would bring me more favorable riding conditions and warmer nights, but I would have to get through today first.

The breath from my exhales was so thick they appeared to be billows of smoke, and my bicycle groaned and creaked at having some of her parts nearly frozen stiff; the chain struggled to move at first as sections seemed to be glued together. Before long, my hands went numb, and I questioned if what I was doing was truly a bad idea. Wanting the reassurance that I wasn't the only one attempting to navigate this weather, I constantly looked around me, hoping to spot someone else, but there wasn't a single person outside for miles. As I continued pedaling, I gazed at the river that I was riding alongside and noticed that ice was actively spreading over its surface. This sight terrified me even more, as I knew that moving water froze at a significantly lower temperature than standing water. While the frozen puddles I passed didn't surprise me, seeing the river actively freezing over caused great fear.

I knew I had to travel just shy of one hundred miles in these conditions to reach my next destination, and while it would warm up as the day progressed, I had no idea how much so. But what I did know is that by the evening, the temperatures would plummet again; if I couldn't make it back to the warmer climate by the sea, I'd risk freezing to death. This motivated me to ride at a fast but even pace, and I didn't stop for anything. I ate, drank, and even urinated while pedaling, the last one turning out to be an awful idea as the ridiculous conditions led me to making a mess of myself, the hot liquid quickly becoming crusty and hard on my pants.

After a few hours, the sun finally rose behind thick clouds, this dull gray haze providing a glimmer of hope as my hands were so cold I worried about getting frostbite and losing a finger or two, the fingerless gloves doing little to protect them. So, I steered with one hand and warmed the other inside my armpit, underneath my jacket, sweatshirt, two shirts, and thermal long underwear, alternating every ten minutes. As snot froze into icicles, my tears crystallized onto my face, my legs painfully stiffened, and my core generating only enough heat to keep my torso warm, I performed routine mechanical movements on auto-pilot.

As this miserable state went on for hours, I reflected on my journal entry from the night before:

I like to be joyous for this festive occasion. But tonight, I asked myself "why?" Winter solstice and Jesus Christ are the origin of this now over-commercialized and consumption-based holiday... The days allow me more time to reflect on the amazing lessons Jesus taught. Dan asked me, "What's the first thing you think of to start the day?" My eventual response was, "What can I do to make the world a better place...?" It's about people taking a conscious understanding of the consequences of their actions; call it a responsibility for what they do. For corporations to change, there has to be nowhere in the world for them to exploit; a long process in raising the standards of living worldwide. But why don't Western people organize themselves as communities anymore? On the grassroots level, a great deal can be done to improve places. People need to care more about the world and each other, instead of being greedy and selfish. "A chain is only as strong as its weakest link." Amazing wisdom found on a bar's cup coaster: "The mind is like a parachute. If it's closed, you crash."

My host lived at the base of the Pyrenees mountains in Southern France, and as I rode out of Toulouse that frigid morning, past Villefranche-da-Laurangais, Casteinaudary, Alzonne, I was afraid for my life. I took my first break in Carcassonne around noon, having continued swapping my freezing hands every ten minutes for the last five grueling hours. As I had hoped, the weather warmed up, and I finally saw other people outside. I dismounted Pearl at a group of cafes and restaurants sharing a pavilion, parked her on one side, and rummaged through the garbage bins, devouring what leftovers I found.

With the worst of the morning's frigid temperatures behind me and food in my belly, I felt relieved and revitalized. While sharing a cigarette with a homeless man, we chatted briefly as we relaxed on a bench, him warning me about an incoming colder storm, motivating me to ride with haste. I relished in this simplest of human interactions and cherished his act of kindness, a symbol of my prayer for survival coming true. I thanked him for the gift of his company, as this brief relationship helped me feel less painfully alone, as I'd be stuck with my fearful thoughts the rest of the day.

The Cycle of Kindness

All morning, I'd followed the same bike path winding along the Canal du Midi, but no longer had such an easy route. I found a clearly marked path leading east out of the town, but before long, it turned into a dirt road and then a single lane bicycle path that was merely grass ground down to the dirt, a divot several inches deep from repeated commuting. I followed it for dozens of miles until I eventually felt lost, with hardly a trail left to ride, before having to walk the rest of the way to a nearby road—carrying Pearl as I did so, her whacking me in the shins with her pedals more than once. The heavy cloud cover and occasional sprinkling of snow throughout the day made it a grim and dreary one, and with little light, dusk set in significantly earlier than expected, only hours after stopping for what you could call my lunch. The light continued to fade, increasing my fear and sense of urgency. I wasn't yet to Narbonne, with another twenty miles to go, on one of the shortest days of the year.

With the temperature dropping as well, I became distressed, recalling the times when I knocked on doors and asked strangers to let me camp on their lawn. So, I started stopping by homes, hoping for a similar outcome. But out of the dozen houses I stopped at, either no one was home or they were and didn't answer. I had no choice but to press on. As darkness continued to creep in, I rolled down one more driveway, knocked with no luck, but noticed another building beyond the house and felt desperate enough to peer inside through the glass. It wasn't a home, but a building that gave access to an underground waterway. I wiggled the handle, finding that the door was loose enough that, with a small push in the right place, it opened.

Inside, I discovered a sort of shed, with a huge manhole covering over water I could hear passing underneath the concrete floor. In a side room, there was a tower of old tube televisions, and as luck had it, a pile of mattress pads as well. I went back outside, straining my eyes to see if anyone was in the distance who could have seen me enter the building, and when I confirmed no one was around, I picked up Pearl, brought her inside, threw my sleeping bag on top of the stack of pads, and crawled inside of it to preserve warmth while I ate a cold dinner of dried fruits, nuts, and the last candy bar I had.

I listened through the stillness to make sure no one was coming to evict me before allowing myself to fall asleep. I felt safe enough that I didn't even bother to lock my bike, as I'd definitely hear someone entering before they had the chance to steal anything from me. Before drifting off to sleep, I reflected on the lone cigarette from earlier, the single act of kindness, and the powerful impact it had made. Not only was it the only human interaction that I had all day, which I craved in my isolation and loneliness, but it was a link that kept a chain of frequent gifts I had received in my travels going. These acts of kindness not only fed me, gave me shelter, and increased my faith in the goodness of humanity, but they were sometimes the only thing that kept me going when I had little to no other reason to continue.

I woke up multiple times that night, restless for long periods as I simply lay there, with nothing to comfort me other than the thoughts rattling around my head, which did not help, as I tried to fall back to sleep. Nights like those felt so long, with over twelve hours of total darkness, but I was thankful to have survived the coldest day of my life.

Without the money or desire to return home, I had been traveling alone for more than a month, feeling abandoned by Dan, my best friend and the catalyst for this chosen path. He had enrolled me in his vision, with goals of seeing the Pyramids of Giza, swimming in the Mediterranean, and living this unique lifestyle off the grid together. All of our other travel companions had gone their own way too, yet I refused to quit. Before this trip, I had doubts about what I was doing with my life and questioned my meaning and purpose. Because of Dan's belief in me and the experiences of the last nine months, I felt convicted in my capabilities and it drove me to achieve something greater than I had allowed myself to dream before. My unwillingness to allow others to tell me when enough was enough and the desire to prove to myself how far I could go strongly motivated me to continue.

I wanted to spread positivity through acts of service, benefitting and uplifting people around the world and supporting humanitarian causes and charities throughout my travels. I was determined to pay forward the generosity I had received and to give others the same faith and hope in mankind that had restored in me. This total transformation of my way of being became a new ethos—a cycle of kindness.

Chapter 2
Genesis

As the middle child of three children, with nearly a five-year gap before my younger sister was born, I grew up on a five-acre family farm in Aurora, Oregon. I loved the open air and helping my parents produce our own food, including raising pigs, chickens, and cows. I often played in the mud and adventured to nearby Champoeg State Park, on the banks of the Willamette River. While I loved my connection with nature, I could not escape the torment of my brother because of this remote isolation. Before I came along, he had all of my parents' attention, love, and affection, and when I was born, he felt deprived of those things and resented me for it, punishing me before I was even old enough to create memories. There is a picture of me at six months old, lying on the floor crying, while he is sitting on top of me with the biggest shit-eating grin on his face. I later wondered why my parents took this photo instead of remedying the situation.

Throughout our childhood, rife with competition, degradation, humiliation, physical and verbal intimidation, manipulation, and perpetual fear-inducing aggression, I wondered how worthless I must be, that there must be no other reason for this awfully inhumane treatment and lack of protection. My mother believed that safeguarding me was my father's responsibility, but as a child, he acted similarly toward his own brother, which led to his inability to reflect and admit this kind of behavior was unacceptable, subscribing to the notion that boys will be boys and that it would toughen me up.

So, my adolescent mind was left to conjure up a false belief that this was my fault, and the only solution it could come up with was that if I was perfect, then there would be nothing to antagonize me for. Subsequently, I continued to strive for excellence in all areas of life. I dutifully assisted my mother with household chores, cooking, cleaning, gardening, harvesting, canning, preserving, mowing, animal husbandry, orchard maintenance, and anything else she needed. At school, I achieved the pinnacle of intelligence, winning a schoolwide spelling bee, geography bee, and a statewide math competition—all in sixth grade, beating the older students in two grades above me. At church, I took part in all the sacraments available to me and read the bible seventeen times before high school, believing piety or sainthood could save me.

When my sister was born, I took it upon myself to be the ideal older brother and protector. In the Boy Scouts, I was determined to earn every merit badge offered to me, rising through the ranks as quickly as possible. I studied many subjects in my free time, absorbing everything I could read. I mastered the MS-DOS prompt, coding, hexadecimal, and every video game I got my hands on, which led me to grow fond of computers and technology. At age eleven, I even purchased my own PC. I was a kind and generous friend to anyone who would be mine.

But even with my effort to be perfect, I still had bullies who made life at school miserable, accompanied by my personal hellspawn at home. I felt disheartened that nothing was changing, so I continued to hide in my books, isolate myself in video game puzzles, and build walls in my mind about how evil individuals are, how unjust the world was as a whole, and that I could trust no one.

If it weren't for my younger sister, I would have likely become a young cynic, bitter and angry at a depraved world. But this tiny bundle of joy warmed my heart with unconditional love and compassion; focusing on her, instead of my misery, got me through many days of hopeless despair. Before she was even three years old, I began crawling into her bed for comfort. I cherished every moment I was close to her. So, when my brother did the unthinkable, manipulated her against me by threatening to torment her if she would not join him in torturing me, the pain was excruciating. At first, I had no idea he had a hand in her changed behavior, and I believed she was doing it of her own volition, which further drove me toward mania and depression. I was slamming doors in frustration with such force that I would break them, compelling my parents to finally pay attention. They signed both me and my brother up for therapy.

To make matters worse, when I was eleven, my parents informed us they were separating, and by age fourteen, the process was complete; three of the most difficult years of my life. After years of conflict, yelling, blaming, projecting, and not taking responsibility, my parents tried Marriage Encounter, a Christian retreat to get their relationship back on track, but without success. As I struggled through the arguments and the volatile and unsafe home environment, I felt lost and confused, insecure and afraid. I don't know how I got through it. Eventually, my father had to sell the farm, which gave me the choice of which parent to live with, removing me from this horrendous situation. The court ordered my sister under my mother's care, as she was still young, and my brother chose to live with my mom and sister. As for me, I waited for my brother to choose; myself selecting whichever parent he did not. Not understanding my reasoning, my mother was so hurt, wounded to her core that I didn't choose to live with her, but I couldn't bring myself to choose her if it meant living with my brother again.

While this all sounds terribly depressing and inducing of the worst victim complex ever, fear not, dear reader. I give this context so you can understand how these circumstances actually set me up for success later in life, as I'd already adjusted to uncomfortable and challenging situations. This story gets much better, and although I don't want to give away the ending, I can assure you that it is a happy one.

After packing up all our possessions, for the first time in my life, my dad and I moved to a small apartment with a view. At the end of that summer, it was time for high school, and I had tested into an expensive, top-tier college preparatory academy in the tradition of the LaSallian priests in the Catholic church. The three months leading up to school, I was alone while my father was at work, and with only occasional visits from my siblings, I had developed an anxiety disorder, further escaping into the magical realm of video games. Just before school started, I was getting a drink of water from the kitchen in the middle of the night when I collapsed onto the floor. I couldn't move. I just breathed in panic for hours as the liquid slowly soaked me and the carpet. When my father found me the next morning, a myriad of doctor visits ensued, and while they couldn't find anything wrong with me, they kept prescribing new medications and practices to try.

At soccer tryouts a few weeks later, I made a new friend, John. My symptoms diminished, as the feeling of total unworthiness within me was relieved slightly from this new bond and being accepted into the prestigious school. As I made a few friends in the first weeks of classes, my symptoms went away entirely. I was no longer bullied, and the other students engaged me on an intellectually stimulating level and encouraged the best in each other, instead of tearing one another down.

I excelled in several honors classes while struggling to maintain a passing grade in English, where my public-school education had failed to prepare me for these high standards. In freshman year, during a conceptual physics class lecture where the professor kept his back turned to us while writing on the chalkboard, a student pulled a prank on the teacher by secretly attaching paper clips to his rear pocket, resulting in the class laughing, which finally caught his attention. He had no idea what had just taken place as he turned around to see what was so funny. I'd never encountered someone so bold, daring, courageous, and stealthy. This small act drove my determination to know this fellow and befriend him. We became as thick as thieves, and when I got my driver's license and a car, we embarked on countless adventures, staying out late into the night, disregarding state laws, our parents' rules, and the curfews they tried to enforce. We eventually became best friends, better than brothers, the closest I'd ever gotten to another man.

Throughout the remaining years of high school, we stayed friends and even when we went to different colleges, we remained close, visiting one another when possible. Dan graduated from a radical liberal-arts college in three years with perfect grades, while I had dropped out of a politics program at a top-fifty liberal-arts school with a job as the only student in the tech center, continuing my childhood fondness of the realm of computers. I'd met a theater student my freshman year, who earned the nickname Red for her fiery dyed hair. She was a manic-depressive virgin who I stayed with despite the chaos of her type two bipolar disorder, feeling some reprieve from being the most messed-up person in the room. Throughout her infidelity and excessively inebriated partying, I lacked any capacity to set boundaries for my health and wellness.

Meanwhile, my old mindset had gotten the best of me, and I fell victim to a system that was vile, seditious, and corrupt and one I was powerless to change. Defaulting to my childhood coping mechanisms, I began playing video games full time to isolate myself from the world. This time, however, I ended up on a highly competitive team and went to the first ever Blizzard Convention to become a world champion at this first tournament.

The success I experienced brought forth new emotions, and my teammates' dedication motivated me to strive for excellence, as we spent countless hours chatting and grinding in this massively multiplayer online role-playing game. After I quit going to classes and work, losing my presidential scholarship and most of my social life, this game became my everything. I would stay awake for days on end, shower less than once a week, and use the food stamps I had received to buy cheap and quick meals or hand to mouth food and caffeinated soda so I could keep playing through fatigue. I began to lose my eyesight from staring at a screen nonstop and gained weight because of my lack of exercise and poor eating habits. This is when my girlfriend of two years admitted to cheating on me and finally dumped me; she couldn't handle my pathetic state of existence.

I felt ashamed of my life and lacked the courage to be forthcoming to my friends and family that I was no longer enrolled in school. I started lying to everyone I knew about what I was doing, and made up excuses not to see anyone who cared about me as I sank into a deep depression. Occasionally, old friends came over and threw me in the shower before forcing me to go out with them. I was barely making my rent by gambling on myself within the game and selling what computer hardware I won at tournaments. Dan was one of the few friends I trusted enough to tell the truth to, and as we played video games online together, he could see how much time I spent in that realm, consumed by my virtual life. When he found out that my girlfriend had broken up with me, he became worried about these unhealthy habits even further and took it upon himself to rescue me from this rut.

Dan had never gotten his driver's license as he was opposed to car culture and commuted around his college town by bicycle through all four seasons. His enthusiastic passion, marvelous determination, and powerful will to live differently was contagious, and during one of his occasional visits, we went for a hike at Silver Creek Falls State Park. When he asked if I wanted to try a dose of magic mushrooms, I figured, *what did I have to lose?* During the same trip, he laid out his grand scheme to travel by bicycle around Europe, visiting intentional communities and anarchist co-ops, being Willing Workers on Organic Farms (WWOOF), and otherwise living liberated lives. When I asked him why that specific plan, he said a CrimethInc book titled *Off the Map* inspired him, wherein two women hitch-hiked and backpacked around the U.S. without money. It all sounded significantly better than my life.

Dan also enrolled a friend from college named DJ, whom I had only met once before our trip. I didn't know him well enough to trust him, but as an extension of my best friend, I gave him the benefit of the doubt. He was an agile and whimsical ninja-in-training with an infectious smile and penchant for smoking, hacky sack, random quotes, and poetry. Each of us prepared in our own ways. I didn't even own a bicycle at the time and was in the worst shape of my life.

Even with this fresh change of scenery, my belief in humanity was still distrusting and apprehensive at best, Dan being the only glimmer of hope that I clung onto. I had hardly maintained more than a handful of other friendships from high school. During college, we had both developed a highly anti-capitalistic mentality and looked forward to a radically different existence. Dan did all the research to locate European intentional communities, co-ops, and charitable organizations to visit. There, we would learn alternative lifestyle methods, especially how to exist without money, not wanting to contribute to commercialism. After communicating with a variety of establishments that extended an invitation for us to visit, he had a vague plan to trade our labor for food, shelter, knowledge, and experience.

We all wanted to minimize our carbon footprint, so DJ and I thought this was a great idea. We left eight months later in the following spring, equipped with what possessions we could carry in a single backpack. I had applied for, received, and maxed out credit cards to afford a backpack, tent, clothes, boots, camping gear, and bicycle repair tools. I had no intention of ever paying them off, as I suspected I would drop out of mainstream culture permanently. So, there we were, about to live in the fringes of society, and as Timothy Leary's quote goes, "Turn on, tune in, and drop out."

Chapter 3
A Clean Slate

On March 29, 2006, Dan, DJ, and I hugged and kissed our families and loved ones goodbye before departing on a four-hour plane flight from Portland, Oregon, to Cincinnati, Ohio, followed by a two-hour layover and then a twelve-hour flight to Amsterdam, Netherlands; or to be more precise: to Schiphol Airport. When people found out I was going to Europe, I got asked, "Why?" dozens of times. I worried how everyone would judge my intentional homelessness, and how they would fear for my safety. So, instead of admitting that I was essentially going to live as a vagabond nomad on a bicycle off the societal grid, I lied and told them I found a job working on computers for international collectives. While I ended up doing just that, I never got paid for it.

I had been on planes before, but the second one was a significantly longer flight than I was accustomed to. At first, we were all eager with excitement to begin our lives anew, to truly travel, to go places and see things we had never gone or seen before, as well as meet people who we would have never met otherwise, and would, in all likelihood, never encounter again. The prospect of each experience being fresh and wanting to savor the moments brought me back to times of childhood, when the world was full of wonder, and I took each thing in with a palpable desire for its newness. All of this exciting anticipation made it hard to sleep on the plane, so Dan, DJ, and I played cards, talked unnecessarily hastily, and overall pumped each other up for our adventure to come.

It was clear that Dan was the leader in this expedition, as he had done the planning, made the connections we would use, and had the most expertise in the areas we needed for this unusual journey, barring one. As for my strength, I am an Eagle Scout, and I am very good at sensing direction, even without a compass, which comes in handy amongst turbulent skies and foul weather when it is difficult to tell exactly where the sun is. As we burned out our overzealous energy over the first several hours, the initial fervor wore down as we retreated to napping, reading books, and watching whatever in-flight movie was playing. When the sun rose over the Atlantic Ocean with a couple hours left in our flight, the realization of our folly arose with it, as we had a long day ahead of us and would need all the energy we could muster to get through it.

I had only flown to Europe once before, taking part in a football, read soccer for Americans, tournament during my high school years in England. We got our asses kicked by the way, receiving the small silver trophy award, given to the team who lost every single game and then lost to the other team who had also lost every single game. Despite having flown over this area as a teenager, I had a renewed sense of wonder and a slightly timid apprehension, as I previously had had chaperones and my father to accompany me on the trip. This time, it was three spry-eyed, twenty-two-year-old friends, straight out of college, feeling as if we had nothing to lose and everything to gain. Once we got over land, our decisions took on a certain weight to them, the endeavor we were about to undertake becoming even more real, and as we got nearer to the airport, the pilot executing the standard landing procedure, we wondered, *where is Amsterdam?*

Day one began with the realization that things were about to get very different from what we were used to. In the United States of America, we often take for granted the fact that airports are located right in the middle of major cities, and if not, then we place them next to public transportation, which offers easy access to them. We didn't realize that in other countries, especially much older ones where they had developed infrastructure before the invention of flight, airports are far outside city centers. Departing our aircraft and arriving in the terminal, everything looked different, and yet simultaneously familiar. We were in an airport all right, but the stores, kiosks, signage, and directions were very different and in a language none of us knew a single word of. We found the baggage claim simply by following the masses through the maze-like international airport, collected our bags, and exited the airport. Now standing outside, we again wondered, *where is Amsterdam?*

Schiphol, for being as large as it is, had the flattest of fields surrounding it, looking as if they were agricultural territory or pastures and had tall and skinny trees to break the wind, which also broke the fields up in rows. We would find that this wind would maintain a consistent presence for our entire duration in the Netherlands. We were dumbfounded, being used to the straight grids of most American cities. As we had agreed to spend as little money as possible, of which Dan handled the finances, a job title which we gave upon the taskmaster so foul that I hesitate to even name it, we realized we were going to have to rely on others to accomplish our goals.

We walked up to our first stranger, and I asked, "Excuse me, where is Amsterdam?" And they replied in Dutch, which we didn't understand at all. The first lesson as a foreigner: never assume that the person you want to talk to shares your language. We asked a second person and received a similar response. When we asked a third person, an older gentleman, if he spoke English, his positive response thrilled us. After he pointed us the way into the city, he further informed us they parked the shuttles into the city in the opposite direction. As we excitedly strode away on foot, I turned around to thank him and noticed the surprised look of amazement on his face. He shouted out that we couldn't walk there, as Amsterdam was six miles away. We felt like someone had slapped us, challenging our capabilities. We thanked the older gentleman again, walking in the general direction he had pointed, exiting the airport and quickly finding a bicycle path that led toward the city. We vowed that if anyone told us we couldn't do something, then we had to do it, as if we needed to prove our mettle and show our strength, willpower, and determination to ourselves. Let no one tell us what we can and cannot do!

By the time we reached the outskirts of the city, six miles later, the monotony of the flat scenery wore on us, as did the headwind we walked into; we realized how much stuff we had brought, as Dan and DJ's possessions didn't even fit in their backpacks, and they had to carry the excess in totes by hand. I had to give it to us; we were prepared for our journey, but perhaps over-prepared. On top of having that weight on our shoulders and having to carry what didn't fit, we were also wearing brand new boots, which wore calluses and blisters on our feet. At first, our lively conversations kept us excited as we shared dreams of visiting Stonehenge, climbing the Pyramids of Giza, and sailing around the Mediterranean, but over the first few hours of walking, our enthusiastic energy and romantic fantasy of the journey faded under the encumbrance we carried and the reality of our situation. The first sight of an old windmill immediately lifted my spirits. As the reminiscent tale of Don Quixote came to mind, I recalled that yes, I am on an adventure, and at just the beginning of it!

We ate the small bit of food we had packed as we continued to approach the outskirts of town, entering these distant suburbs, and wondering aloud, "Now what?" Without an understanding of which way to go, and a complete and utter incapacity to read the street signs and directional markers along the bike path, our simplest choice was to continue forward. As we did, the buildings became larger, and it felt more like a city. By the time we came across our first dyke, with a beautiful stone bridge crossing it, we could see coffee shops advertising marijuana, which is legal in Amsterdam. The three of us shared a sense of triumph; we made it! But truly, we still had no idea where to go from there, and only knew that we needed to acquire bicycles for our journey and find a place to sleep for the night. From Schiphol to the outskirts of the city, into the city center, through Vondelpark, and then wandering around, we trekked nearly eighteen miles that first day, carrying backpacks stuffed to the brim and whatever didn't fit in them in our hands.

City streets didn't follow straight lines, and attempting to find our bearings confused us, as we struggled to fathom the reason for constructing a city in this manner. We hadn't purchased bikes yet, let alone found a cycle shop, and also failed at finding somewhere to put up our tent, and this defeat further dampening our spirits. Weeks later, we saw an overhead-view map of the entire city, and it was amazing to see how contractors built the city around a central point and then somewhat circularly around it, including the dykes, creating the waterways for people to navigate through. We backtracked a few miles to Vondelpark that night, believing it to be the safest place to rest. After finding bushes that offered privacy, we agreed to sleep in shifts during the twelve-hour night, watching for the police and other homeless who could attempt to rob us. This was a new experience for me, and as I got the middle shift from midnight to four, I struggled to stay awake, using every tool I had learned to keep myself alert while driving, from pinching or slapping myself to singing quietly or playing mental games; nonetheless, I'm sure I dozed off. The time seemed to drag on, ever so slowly, until it was finally time to awaken DJ and pass out again.

Meanwhile, the temperature had plummeted to twenty-nine degrees Fahrenheit, and we had all bundled up before crawling into our sleeping bags, now thankful for the extra resources we brought with us and laboriously carried all this way. However, our bodies still ached and shivered as we arose, stretched, and vacated our spot the next morning. DJ groaned about wanting coffee and Dan reminded us we weren't going to frivolously spend money on such luxuries.

Back on our mission to purchase bicycles, we roamed the city with little more than our intuition to guide us, intrigued by our surroundings and occasionally popping into a church or cathedral to inspect the incredibly ornate and awe-inspiring decor. They built these structures in a wealthy period hundreds of years ago, where the tithes that were collected led to stained-glass windows, pearlescent and gold-foiled candleholders, intricately carved wooden doors, exquisitely chiseled statues, and magnificent marble floors. The difference in architecture throughout the entire city was a stark contrast to what we had seen in the United States, especially in the West Coast, where hardly anything is more than one hundred and fifty years old. Most of the buildings were a minimum of three stories high, and without a way to access a high vantage point, we could rarely see any length of distance in any direction, and the street names seemed like pure gibberish, hardly distinguishable from one another, difficult to remember, and nearly impossible for us to pronounce.

As another means to save money, Dan taught us to dumpster dive, which was a totally new concept to me, and while I was fully willing to wholeheartedly adopt his plan, this practice left me uneasy at first. I was weary of getting sick and felt slightly disgusted at the unknown amount of time the food had been sitting out prior to our finding it. I didn't consider that the cold nights were as good as refrigeration and still thought of the discarded food as waste. When we passed trash cans in areas near restaurants, cafes, and grocery stores, we looked in and dug around for anything edible, which we promptly stuffed into our faces. Sometimes, we went into an establishment to ask if they had any food they planned to throw away or had thrown away recently and if they would give it to us instead. Most of the time, people shook their heads, spoke angry Dutch words, and pointed their fingers toward the door. These initial attempts diminished morale and further reinforced my mindset that people sucked.

That afternoon, with hungry bellies and a complete failure to accomplish our objective, we switched strategies. Actually hoping to buy something now, Dan began busking in a heavily trafficked pedestrian path by laying his hat down on the ground and showing off his juggling skills, earning several euros. Busking is a form of avant-garde street performance, deriving from the Spanish word 'buscar', which means to search, as in searching for one's profession by trying it out on the street for the public to judge, based on their willingness to tip. We saw one gentleman who had mastered the art of busking. He stood on a bucket, holding one flaming juggling torch over his head, yelling, "I am a terrorist!" While people stopped and observed what he was doing, he would encourage and sometimes literally pull people toward a chalk line he had drawn. His ability to draw in a crowd with lines like, "Hey! He stopped. Why didn't you?" enamored me.

Before he even started his show, he had a group of people shoulder to shoulder, three deep, surrounding him. This only grew his crowd as more and more people became interested in what everyone else was looking at. I admired his capability and the tactical brilliance of his form of crowd control. I saw this same performer several times throughout Amsterdam, later learning that he could make up to two thousand euros per performance and that he would do up to four shows per day, truly making an impressive living as a street performer. He also performed with crystal contact juggling balls, which he passed effortlessly along his body, appearing like magic, as if gravity didn't exist. He could get up to four in each hand and would end the show by doing body rolls with one ball made of Kevlar lit on fire. We had a lot to learn.

Our sole goal within our time in Amsterdam was to find the bicycles of our dreams, the perfect bike touring machines that would facilitate the best trip possible. We saw gorgeous bikes everywhere, as the bicycle lanes were more prolific than car lanes. The streets were a whizzing *buzz* of cyclists obeying street signs and laws totally foreign to us, following arrows and signals. The traffic patterns made little sense to us, watching bikes of all varieties zip by alongside the cars, narrowly missing collisions with one another in their own separated lanes.

People had cruisers, recumbents, tandems, electric-assist motors, road bikes, and an impressive variety of bags, carts, carriers, lights, and attachments. Some of them had the most incredible custom-made frames, often to carry children in the front or rear inside wooden compartments. There were bicycle delivery people, known as couriers, carrying everything from food and beverages to plants or legal documents. People also drove mopeds and scooters, as well as the smallest cars I had ever seen. Economics, and the lack of a powerful military heavily invested in oil-producing companies, meant extremely high gas prices—over nine-dollars per gallon—leading to a culture less invested in cars. Dan immediately fell in love with this bike-centric approach to urban development. This massive infrastructure throughout the nation and not having to share a lane with vehicles was a joy to us all. One of our hosts that we would later stay with even told us a statistic that in the Netherlands, there were sixteen million people and eighteen million bicycles.

At train stations, there would be hundreds if not thousands of bikes all locked to long rails. They respected each other, and were very courteous riders, looking out for one another and hardly ever running into another bicyclist. And there was truly a special place in hell for bike thieves. Even cars gave them the right of way; this place was a bicyclist's paradise!

As we wandered the city, we stopped in at every bike shop we came across and leave defeated, not finding what we were looking for, at a price we could afford, anyway. The top-of-the-line bikes we wanted cost six-thousand dollars. Before departing every store, we would ask for a recommendation for another shop and then spend hours lost around the city trying to find our bikes. This search consumed six days, and as each one passed without yielding results, we felt more despair and concern. We became disheartened and downtrodden, realizing with plummeting morale that it would have been better to buy them in the U.S. and pack them into bike boxes, bringing them on the plane with us.

Within the first week, we explored most of the city center on foot, continuously returning to the central train station, where there was reliable dumpster'd food. We regularly discovered cute little parks, in one of which was a field trip for elementary kids. When they departed, each child dumped their sack lunches into one bin; I picked through every bag for any edible things they discarded. In our hunger and desperation, we would also pick up half-smoked cigarettes or sometimes half-used pouches of rolling tobacco and light those up to stave off the hunger. We returned to Vondelpark to sleep, although fears of getting caught and fined increased, as did our wish for more protection from the cold. We had received word from a random homeless man of a campground outside of the city center called Camp Zeeburg, that was under a bridge, in between two sections of river. So, we trekked out there one night. Since we didn't have a vehicle, we were much more incognito and could sneak in on foot without paying the fee.

We found an open spot and pitched our tent, and as the cold crept in, the wind picked up and howled something fierce. We worried that the wind would tear our tent to shreds as it constantly blew the side closest to our heads into our faces. The first time we ever used the tent became a comical farce of errors trying to put it up in nearly sixty mile-per-hour winds. By the following morning, the wind had pulled our stakes up, and although there were over four hundred and fifty pounds of human weight plus gear inside the tent, the tent had moved about six feet. We had hardly slept a wink with the incredulous sounds and the whipping of the walls, and as we packed it up, we realized that one of the brand-new poles had been bent and would stay that way for the duration of the tent's life.

We did our best to keep morale high as we continued our search for bicycles, often with empty bellies. I could tell I was quickly losing weight between the continuous exercise and the lack of caloric intake. On our third day, Dan spotted a case of full, large Carlsbad beer bottles sitting inside a lower patio with a metal protective guarded railing, and while we couldn't get inside, his long arms could reach half of the case, so he grabbed them one by one while we kept lookout. Slightly inebriated later that day, we ventured into one cafe to get warm and realized how easily they sold marijuana in all sorts of baked forms and flowers by the gram. We ended up splurging and spent about eight dollars on three and a half grams of what turned out to be some very potent weed. I hardly had a tolerance, and the effect felt immense and overwhelming.

On another evening, we walked through the red-light district, known for its prostitutes advertising their scantily clad bodies in seductive poses, with come-hither looks on their faces, alluring passerby, from display windows backlit by purely red bulbs, accentuating their skin tone and provocative features on dimly lit streets—something I had not experienced before in my life. It felt odd that these women were comparable to department store merchandise, a commodity to be bought. I've struggled with the concepts of strip clubs, escorts, and paying for sex my entire life, but this brought it right in front of my face. I understand that there are different strokes for different folks and that this was the oldest trade known to humankind, but I felt flabbergasted, nonetheless. The drunken belligerence I found in that area was also intriguing, as I later learned that the red-light district was infamous worldwide and attracted the globally affluent wealthy elites that had money to spare. This entire scene sickened me. I snubbed the idea that the wealthy could buy people and likened it to slavery.

After several days of exploring the city, we got the feeling that we could be stuck in Amsterdam for a long time if we could not find bikes. After our windy night of camping, the frigid nights, intense gusts, and consistent rain began to affect us, stagnating our momentum, and we desperately needed to reinvigorate our initial excited energy. The repetition of getting lost or sidetracked, picking through trash cans, and visiting bike stores without success had us in a rut. I dreamed of exploring the Rijksmuseum but didn't dare ask for the funds to do so. While wandering one curving street, we finally got a stroke of luck.

Upon passing by a little hole-in-the-wall bike shop, Dan positively expressed an intuitive feeling, encouraging us all to enter. With nothing to lose, we went inside without question. The proprietor was lazily sitting, waiting for his kettle to boil some hot water for coffee, and he asked if we wanted some, which we gratefully obliged. Around his dank and poorly lit, lower-level shop was a disorganized mess with bicycles hanging from the ceiling. Within the chaos, two mountain bikes caught our attention, as we had hardly seen any inside other shops. Upon requesting the price, we discovered they were within our budget! Alas, there were three of us and only two of them. As Dan searched around, he spotted a three-speed Dutch cruiser with an internal shifter that was love at first sight, but sadly outside of our price range.

After deciding to talk it over outside, a pigeon interrupted our brief meeting by defecating on me! I felt the wet *splat*, immediately followed by the uncontrollable hyena-like laughter that came out of my companions. Wondering what all the commotion was about, the bike shop owner came outside, and when he saw what had happened to me, he told us that this meant good luck and fetched a rag to help clean up my hair. The omen was the first heartfelt laughter in days, as we thought perhaps, he was right. So, Dan went back in with the shop owner and haggled him down on the price. After sealing the deal with a handshake, he handed over practically all our cash that he had safeguarded so cautiously; nearly two thousand dollars. The owner seemed elated to get rid of the mountain bikes, as they'd been in his possession so long that dust covered them and they needed the inner tubes inflated. With our new wheels, and with them the mobility and freedom to leave Amsterdam, we left the store feeling triumphant. I questioned the deal we had just gotten and didn't trust the store owner about the durability of the bikes, but nonetheless, it was the best solution we had found thus far.

Excitedly, the three of us strapped, duct-taped, and zip-tied every bicycle light, blinker, sticker, and decoration in our possession onto our new metal chariots of freedom. Like birds with cage doors left open, away we sped, directly to the shop of an incredible company named Amsterdam Bicycles where we had previously ordered a suitable cart and put it on hold until we acquired our bikes. Unfortunately, purchasing our new steeds reduced our funds below the agreed cost, and upon informing the clerks of such, they became understandably angry. Yet, without the extra space to store it, they reluctantly sold it to us for literally every euro we had. With elation and gratitude, we attached our precious cart to the yellow mountain bike and wheeled away from the shop. After stopping at a nearby library to print a local map, we plotted the next steps of the journey to our first community destination.

Dan, DJ, and I were finally ready to get on the road and incredibly eager to leave Amsterdam behind. Regardless of it being around four-thirty in the afternoon, with the sunlight already weaning, we got moving with haste toward our first stop, a community called Het Carre, in Delft, about forty-two miles away.

Chapter 4
On the Road at Last

After a week spent finding our bikes in Amsterdam, we had a renewed energy and eager excitement to sleep indoors at the upcoming community, so, as quickly as we could, we packed our possessions into the cart and bike bags, known as panniers. We then named our stallions, in true fashion after stories of old, Dan bestowing Junior upon the Dutch cruiser, DJ assigning the yellow mountain bike Lord Pancake, and the cart given the name Hangar, as it held over two hundred pounds. I struggled with this exercise, and finally, Dan told me I was overthinking it and asked me what was the first pure emotion I ever remembered feeling. The red bike earned the name Fear.

Dan was the strongest and volunteered to bear the heaviest burden, thus carrying the cart while DJ rode the cruiser with two saddle bags permanently affixed, and me, being the least experienced, rode the red mountain bike with no weight. The Netherlands is a fantastic place to start a bicycle tour. Being so flat, it liberated us from the struggle of climbing hills. We still did not know where we were going as we attempted to follow confusing street signs. I had maybe picked up fifty words of the local language by this point. On that first day of riding, I felt truly alive, and it seemed as if things were moving in slow motion. I simply followed while in deep contemplation: did everything happen for a reason? Was I meant to go through these challenging experiences to be a stronger person? Or was it just luck of the draw, random chance, and circumstance? Fate or free will? Thus, my philosophical, esoteric, and metaphysical ponderings while cycling began, often comparing Eastern and Western religions, thoughts of karma and reincarnation, as well as life after death.

As we passed through towns with baffling and comical names like Amstelveen, Uithoorn, De Kwakel, and Zevenhoven, on multiple intersections, we were stumped about which way to go, pulling out our compass and deciding; continuously perplexed by the signs of 'Doorgaand Verkeer' with no matching location on the map. After a few hours of riding, dusk turned to night, and we illuminated our blinkers accordingly. We were even more hopelessly lost in the dark and lacked the certainty that we were closing in on our destination. My directional sense wasn't as accurate at night, especially in unfamiliar territory, but we trudged on regardless.

Fortunately, the pleasant weather kept spirits high, yet after twenty miles into our forty-two-mile goal, I didn't know how much more I could do. I limped on by the sheer support, optimism, and enthusiasm from Dan, who continued to encourage DJ and me, while sometimes pushing against my lower back with one hand, propelling me forward at the cost of his own inertia. His energy was contagious, and he conjured up enchanting ideas and regaled us with his fantasies about the places we would go and the deeds we would accomplish, creating a camaraderie between us. It effectively worked to harden my determination to not be the first person in our triad to give up. But my left Achilles was tight, and I couldn't get it to relax and loosen, no matter how much I stretched at every stop.

At some point, we made a wrong turn, and after a few miles without a bicycle lane and cars honking at us, we heard sirens. Behind us, the familiar spinning blue lights accompanied by a spotlight informed us the Dutch Politie wanted us to pull over. They approached while yelling at us in Dutch. Thankfully, I had learned how to reply with, "I don't speak Dutch," and, "Do you speak English?" so they knew we were tourists versus not being cooperative. They cited us for illegally biking on the shoulder of a car-only road and without proper lights. Despite attempts at a rational logic debate, and having spent every cent on the bikes and cart, they forced us to hand over our passports until we could pay the twenty-Euro fines per person, which taxed our spirits and our funds. Dan had reached his daily maximum withdrawal limit, and the police station was closed, so we had to wait until morning. A journal excerpt I wrote later that night reflected:

On the Road at Last

Within six hours of having our bikes, we already got pulled over, and for what, you might ask? Not for biking on the road, not for reckless endangerment, riding without a seatbelt on, or defecating in public, but for not having ENOUGH bike lights! We spoke with a very rude and pompous policeman who lied to us, claiming we needed three front lights and four rear lights per person! This is absolutely absurd because it is not the law here in Holland and is pretty ridiculous in general.

The entire situation was jarring, demoralizing, and further reinforced our belief that the police were corrupt bastards. My faith in humanity continued to waver and lessen, as even across an ocean in a different culture, the same issues we fought against back home prevailed. Dan, at least, had the wherewithal to get their names and badge numbers, and the exact address for the police station. They forbid us from riding our bicycles without the proper number of lights and warned us they would fine us again if they caught us.

Knowing we couldn't go far without our passports, the police directed us to a church for a place to sleep. We emotionally limped into the next town through the cold, Alphen aan den Rijn, pushing our bikes alongside us late into the night. Of course, when we arrived, the church was closed, and knocking on the doors and looking around for people yielded no rewarding results, so we went to a nearby hospital instead, chained our bicycles together out front, and pleaded with the receptionist for shelter, informing her of our plight. After calling around town looking for a place for us to sleep, she had no good news to offer us—her supervisor even rejecting her request to help us. Thankfully, she said that she would let us sleep there, anyway, and led us to an unused X-ray room where we passed out on the cold, hard floor, grateful for this receptionist's kindness.

Having told us to be out by six the next morning, we arose stiff a few hours later with lactic acid still flush in our muscles. We gathered our meager belongings and headed back outside. A frigid blast of air greeted us, and below-freezing temperatures removed any heat that remained in our bodies. The weather even froze our bicycles, the locks needed thawing just to be removed. Nonetheless, with how the morning greeted us, the woman had been a blessing, a glimmer of hope in the human race, and we gave her our gratitude as we left. We ventured into the center of town, found the police station to make sure we knew where it was, and then backtracked to a park to stretch our aching bodies while we waited until a bank was open to withdraw the funds. Afterward, we went back to the police station to pay our fine, got our passports back, and left! Our muscles ached from the fatigue of the day before, only to be taxed and tested again. Yet, we were moving, and something about the unfamiliar territory kept our eyes rapt on the landscape, a heightened sense of perception accompanying us throughout our journey.

After biking through a string of towns over twenty miles and four hours of confusion with poor way-finding, we arrived at Het Carre, a community in a Delft suburb, where we encountered our first host: a non-traditional family led by a man named John, whose spiritual beliefs, following Sathya Sai Baba, shaped their lifestyle. John's partners, Anne and Hilde, along with their three children, welcomed us warmly, showcasing their selfless generosity through communal living. While I couldn't tell which children belonged to either woman, they all treated each other as family.

Despite legal and social challenges, they embodied resilience and compassion, overcame adversity with grace and selflessness, and lived in service to others and their healthy children. I opened up to meditation and charity work there, sharing my skills as a computer specialist within the community, engaging in a work-trade arrangement, while learning about their unique way of life. Witnessing John's legal trial and the community's struggles moved me, and I reflected on justice and my role in effecting positive change. We filled our days with exploration, workouts, and beach trips, the company of our hosts and their children enriching every moment. We learned practical skills like bicycle repair and indulged in hobbies like juggling and a Tai Chi game called push hands. This period formulated deep connections as we bonded as a team through shared meaningful experiences.

A week in, we made a special trip to Scheveningen, a delightful beach town with a lovely promenade and acrylic barriers that protected it from the wind. On our ride home, there was a tubular pole sticking straight up to prevent vehicles from entering the bicycle-only area, and everyone dodged it, except for DJ, who somehow managed to not see it. In the most brilliant propensity for accidents that I would soon learn he had, DJ perfectly rode the front wheel straight up the pole, flinging himself over his handlebars, the bicycle landing with the pole directly in the center of the triangular bike frame; I was beyond stupefied! DJ was one of the most adept, swift-footed, and sprightly people I had ever met, yet he had an incredible aptitude for folly and clumsiness, as if he were ill-fated; like a Dungeons and Dragons character who gets an extra point in one statistic for taking a character fault or flaw. He had sprained his ankle in the affair, and one of our hosts helped him walk the rest of the way home, while I walked alongside in moral support, pushing both of our bicycles. Amidst it all, the warmth and kindness of the people I encountered struck me, leaving a lasting impression of the power of compassion and community.

During this time, I began my lifelong juggling practice under Dan's tutelage, starting with just one ball, practicing for an hour straight. Then, I moved to two, doing a little passing with DJ, who was also learning. This was very difficult for me, and I was a slow learner as I lacked hand-eye coordination. Previously, I played soccer and ran, neither of which required this type of skill. As a child, I got picked last for teams in physical education, as I could not catch, throw, or shoot any ball well. I quit after one season of basketball and half a season of baseball, both of which my father signed me up to try. Yet, I enjoyed juggling. There was a real difficulty within it. I did my best to learn, albeit slowly, as I wanted to be included as a part of our group.

In the evenings, we sat around reading and trained in juggling and other skills. All three of us checked emails, corresponding with our families and friends. I was surprised and thankful that Red, my college girlfriend, kept in touch, saying that what we were doing inspired her so much that she was contemplating joining us. Each of us also wrote in separately maintained online blogs that we started prior to the beginning of our voyage, for our respective audiences. I would occasionally get nostalgic or homesick, missing people and my old, comfortable habits while reflecting on how quickly my life had changed. And the change wasn't about to stop; after weeks, our time at this community had nearly come to a close, and we were preparing for our departure in several days' time. While finishing up on one of the last computers for an older gentleman named Eddie, I received the most incredible, life-changing gift that would come to alter my existence and how I live for the rest of my life.

Eddie told me stories about his experiences during the grueling six hours of fixing his computer. He told me of past lovers, how he had taken ecstasy, and how it had transformed his perception and heightened sensations, specifically, how amazing his body felt while on it and while having sex. He warned me never to do this, as it would permanently alter the way sex without it would be. Yet, he described looking into the eyes of his lover and witnessing the entire universe, with all its depth, breadth, and beauty, in an effervescent and ethereal moment of divine singularity. He said he felt connected with all things, experiencing a sense of unity with the cosmos. After I had finished with his computer, he unexpectedly gave me three pills and told me not to tell anyone that he had done so.

He then offered for me and my travel companions to join him at a church on Friday night in the Santo Daime tradition. He told me the origin story of the church and how in the 1930s, a man was dying of starvation in the Amazonian jungle, and in what he believed to be his final moments, he got down on his knees and prayed to God. In return, God came to him in a vision, telling him to eat a specific vine and root, so he did. These two different plants combined inside of him became Ayahuasca, which is a plant-based psychedelic substance that provides a flood of dimethyltryptamine (DMT) to the brain. This led him to have a transcendental metaphysical experience. During this altered state, God instructed him to form a new Christian religion, based in the Portuguese language, to share this experience with all of its followers, so that individuals could have a deeply connective relationship with God and to know divinity first-hand, instead of through a Priest, Rabbi, Imam, Sangha, or Guru. He did exactly as God instructed, creating a religion that has grown to be recognized nearly worldwide today. However, some countries banned the elixir.

I only had one day to decide, and one full day of fasting before the experience, if I chose to partake. I discussed it with Dan and DJ, the former being excited, the latter being doubtful. Dan's willingness thrilled me, as the thought of going alone made me nervous. I had no idea I was about to embark on the most profound spiritual experience of my life up to that point.

On Friday, Eddie picked us up in his little car and drove us to a central part of the city, where we climbed steps to the inside of an old stone building, the top floor opening into a heavenly room, complete with giant mandala-shaped stained-glass windows inlaid into the west wall in an elaborate and ornate pattern. There were two musicians in the center, both with guitars, a circle of eight around them, another circle of eighteen further out, and lastly, a larger circle, which did not get completed, as our numbers were around forty in total. The instructors arranged us intentionally, and if you were to look down upon us from above, you would see a pattern, like a circular pendulum, that rotated around a central axis point in between the musicians. They gave each of us a small booklet, filled with all the songs that we would be singing, and while listening to the instructions in Dutch and English, I flipped through it, realizing it was entirely in Portuguese. *Great!* I thought. I didn't know a word of the language, and I would fumble through not being able to read sheet music, either. The other people primarily spoke Dutch, German, and English; I was thoroughly confused about how this would work.

The facilitators introduced themselves, sitting off to the side with five-gallon buckets in case we required help or needed to vomit. They told us we didn't need to worry about cleaning up and that they would take care of everything for us. They even placed yoga mats out with blankets atop them for us if we wanted to lie down and rest. Then, they showed us the footwork, giving us an opportunity to practice the dance we would do throughout the ceremony: three steps to the left, crossing the feet, and three steps back to the right, while singing; I had no idea that this was going to last for around six hours. We began by entering a deep, meditative space, attempting to clear our mind of thought, with the ability to be present and single-minded on one thing: our love for our creator. Finally, we ingested up to three small cups of the Ayahuasca brew, one at a time, with one-hour intervals in between, allowing everyone to intake as much as they felt called to, requiring no extra ingestion. Afterwards, we all sat in silent meditation. As the sun set, I saw the brilliant rays of sunlight through the stained-glass windows, and I began to perceive the energy within them.

It felt as if I were bathing in divinity itself, a warm, tranquil, peaceful, energetic vibration sweeping over me, my body sensations increasing. I felt my heart beat, steady and even. I felt the Ayahuasca concoction coursing through my body, which had tasted earthy and alkaline, navigating past my stomach and into my intestines, dispersing into my blood and activating my nervous system. I perceived another sensation so difficult to describe, but it felt as if there was a spirit within the medicine that reached into my soul, or the essence of my being. From that place, it gathered my trauma and all the pain, suffering, animosity, rage, hatred, as well as the fragments of my spirit that had shut themselves off, hiding within the deepest crevices of my psyche to avoid further agony. It brought them out again, reincorporated and integrated them back into my being, while shaking off the past to allow myself to be present and whole. I found myself in awe of the sensations, with a slack-jawed, open-mouthed amazement, and this was still just the beginning.

While all of this was happening, there was a cue given to the room to stand up as the ceremony was about to begin. They moved the chairs out of our way so we could dance and sing our praise to God in heaven, Jesus Christ, his only begotten son, and most of all, the Virgin Mother Mary, for whom we dedicated most of the songs to. I found it difficult to stand, let alone keep track of what page I was on, or read and decipher sheet music while simultaneously keeping my movements in rhythm with the group. But shortly into the program, I got the swing of it, and my body became agile, the motions flowing smoothly, and I could sing in Portuguese! My newfound capabilities perplexed me, and as the tempo and cadence of the music increased throughout the ritual, the buzzing of energetic vibration in my body arose to match it.

As a child, my brother and father often told me to be quiet and to stop singing in church, that God did not want to hear me, as my voice threw them off from their wonderful singing. However, at that moment, my voice felt in harmonious pitch with the rest of the group. I could feel the differences between the notes and found the specific area inside of me they resonated within. The music was blissful and reminded me of the parable in the Bible that said, "In the beginning, there was the Word," and that the word would be sound. Did that mean that everything we know of in our perceivable universe began as sound? I can only assume that the big bang must have made an enormous explosion, encompassing all pitches and frequencies simultaneously. Or was it one large Om?

During the ceremony, I didn't think of these things as I was totally present, solely focused on the here and now. Throughout hours of this rhythmic movement and singing praise, I felt changes taking place within me, and as the music reached a crescendo, I needed to vomit. The realization came over me quickly, and I dropped my pamphlet and rushed over to the facilitator, who was ready to receive me, bucket in hand. I was not the first one to do this, and whereas the sounds of others purging didn't affect me before, suddenly, the sole focus of my ears seemed to be on these putrid, odorous expulsions. It surely didn't help that I had my head in a bucket, causing my own sounds to reverberate back into my ears. I was already nauseous, and this amplification didn't help my condition.

Afterwards, I washed my mouth out with water, and then drank some. It seemed sweeter than water has ever tasted in my entire life. Like the nectar and ambrosia that I had read about in Greek mythology books—it was truly the stuff of life! To recover from the purging, I laid down in one of the few beds available for those too overwhelmed to sing and dance, and someone placed a blanket over me. From there, I could focus on the sensations that were taking place within me. It felt like magic, unlike anything I had experienced, and I much preferred it to the activity; the stillness allowed me to presence and introspection. A little while in, Dan came to check on me, as did the facilitator, letting me know someone else needed to lie down and that if I was alright, I needed to get up and rejoin the group. I consented with hesitation, still enjoying the experience of just being.

As the night became early morning, the pace of the guitarists slowed until the end, where the final incantation was smooth and elongated, like the consistency of molasses. There was a collective sigh of relief as we all took our chairs and sat back down. The ceremonial leader said a few things, encouraging us all to ground ourselves before sharing what kind of experience we had had with the group. We took a few minutes to gather our thoughts before going around the circle. Some folks talked about the sensation of being connected with God, appreciative of their existence and grateful for their creator. Others reflected on their childhood, or their life in general, giving particular importance to their relationships. One woman even spoke of having an out-of-body experience that was incredible to hear about.

When it was Dan's turn, he hardly said anything except for being thankful to be involved in the ceremony. When it was my turn, I spoke about how, before, I didn't know what was going to happen, but that the experience amazed me. I told the group that I could see energy rays and my inner feelings, and how the connection with divinity was beyond healing and therapeutic, allowing me to let go of a great deal of trauma, hurt, and pain. The ceremony refreshed me, bringing a sense of renewal and giving me a new centeredness within my being. I felt more whole and complete overall. Everyone attentively focused on my words with deep compassion and empathy, showing they understood. For the first time in my life, I felt truly heard and that my words were as important and valuable as I was. As I listened, I deeply connected to everyone else's experiences, and even more so when I shared my own. After me, a few more people went, commenting that Dan and I were like heroes, saints, or angels for taking part in this ceremony at such a young age. Everyone around the room nodded in agreement.

After everyone finished, we went into the area where we left our shoes and possessions and found an abundant feast waiting for us! I hadn't eaten in about sixteen hours and sampled every food present, taking my time in savoring the immense flavor within each dish, my taste buds more alive than they had ever been. Everything tasted as if it had divinity infused within it, and I slowly indulged myself into a satiated bliss. I was hardly tired as Eddie drove us in his car back to Het Carre, but I struggled to be in a vehicle, feeling uneasy and a bit motion-sick. When I finally laid down to sleep later that night, reflecting on the wondrous ceremony I had just experienced, I was immensely appreciative to be alive.

The next day, I was a new man with a lot of energy. Wanting to fully connect with myself, I desired solitary time in nature and rode Fear all day. We would leave the community in a couple of days, so I didn't want to miss out on finding these glass houses that people had told me about. Without a care in the world, I embarked, wondering what these domiciles made of glass would look like. I roamed along dykes and through fields of agriculture with a newfound sense of balance. Before yesterday afternoon, I was awkward and clumsy on a bicycle, but now, I found poise and grace, a connection with my metal steed. The medicine journey had brought me in tune with my body, and that alignment carried enhanced abilities with it. Yet, through my hours of riding, I found no glass houses, just an abundance of greenhouses. It was only upon returning that I realized the mistranslation.

While I had been riding, I pondered whether Ayahuasca was a sort of learning enhancer, and if humans worldwide could use it to facilitate a better connection with ourselves, our spirit, and God himself. This was a question I kept with me for a while until I could finally research it and hopefully find the answer. Through my learnings, I discovered we receive a flood of Dimethyltryptamine (DMT), which is a naturally occurring substance in our brains, when using Ayahuasca, when we are born, when we die, and in smaller quantities when we dream or are in solitary confinement with sensory deprivation for more than a week. Our pineal gland produces the chemical, which many people believe to be our third eye. I wondered what it meant that our brains can create this substance and have the receptors to receive it. The discovery that this chemical is found in nature by combining certain plants together shocked me. The roots and vines that contain it often resemble the spiraling double-helix of our DNA, which I took as a sign, as I'd experienced an internal feeling as if parts of my DNA were shifting or healing.

I found a desire within me to be more honest and transparent in my communication, especially about my feelings, which I was more in tune with than I had ever been before. I also wanted to come clean about past lies that I told my family, specifically about having a job in Europe. Despite the distance, I gained more compassion for my parents and siblings than I had in years, maybe ever. I also felt immense gratitude to my parents and ancestors for all the hardships and suffering that they had endured so that I could have the gift of life. I knew they all did the best they could with what they had, and me holding resentment against them for the traumatizing treatment as a child was akin to harboring a poison inside of my body that was eating me from the inside out, yet one I could release anytime I wanted to. In the proceeding days, I saw improvements in a variety of ways. My juggling skills progressed more rapidly than they had before. I was mindful of my eating and was very present with others in conversation. Even my ability to listen had sharpened.

I felt thankful for this time within our first community to be grounded and integrate the lessons from Ayahuasca, but at the end of our three weeks at Het Carre, it was time to leave. I gave a warm embrace to each of the adults and children whom we had lived with and learned a great deal from, especially about Dutch culture and government, alternative approaches to spirituality, and living life as an act of service to others. They had so many jokes about things being orange and while I still couldn't understand why, I felt more connection to their way of living and society at large.

Alas, it was time to get on the road again. The three of us would leave the comfort of sleeping indoors and embrace the unknown of our next adventure.

Chapter 5
The Journey Is Greater than the Destination

It was nearing the end of April, marking almost a month of being in Europe, and we hadn't gotten a single stamp on our passports yet. So, after leaving the community, we traveled with haste to the nearest border, which was Belgium. The night before, our hosts had filled our food reserves for our journey, and at four in the morning, we ate breakfast and said our goodbyes. Luckily, our understanding of how to read signs and maintain a correct directional sense had improved over the last few weeks.

We learned a lot from our first community, even though it was far from ideal. We observed many problems that arose while living there, such as their consensus-based decision-making model. This model meant everyone needed to unanimously agree in order for something to happen, which got especially bogged down as any individual could effectively veto a group decision. Because of people having different beliefs and ideals about the best path forward, they also struggled with where to allocate funds, who to let into the community, and when to have meetings. But overall, we learned a lot from our hosts, especially how imperative it is to have a clear manifesto that everyone agrees to. With many more intentional communities to learn from later in our voyage, my journal helped me recall:

We departed around five and started heading south toward Rotterdam. It was foggy, which was very beautiful as it was dark... While we rode in between a couple rows of trees that extended as far as you can see, streetlights illuminated the fog in between, restricting vision because of the reflection and making the path seem to go on forever; quite a sight to be seen. It was funny to us when the streetlights went off around six a.m. before the sun even rose.

Bicycle traveling became easier for us, and our camaraderie had grown as well. After my profound experience with Ayahuasca, my mindset changed; gamifying every aspect of existence, becoming the best character I was capable of. I had played so many video games in my life that were about role-playing, so I thought of myself as a character, and I was leveling up all the unique attributes and skills that I could. I used the tactics and techniques that I learned from gaming, and my path to becoming an Eagle Scout to refine my teamwork, communication, and leadership skills in real life. The hours spent within the rote monotony of bicycling and juggling improved those skills. And like any epic game, our story developed a soundtrack. John Denver's "On the Road' and Tom Petty's "Time To Move On" became our favorite anthems as we set out each early morning or when we resumed cycling after a break. We rarely ate breakfast, and instead, we stealthily packed up our tent and belongings before anyone else was awake and quickly got to pedaling. Once we became hungry, we would have a quick morning snack. Only after about six hours would we take a long break for lunch.

To help the time pass even more, we practiced ninja skills like stealth and sneaking, and created little games to test our skills. We improved our balance, agility, and dexterity through a myriad of training exercises and contests, matching our skills against one another. Push hands remained one of our favorites to gain better stability, equilibrium, and grounding. Dan taught DJ and me about "sky-lining," or how to avoid being detected in the dark. If we were in exposing positions, someone could see our silhouette against the sky, so we avoided detection by staying hidden in proximity to other objects acting as backdrops. We were improving in a variety of areas, training in all ways. We were far from being seasoned bicycle veterans, but we weren't inept novices any longer.

Our journey southward from Het Carre to Belgium felt smoother, perhaps because of a slight tailwind, our tuned-up cycles, or the illusion of downhill slopes. We had fixed our bikes after they hung unused from the rafters of the Amsterdam shop for who knows how long. The chains demanded lubricant, the shifters needed tightening, and the limit screws on the front and rear derailers were out of place. On top of all that, the brake cables required loosening or tightening, so our wheels weren't rubbing while stopping. We also improvised a cover for our cart out of some spare PVC pipes and an unwanted canvas cloth to keep our belongings from soaking in foul weather. Last, we hung Tibetan prayer flags so motorists behind us would see our declaration of peaceful and positive intent. We encountered the first rain shortly after leaving that initial community and wished for waterproof gear. Nonetheless, spring brought longer, warmer days, lifting our spirits as we pedaled and engaged in philosophical discussions about life's meaning. We debated concepts such as fate versus free will, which government structure benefited mankind the most, the difference between commercialism and capitalism, or whether there even was one, and similar topics until we ran out of points to make and things to say.

We marveled at Dutch bridges and unique architecture, including a bike tunnel under a river as we traveled past towns with names like Hazerswoude-Dorp, Zoetermeer, Bleiswijk, and Prins Alexander. Rotterdam's modernity impressed us, as it was rebuilt post-World War II. We rarely traveled in a straight line and would alter our course on a whim to catch a viewpoint or examine something that sparked our interest. While it elongated our total mileage, this unconventional approach led to many pleasant surprises, like a small town playing American eighties music, giant metal windmills, beautiful vistas, and resting places alongside dykes and countryside unlike anything we had ever seen. We traversed through Charlois, Barendrecht, Puttershoek, Moerdijk, Zevenbergen, Oudenbosch, and Rucphen before reaching the border on our longest day of riding yet—seventy miles.

It took pedaling all day to reach Belgium. The absence of customs formalities surprised us, having expected inspections at control points. With nothing to celebrate, no stamps in passports, or a feeling of triumph and accomplishment, our morale sank with disappointment. We suddenly lacked direction or purpose in visiting a country just to say we had been there. Our malaise didn't last long as DJ soon realized that he had forgotten his sleeping bag back in Delft, so we reluctantly backtracked the following day, all ten hours of cycling to retrieve it. We thoroughly disliked going backwards and practically had a pact against it, but we decided it was worth the hours of cycling instead of having to buy a new sleeping bag. Evening was upon us by the time we reached Belgium, and we were all exhausted and downtrodden. Thus, we stopped and set up camp not far from the nonexistent cultural partition, sharing sleeping bags in shifts every four hours that night like a ridiculous game of musical chairs. I felt frustrated but recognized it was for the group's benefit, despite the discomfort of sleeping without proper gear. One blog entry summarized the teamwork of sharing tasks and specializing in others:

Over the course of the day, we all switched using different bikes. We each took the cart for a bit and then traded off... I go up to people and ask them directions, and if we can fill our water bottles in their faucets... I've learned some key Dutch phrases like, "Do you speak English?" or, "Where is _____?" and, "Thank you very much!" I carry all the town names on a piece of paper, as well as my trusty compass! I am also the company chef, and I feel like the company micro-manager. I do the little day-to-day or moment-to-moment things and organize for the group, while DJ is our chief merry-maker and morale-booster, a versatile cyclist and contributor, as Dan more or less oversees the whole operation.

We were becoming a team, learning each other's strengths and weaknesses, and each becoming specialists in our own niche. As an Eagle Scout, I handled navigation. Dan, the muscle, took the heavy Hangar more than his share. DJ, agile and quixotic, often accomplished sneaky feats or created loud, distracting commotions, affording Dan an opportunity for thievery. Every day of our travels was special, some easy, others vastly difficult.

Setting off early the next morning, we aimed to make good time, battling against the headwind on our journey back north. The sunrise was immaculate that morning—sheer, natural perfection. It created magnificent sun rays that appeared like the crown of God and felt like a gift to us for waking up so early and for being exactly where we were in life. It was hard to keep my eyes off of it as I pedaled. I almost crashed multiple times because I wasn't looking where I was going!

After a couple of hours, we stopped for breakfast near Dordrecht. I entered a bakery to beg for whatever they would give us, and the worker gave me a loaf of day-old bread. Smiling, I returned outside triumphant, eager to share my bounty with Dan and DJ, when the same bakery worker emerged, handing me three more loaves, not initially having realized there were three of us. The kindness and generosity of people who didn't know us at all continuously amazed me.

We found a nearby park immediately thereafter, and it was my job to spread one avocado into six sandwiches, using the bread from the bakery. In the middle of this task, a very cordial and friendly man approached us, asking to recite a poem by Dante Aguilera in Italian. All I could make from it was that the poem was about something divine, and while I didn't understand a single bit of it, its beauty reminded me of the scene from *Shawshank Redemption*, where Andy Dufrene sneaks into the warden's office and plays a piece of magnificent music for the entire prison, saying, "No one knew what those two Italian opera singers were saying, but it was one of the most beautiful things we had ever heard."

As we left the park and pedaled through the town, there were orange, white, and blue flags and decorations everywhere, as townsfolk emerged to further decorate for a day of festivities. We realized that the morning's peculiar and fortunate experiences were all due to it being Saturday, April thirteenth, All Queen's Day, one of the biggest holidays in the Netherlands. In every town we visited, main streets were alive with vibrant celebrations, full of people singing and dancing in revelry, donning outrageous orange costumes, a nod to the royal family, present in the original National flag and local culture.

The joyous occasion increased my belief in the goodness of humanity, especially when people were in a jovial and jubilant mood. Despite sore muscles and persistent headwinds, we returned to Het Carre faster than expected, enjoying brief breaks amidst the festivities. In one village, locals stopped us as we rode through the center of town, encouraging us to party with them. They offered us free beer and food, which we gratefully accepted. During another pause from riding, as we wound our way north, not yet having recovered DJ's forgotten sleeping bag, we switched bikes, and five minutes into cycling, DJ didn't take a wide enough berth around a pole and smacked into it with the cart, sending himself and it to the ground; his knee swelled up something fierce, and the bone had a small indentation. It bewildered me how he managed to injure himself again, fairly seriously, and within a quarter mile of his previous accident. To let his knee rest, we busked in

Scheveningen the next day, looking forward to a lighter day of riding, after completing seventy miles for two days in a row.

The next morning, we slept in, ate some leftover Chinese food someone had abandoned in the park where we camped, and slowly got underway. Less than one-half hour into the ride, DJ had to stop, dry heaving from intense knee pain. "This is the worst pain in my life," he said in between breaths. Judging by the gnarly scars on his arms, I knew it was serious, so to ease his discomfort, we broke into our emergency supplies and gave him some pain meds and vitamins.

We arrived at the beachside boardwalk we had previously visited and found a spot near an entrance with lots of foot traffic. By lunchtime, tourists were out in force, and Dan was juggling like a speed demon, attracting attention and money from onlookers. He seamlessly flowed between impressive tricks, creating a mesmerizing visual display. Occasionally, he would drop a ball, but rarely enough that the hat grew heavy with coins and bills. Within an hour, he was tired, and I was ready for my first attempt at street performance. With my limited yet growing ability, I juggled for an hour and a half before receiving my first tip—a fifty-cent Euro piece! I felt elated. DJ then took over for a couple of hours before Dan resumed for the biggest rush of the day: people watching the sunset.

While DJ and I took our turns busking, Dan snuck away to a grocery store and returned with a bottle of Scotch and a smaller bottle of brandy. I didn't care what Dan purchased or stole; it delighted us, and we celebrated our first booze since the beginning of our journey. At one point, DJ drunkenly knocked over the Scotch, and I quickly slurped up what had spilled on the sandy concrete walkway. Aerating the alcohol while utilizing my mouth as a vacuum, combined with ingesting sand, was a disgusting combination. But I refused to let it go to waste. We became inebriated and giddy by sunset, having made the most money so far, and were enjoying ourselves immensely. Hardly able to walk straight, we decided it was time to get on our bicycles and ride up the coast, beginning our search for a place to camp for the night.

Knowing it was illegal to camp in public parks in Holland, we had become adept at 'Ninja Camping,' finding dark, out of the way spots that were hard to see, ensuring no car headlights would illuminate us. Not long after, we stumbled upon a park that offered the perfect spot with rolling hills, and I scouted ahead and found a secluded area, though rabbit feces covered it, which earned it the nickname Rabbit Run. We set up the tent, gathered firewood, and lit a roaring fire. Dan surprised us once again with three bottles of quality Chimay beer, which we enjoyed while watching a stunning sunset over the sea. Dan and I ran and jumped over the blazing logs in sheer joy as DJ watched, resting his knee while enjoying the show. The nights were warmer than in Amsterdam, making it more pleasant. Later that night, we all fell asleep for a good night's rest, happy with ourselves, thankful for the warmth, companionship, and adventure.

When we awoke, we found ourselves surrounded by the cutest little bunny rabbits nibbling on the grass. We shrugged off minor hangovers by nearly exhausting our water supply and having a meager but welcome breakfast. As we wound our way back through the rolling hills, searching for the bike path, we were still feeling grateful for the gaiety of the past night and the jovial life we were living together. Starting a day's ride on a bicycle path, as we did that morning, felt like a serendipitous sign of good things to come.

We got moving amidst an early morning drizzle on the Dutch government's vast network of bicycle infrastructure. We had already ridden approximately four hundred miles total and had another full day ahead of us, DJ's knee being rested for as long as we could afford. The path along the beach, complete with sand dunes and patchy grass, held a lovely view as we biked through Strand Wassenaarseslag, Katwijk aan Zee, and Noordwijk. Within the first hour, the wind picked up and brought heavy rain. The North Sea's treacherous nature, with its instantly changing winds, made the day dismal. Heads down, friendly chatter to a minimum, we tried to keep the rain out of our faces. Around lunchtime, the wind turned, the sky cleared, and a warm breeze appeared, which felt incredible. Our long underwear and multiple layers were no longer necessary, making biking more comfortable and aiding in drying us out.

The magnificent beauty we witnessed that day was unlike anything else so far. Famous for their splendor, the tulip fields of Lisse appeared like a mirage when we spotted them from afar. Upon approaching, the distant specks of color turned into rows of vibrant hues, shades, and tints of every part of the rainbow. Perfectly blossoming flowers stretched as far as the eye could see. As these tulips only bloom for a few weeks out of the year, we felt incredibly fortunate in our timing. Soon, workers would come to pick and transport the flowers, distributing them throughout the region. Seeing all the new growth made me consider my personal philosophy of why we give flowers to loved ones, besides their obvious beauty, which can be cynical and comical. Flowers are the genitalia of plants, and giving them as gifts is a subtle reminder of the fleeting nature of beauty and fertility.

The gifts will sit in a vase, and people will enjoy them temporarily, but as they are no longer connected to their roots and source of life, they will inevitably wither, grow old, and slowly lose their petals and decorative luster. After their beauty and aroma fades, people discard or compost them. They are a reminder for the woman, that she, too, will inevitably have her beauty fade, her reproductive organs will only remain fertile for a window of time, and that she ought to use them quickly, before it is too late—preferably with the cordial and friendly giver of said flowers. Nonetheless, the experience of bicycling alongside fields of immaculately maintained blossoms was incomparable to any other view we had had up to that point. It was as if our vision was gorging on the vivid and vibrant smorgasbord of eye candy, lapping up the luscious aromas with our nostrils, perfectly entranced by the all-consuming effervescent experience.

By the time we reached the town center, we felt as drunk as the night before, but this time, on the intoxicating beauty of the tulips. Everywhere, people were smiling, as if the flowers themselves brought happiness and love into the air. We couldn't help but feel the same, escaping hunger and thirst for a brief period. As we continued into the afternoon, we bid a fond farewell to our new floral loves, but the road called, and away we went, pedaling through Nieuw-Vennep, Hoofddorp, past the Schiphol Airport, where our journey began, and lastly Badhoevedorp, all the while, seeing the same signs for Doorgand Verkeer, the meaning still eluding us. After a long day of riding, we found a church awning to escape the rain and sleep under.

We wouldn't return to Belgium for over three months and set our sights on our next host location, a community just over the German border, turning east back toward Amsterdam. Every new location brought intrigue and uncertainty around what we would learn and get to experience. We didn't know where our next meal would come from or where we'd sleep, keeping us on our toes and sharpening our senses for resources we could safely pilfer. Experience taught us to scavenge trash bins near restaurants, cafes, and grocery stores, which often threw out food near its sell-by date. Begging for day-old bread and other discarded food became part of our routine. One day, we turned onto a cobblestone road strewn with onions that had likely fallen off a truck. Hungry, we ate them raw, eyes watering and stomachs rebelling. We later nicknamed it Onion Road.

Churches were usually safe places to sleep, offering overhangs to avoid the rain, though the cobblestones were uncomfortably hard. We constantly kept an ear open for would-be thieves, hoping for the best but preparing for the worst, with Dan always carrying a quick-release knife, fortunately, never used. We developed a set of protocols to live by to help us avoid trouble, the police, and hazardous situations. The foremost being: don't get caught! We prepared meals in turns, but we rarely cooked to avoid attracting attention. Coffee and tea became delicacies, and DJ often rolled and smoked cigarettes, a habit Dan picked up, and then, eventually, I, too, joined in, wanting to feel like a part of the group.

The next morning, as the sun rose, we dusted off our sleeping bags and slinked away to a nearby public park in search of bathrooms. The brief warmth of the morning sun eased our aches, but soon, dark clouds and heavy rain left us sopping wet while pedaling against the wind. Similarly to previous days, harsh weather shortened our tempers, so to avoid arguments, we knew to keep to ourselves as we trudged toward Amsterdam. When we cycled past any pleasant park, we'd assess as a team if it was a good time to stop and rest. We racked up hundreds of miles to our running tally as time went on.

Back in Amsterdam, familiarity felt foreign after so much traveling in unknown territory. We knew where to sleep and find food, as well as local resources, such as the library and central train station. Most importantly, we remembered the layout of the city and spent significantly less time frustratingly lost. Despite our frugality, I finally visited the Rijksmuseum, with DJ joining me while Dan stayed outside with the bikes to busk. There, he met other professional street performers who taught him new tricks and the importance of gathering a crowd. After waiting in line to enter the museum for ninety minutes, DJ and I rushed through the first wing, hoping to see as much of the massive museum as possible, only to find most of it closed for renovation. We did get to witness a hand-selected collection of the best pieces, though, but it was far from the full museum experience.

The uncertainties of each day honed our resourcefulness and strengthened our bond as a team. Our journey became less about the destination and more about the adventure itself. The camaraderie we shared in overcoming hardships as a team, combined with the thrill of the unknown, made every challenge worthwhile and every day an exciting escapade. I'm thankful for the journal entries that help me relive the incredible experiences:

In this scaled-down Rijksmuseum, we found eight Rembrandts, as well as many of his different pupils' works of art... There were still-life tabletops, portraits of wealthy merchants, and landscape artwork, one being an amazing stormy night at sea. A lot of old vases, porcelain, pistols, guns, and rapiers ornately adorned with precious metals and gems were there, too. They were part of the exhibit about the Dutch East-India trading company and the Dutch West-India trading company, which was more of a warlike group that was intent on driving Spaniards and Frenchmen out of the Americas more than developing the trade route. There was quite a lot of history and paintings of naval battles and whatnot to be learned from the museum. I feel like I am slowly developing a major in European History.

Although I hadn't studied art history, the masterpieces in the Rijksmuseum captivated me, especially the canvases that covered entire walls. The scale and detail left me in wonder at how long such endeavors took and what prompted an artist to deem their work complete. Engulfed in admiration, I meandered through the museum like a glutton at a buffet, savoring each artwork, frame, and detail. By the time the museum closed, I realized DJ and I had spent the entire afternoon there, drifting around separately, forgetting even my hunger. I neglected to consider how Dan was doing; I was so completely entranced by the magnificent masterpieces.

My curiosity had gotten the best of me, so I approached the service desk and asked the attendant an unusual question about the sign the three of us kept seeing all around the Netherlands: Doorgaand Verkeer. I still hadn't found DJ, but hoped he would find me on his way out. Either way, I would at least be able to reveal the meaning of this sign when we finally reconnected. After a few failed attempts at pronunciation, I wrote the phrase down, prompting the attendant to burst into laughter. This created a scene, drawing attention in the otherwise quiet lobby, and she self-consciously muffled herself by placing her hand over her mouth. Upon composing herself, she explained it meant 'through traffic,' essentially showing we were on the right path. I felt simultaneously overjoyed to have solved this puzzle and frustrated at the simplicity of the elusive phrase. Amused, I exited the building where I found DJ sitting with Dan and told them both the story. Similarly, they greeted me with uproarious laughter. It became our inside joke and mantra: just keep going—we were exactly where we needed to be.

That night, we snuck back into Camp Zeeburg, which, thankfully, was less windy. The next morning, Dan surprised us, making me think this was becoming a routine of his. This time, he had a special treat: three doses of 2CI, a psychedelic substance, that he had hidden among his vitamins. With our food supply low, he suggested this would provide energy and enhance our day. We also had the three doses of methylenedioxymethamphetamine (MDMA), commonly known as ecstasy, the colorful pressed pill Eddie gave me for the computer repair work I did for him back at Het Carre. Despite having never tried either substance, I trusted Dan's judgment and was eager for new experiences. We agreed to ride for a while and take them on our morning break.

We left before dawn to avoid the camp managers and headed east. We all simultaneously took both pills around nine in the morning, DJ not showing the same reservation he had with Ayahuasca, and within thirty minutes, the combined effects were potent, especially with our empty stomachs. I had no idea what the experience would be like, having no exposure to either substance, let alone together. The day promised to be extraordinary, filled with enhanced perceptions and boundless energy. This journey had become about embracing life, saying yes to new experiences, and being open to what came our way. Rarely did I reject anything, and this day was no exception. As the substances took hold, we set off once more, ready to explore and revel in the adventure ahead. That day's blog provides some rather comical remarks:

We stopped in Amersfoort, right in the shopping district, to clean the bike chains which had gathered rust from the North Sea... We got quite a lot of fanciful eyes from young lasses... After getting lost in a park and having

45

to ask for directions, we came to a crossroads with a lone man sitting on a bench. It felt like destiny. The older man was sitting with his legs bowed out to the sides, wearing old jeans and shoes. It looked as if his legs were about twice as long as his torso, and he wore thick glasses and had a small pack. I asked if he spoke English, and he said, "Just a little," so I asked in Dutch where the next town was. He asked me in English if I had a map, which I replied, "No." He brought out his map and revealed the overall lay of the land, which showed me that the next town was southeast of us, the direction we had been traveling all day. But there was no concrete path to get there, so I just busted out my trusty compass and took the path that went most southeast!

The man twitched as I talked to him, bringing his lower lip up over his upper one in almost a 'bitter beer face' look. We laughed so hard as soon as we were out of earshot. The park was so gorgeous, with tan, red, and brown leaves from the last season and fallen sticks, twigs, and wildlife... Later, we found a street as we came in that was the most postcard-perfect Dutch street you had ever seen. Little orange flags from the Queens' Day celebration still lined the street, and all the houses had brick and quaint orange clay roofs. Two of the residents of a house nearby were looking through their window at us before coming out and offering to take a picture. By residents, I mean two sexy women with nice curves, stylish clothes, makeup, and OGLING us like we were the hottest shit they had ever seen, which we probably were! I was already getting darker with the sun. Dan and I both had our shirts off while DJ had his badass rugged getup on. We were kind of surprised that they didn't invite us in after they took a couple photos for a little of the old 'in out, in out' if you know what I mean!

We covered sixty miles that day, passing through Muiderberg, Naarden, and Eemnes that morning. While cleaning our bike chains around lunchtime in Amersfoort, it only took a single look between DJ and me, with our dilated pupils, to confirm my suspicion that we were in for a wild ride. The initial onset of the experience, otherwise known as coming up, was quite challenging, as the sheer and complete difference of our perception of reality had changed so drastically that it was nearly impossible not to be perpetually smiling. As if the shit-eating grins on our faces and our eyeballs weren't enough, the warmth of the day and the body-high sensations caused us to strip down to shorts, socks, and shoes. Immediately feeling self-conscious over our unusual appearance, realizing how stripping down in a town square had drawn the gaze of many strangers, we quickly mounted our bikes and got back on the road. All of this and the intense energy flowing through my body urged me to keep moving.

We had pedaled slowly earlier in the morning because of DJ's knee, but by the afternoon, it didn't seem to bother him at all as we traveled through the towns Barnevold, Wekerom, Otterlo, Schaarsbergen, avoiding central Arnhem by way of Rozendaal, Velp, Rheden, and De Steeg. We had found a love for being on the road, and that day, it multiplied infinitely. We greeted others on bikes as we passed or overtook them with glee, although they rarely returned our level of excitement—as it turns out, the English, "Hi," which sounds like, "Hai," in Dutch means shark; the looks and facial expressions in reaction to our greetings had a peculiar appearance about them, as if to say, "There isn't possibly a shark here. We are on land!"

We were flying, our wheels turning into wings as we soared along the smooth, even pavement, our elated energy propelling us forward. We covered more ground in a single day than we had up until then, by far. On one straightaway, Dan suddenly took off, sprinting on Lord Pancake, carrying hundreds of pounds in the cart, and try as we might, DJ and I could not even come close to matching his pace. Yet, we didn't worry at all as he became a speck in the distance. Both substances brought us to a place of utter bliss, without a care in the world, only needing to stay hydrated as we sweated profusely, our bodies doing their best to handle these foreign particles, this alien matter our cells dissected, dispersed, processed, and eliminated. DJ even discovered an entire pouch of tobacco that someone had discarded on the side of the road, which made him ecstatic as he had run out a few days earlier.

As the giddy afternoon wore on, our perception of time significantly altered, with hours stretching on endlessly. Our sides hurt from all the laughter, and our cheeks ached from all the smiling. Colors became marvelously enhanced and brighter, smells more aromatic. While I normally needed glasses, because of video games deteriorating my vision, my eyes felt sharp and capable that afternoon. Everything I passed had an aura or hue about it, suggesting an ephemeral quality. I didn't want to wear my boots anymore, so DJ and I pulled over so I could take them off, adding them to our gear, and pedaled barefoot for most of the afternoon. I felt my skin come alive like the living organism it is, as all my senses were enlivened. I could feel the bottom of my feet pressing against the pedals, the pull of my forearms, triceps, and back muscles, and the full connection within my body to the strenuous exercise of creating non-stop forward motion. Above all, I felt engaged by the wind as it passed along the hair on my arms, legs, and head.

This was more of a body high compared to the sensation on Ayahuasca, after which I felt extra connected to my spirit and soul—although the combination of 2CI and MDMA further solidified that presence. I was so connected to myself, present in every moment, while waves of bliss and elation coursed through my body. I smiled all day, often laughing like a child, as I enjoyed every sensation.

As the late April afternoon rolled on, we cycled closer to the border of Germany. Our group desired a more secluded camping spot, not wanting to hide as we continued to enjoy our revelry. Upon passing a military base, there was an eerie field surrounding it where nothing grew. Even the trees on the edge seemed to be dying. Not wanting to be anywhere near it, we kept riding until there was a deep forest, a perfect place to spend the night. As dusk became twilight, we walked our bicycles over lush grass and leaves, shrubs and brush until the lights of the cars along the road disappeared altogether.

I found a very old sock, in military fashion, and several bullet casings, as well as holes in the trees. I realized that this was where the battle of Arnhem took place in World War II, and that seventy years prior, blood and death would have filled this forest. Immediately after selecting our campsite, I gathered sticks, logs, and fallen branches from the forest and carefully prepared a safe space to light a fire, not wanting to accidentally burn the trees down, and us with them. As the nighttime darkness engulfed us, it seemed like there were shadows beyond our own. Yet, our day was so epic and stupendous that we felt no fear, and nothing depressed our merry mood.

Despite not having eaten for over twelve hours, we weren't all that starving but prepared dinner, anyway. Earlier, we begged at a butchery and received sausages, which we cooked with the last of our road-side onions and the few remaining bread rolls for dinner, along with brewing some coffee grounds we had dumpster'd for the following morning. Then we told stories around our campfire. We regaled each other with our finest tales, sometimes from our childhood or teen years or the most recent period at college, where we had all discovered ourselves in very different ways. DJ told us about growing up in the Dakotas and feeling like an outcast, beginning a mischief-filled and counter-culture lifestyle in his teens. Dan told us about his passion for writing, the volumes of books he had read, many from CrimethInc Publications, as well as concepts gleaned from the *Anarchists Cookbook*. We took turns asking each other questions about favorite movies, superheroes, and destinations we desired to visit. Many of these queries led to short debates, rebuttals, and witty banter.

As hours passed, the attentive focus faded as night deepened, and eventually, my companions were ready to sleep. However, my elation and energy left me awake. I borrowed DJ's copy of *The Hobbit* and read that glorious tale of adventure and excitement, danger and lore by the firelight; a reflection of my own journey. I read until I had finally come down from the high of the experience and the exhaustion of the sixty miles of biking, which felt like one hundred. Once fatigue overtook me, I quietly put the fire out, swatted at the increasing and encroaching mass of biting insects, and nestled into my sleeping bag, letting sleep sweep me off to that serene and unknown place where I dreamed beatifically.

Ever since the Ayahuasca journey two weeks prior, I felt more appreciation for the twilight hours. As we awoke in the picturesque and tranquil forest the next morning, that moment was no different, even though the sleep deprivation, sunburn, and dehydration from the experiences of the day before were painful. Nonetheless, I felt grateful for life itself and our ability to have such powerful and transformative experiences. Our cheeks still hurt and our sides ached from all the smiling and laughing, and on top of that, we had a voracious appetite after a full day of activity while consuming little food for twenty-two hours.

Despite going to bed last, I was the first one awake, and feeling my appetite returning, I rummaged through our supplies to see what food we had remaining so I could be prepared for when the other two arose. We had brought some high-density supplies from the States and ate everything we had left; our dried goods, superfood bars, and trail mixes. I'd gotten used to rationing our already meager supplies, so this felt like a poor decision. But hunger consumed us, and we were determined to reach our next community that day: a communal farm where we were certain to find an abundance of food. We finished eating and got a move on, packed up camp, and walked our bikes back to the road. The pace was certainly relaxed compared to the day before, and it took some time to warm up as the sun started to glint and glisten through the dew in the forest.

We turned south toward Nijmegen, which was the last town on my written list on the printed map before the border. I started the day on cart duty and began too hastily, causing myself to be worn out after ten miles, lagging behind the others afterwards. We traveled through Rijkerswoerd, Bredelaar, Waalspront, and Lent as the temperature climbed to eighty-six degrees Fahrenheit, the hottest it had been so far. While nothing bothered us the day before, including the nearly empty food reserves, lack of water, and intense sun, that morning, we were hungry, sunburnt, and dehydrated. After a successful dumpster dive behind a grocery store, which prompted a lunch break, we went east through Beel-Ubbergen, Zyfflich, Leuth, and Millingen aan de Rijn. Fortunately, soon thereafter, we were at the border of Germany, and just across from it was the small town of Keeken Kleve. Our second major community destination, named Vlierhof, was right outside it. We got lost at this point while trying to find our destination and added an extra eighteen miles to the thirty we had already done. The depleted serotonin levels and minimal sleep, combined with that day's challenges, left our energy levels flat and our morale diminished.

By the time we finally arrived at the community, it was past six in the evening and people were already preparing dinner. They greeted us warmly and heartily before inviting us to join them, which we did with great enthusiasm. We had just enough time for a brief tour of the community and to set up our tent before the meal was ready. I'm surprised we didn't startle and surprise them with our voracious appetites, which eventually became a running joke amongst our new friends.

We had just reached our third country, after navigating most of the Netherlands, from the biggest city, to the Southern border, along the coast, and all the way across it, all on little printed maps with some notes and a good sense of direction. There was no doubt that we were getting better at this. As we relaxed in the late evening sun, chatting with our new hosts and getting to know the nearly two dozen people who lived there, we took in the peaceful vibe of the space, enjoying the flat-land views of nature and distant farms. We felt welcomed and at home in a way that we didn't during our first communal experience within Het Carre. We liked our new surroundings greatly and were eager to contribute and learn everything we could.

After dinner, we felt satiated and successful, accomplished and emboldened. I couldn't help but feel triumphant as I took a shower and went to bed, despite my grumpy demeanor from the sunburn, dehydration, and two hours of sleep the night before. We had now cycled over four hundred miles in the last week alone, by far our longest stretch with minimal breaks. The realization hit me we were actually doing what we set out to accomplish, and things were working out for us. We improved at all the various traveling skills learned and had experiences we never expected. Frequently, total strangers aided us, giving us food, guiding us along our path. The moments of authentic generosity and connection moved me toward changing how I lived my life, wanting to be more in service to others; thus, the cycle of kindness was born within me.

Chapter 6
Willing Workers on Organic Farms (WWOOF)

To find our hosts, Dan used a variety of online networks that linked cooperatives, communities, individuals, and groups together. Through them, people wanting to learn new skills could exchange their labor for room and board, education, and connection. We visited Intentional Communities and Ecovillages and learned about WWOOFing, which connected us with like-minded people, most of whom were on spiritual paths and taught us valuable lessons. Vlierhof was unique, managed by an older financier and a small board, while most residents were temporary volunteers from across Europe and the U.S. Among them was a former Flemish boxing champion, a young Dutch DJ, an American man known as Voputu, and his girlfriend. The community also included a few skilled Polish tradesmen specializing in COB building, an ancient technique using a mixture of clay, sand, straw, and water to create load-bearing walls. They transformed old barns into sustainable Earthship-style homes and inlaid tubing within the walls in order to heat or cool them with pressurized water systems.

The land housed a horse, a sheep, goats, chickens, greenhouses, and fields arranged in artistic sunburst patterns. The surrounding ditches were wide and deep enough to contain the livestock without the need for fences. The residents were the primary source of manual labor, with the occasional use of the horse to pull a plow. Goats worked as natural lawnmowers, devouring weeds and bamboo roots. We filled our days

The Cycle of Kindness

with hard work, land management, and food preparation. In the evenings, we often spent our time by a fire, reading or talking with residents while someone played an instrument.

One of the community goals was to rehabilitate disabled, handicapped, or emotionally unstable people in nature to remedy their ailments, often receiving individuals from hospitals or mental health wards. These volunteers, subsidized by the government, never caused issues and worked alongside us in the fields. The climate was harsh in winter, wet in spring, warm and sunny in the summer, and returned to precipitation in fall. The community grew a variety of hardy fruit trees and crops, especially corn, legumes, squashes, beans, carrots, potatoes, onions, leeks, garlic, and brussel sprouts in rows extending from a central circle. This created a beautiful crop design if viewed from above. Our days followed the Farmer's Almanac and lunar cycles, planting and tending to vine plants, leafy greens, and root vegetables based on these systems.

The agreement was simple: work for food. Dan often preferred to live more leisurely, so he would fast for days to avoid having to work, exploring the local vicinity and riding Junior to his heart's content. Prior to our arrival, he desired to gain insight into social interactions based on language, specifically about the lack of ability to communicate. This prompted him to create a social experiment, within which he told the community he was mute and acted as one. Despite slipping up and accidentally speaking a couple times, luckily no one was nearby enough to hear him, he amazingly never got caught. He even impressed DJ and me with his determination in the experiment, communicating through a pen and notepad, even alluring a young woman, Elizabeth, into a romantic attraction without even uttering a word to her.

After three weeks, he and I went for a long walk away from Vlierhof so he could express his thoughts aloud and have some time speaking where no one would hear him. The observations he made about pretending to be mute were profound, as he spent so much more time studying the interactions of others and how they varied in their minutiae of detail, especially how people spoke slower to him, used more expressive and animated hand gestures, had more patience with him, and treated him slightly less-abled than DJ or me. The palpable contrast in my connection with him was significant while in this community. Only within this candid connection, while Dan recapped his time at the community, did I realize how much I missed our incredible kinship that had formed through our discourses in philosophy, religion, anthropology, and a variety of other subjects.

My best friend's willpower and resilience were inspiring, but his thin frame worried me. Yet, he continued to ride most days, sometimes multiple in a row, without eating. The journey became more about connecting with others and the land than riding for me, as I embraced every challenge and experience that came my way. Meanwhile, Dan used his experience of being treated differently as a mute to create a 'Magic Note' to hand to store owners and clerks where we begged for food. He hoped it would yield better results than we had achieved thus far, and it was easier on our pride than mustering up the courage to vocalize our humble requests. It read: "Hello, I am a traveling mute. I am riding a bicycle around the world without money. Any food that you can give me is greatly appreciated. Thank you, and God bless you." We had this translated into Dutch and used it as we rode around with mixed success; but nothing ventured, nothing gained.

One day, a few of us from the community, including me, Dan, and DJ, were outside playing hacky sack and practicing juggling, when someone suggested a game of mercy. I was not a fan, but agreed to play anyway, and ended up bowing out after losing the first game. The final match was a gruesome battle between Dan and the boxing champion, Hauke. On Dan's face, I could see him wincing in pain alongside the simultaneous giddy smile of only a true sadist, his hands bent at such an angle I could hardly bear to watch. I swear I heard bones or joints popping, and before it was over, Hauke picked him up by his hands, flung him over his back, and walked around carrying the poor guy; Hauke defeated Dan, yet the word mercy never left his lips—he was a mute, after all. He exited the playing field triumphantly, shining in his commitment to the facade, seemingly unfazed by the pain. At this point, I was inspired by him more than ever. I gained a newfound respect for my best friend, who dedicated himself to his plan with unwavering resolve. If he could do this, what else was he capable of?

Over our four-week stay at Vlierhof, our days blurred together as DJ and I would work six days in a row, as the normalcy of routine left few differentiating memories. Each Sunday, in reward for our efforts, we were allowed to rest and eat without expectation of work. Dan sometimes joined us, other times he was absent on an adventure. I frequently felt bad for whoever did the grocery shopping, as the amount of food that we could eat was immense; often having five full meals a day, and portions such as two sandwiches, a bowl of muesli, coffee, juice, and fruit for our breakfast. Despite being able to eat as much as we wanted on a working day, I had slimmed down. My new way of life already reduced my weight by thirty-two pounds, yet I was feeling healthy and strong in my body. Besides bicycling, the workouts were farm work and heavy lifting, which built up my back, shoulders, and arms; even my six-pack abs from high school returned.

I nearly always wore just a single pair of shorts, sans underwear, and socks with shoes to protect my feet from the tools, and even then, I sometimes went barefoot. It showed as the long work days tanned my skin. Exercise became a regimen: pushups, pull-ups, running, and farm work. Dan and I also went on long runs with Hauke, on a picturesque dyke alongside a nearby waterway. It was during this transformation that I received one of the most perplexing and interesting compliments when Voputu's girlfriend kept staring at my torso, just above the waistline. She expressed how her eyes were unconsciously drawn toward my groin, similar to how a man's eyes gravitate toward a woman's cleavage, and how the angular lines along my iliac crest captivated her gaze like a sexy tractor beam. Her comment flattered me and gave me a renewed confidence in my body.

Mornings always began early with the call of the native cuckoo bird, followed by stretching and a community meeting to delegate tasks. One morning, I arose at four in the morning to learn how to bake German bread in a stone oven and apple pie made with a lattice crust, both of which turned out delicious. Our days continued to be filled with farming, cooking, cleaning, other chores, and finding time to relax so we didn't completely burn ourselves out. We spent many evenings by a fire in the great room. DJ continued his smoking habit while Dan was gone most days cycling. I repaired computers, updated software, and taught tech skills.

The days stretched with the sun rising toward the summer solstice. Seeds sprouted into plants, and Dan's silent courtship with Elizabeth blossomed through gazes and subtle gestures. He had also intensified his fasting, going eight consecutive days without food. DJ was dedicating more time to meditating, but one afternoon, while balancing on a tree branch, he fell and sprained his ankle. Despite my attempts at understanding, I continued to be baffled at how and why his accidents happened.

As for me, I finished reading *The Hobbit*, then tackled *Machiavelli* and *Ayn Rand*. I improved my baking skills, crafting perfect apple pies. I also noticed our runs growing longer. On one run, to the nearby town of Millingen, I wandered into a festive bar but left quickly, lacking money or identification. Another day, I accidentally entered a military encampment and, fearing I was trespassing, sprinted back to Vlierhof. Our days were an ever-evolving mix of hard work, learning, and unexpected adventures, which grounded us in the journey rather than reaching a destination. A journal entry tells the story:

Back at Vlierhof, the Polish guys had a friend over for a barbeque and Polish vodka! They invited me inside, and I joined them after letting my body cool off outside so I wouldn't stink up the place, even though the smell of cooking meat was probably stronger than me, anyway. I had Polish sausage, pickles, peppered tomato slices, chicken, and BACON!!! I had one piece cooked and two pieces RAW! I guess it's a common thing in Poland to eat raw bacon, a delectable treat that I savored greatly. They had a cool tradition of having one shot glass on the table and pouring the shot for the next person, but never pouring your own. It was so much fun to communicate with these guys! They knew so little English, and I got to use a lot of other communication tools to express what I wanted to say. I've learned a lot of Dutch, German, and Polish words; my favorite being, "Nas Drovia," which is like, "Cheers," or a toast. We polished off two bottles between four guys. I learned some fun drinking tricks and witnessed one-handed pushups done in a fist! It was impressive. We also did triangle pushups, knuckle pushups, and clapping pushups. I cannot believe how enjoyable my life is. I truly want everyone's life to be this good. I don't want this to be extraordinary—it could be merely ordinary!

One afternoon, I had one of my most cherished experiences of my entire trip, as the young disk-jockey, Herman, brought back three-eighths of magic mushrooms; a.k.a. Psilocybin from the Netherlands, a specific strain of Cyanescens that had small purplish-blue caps and long, thin stems. As he was around our age and felt a connection with us, he took one bag for himself and gifted the others to Dan and me. DJ was still recovering from his most recent injury and sat this one out. The community at Vlierhof was against consuming drugs on the premises, so we went into one of the trailers and did it sneakily, hanging out there while waiting for the mind-altering effects to begin. After a half hour of playing board games and building puzzles, we looked up at each other, and with a slow smile that creeped into a massive grin, burst into laughter, falling over onto the floor in sheer amazement and disbelief by the sensations and distortions taking place.

It felt so overwhelming I could hardly talk. Herman needed to go lay down, and Dan could not stop smiling and laughing. We spent a few hours inside, having many hallucinations, which I'll attempt to describe: the walls reverberated in and out, almost like waves were passing through them. They weren't solid but flowing, or they would shake, appearing to move closer and further away from us, most noticeable at the corners and edges. Colors changed and became muted or brighter, and patterns existed everywhere, as if a visual overlay was on top of, or revealed, because of our enhanced vision. The sunlight was brighter and shadows bizarre, taking on qualities of movement that made them feel quite alive.

At one point, I laid down on my stomach as the physical sensations were intense, feeling like my skin was vibrating. I heard popping and other noises in my ears, which was my introduction to auditory hallucinations, an element that was quite surprising and perplexing. I put my hands out in front of me, and they appeared to melt into a puddle, slowly oozing and spreading out in all directions as long as I kept my eyes relaxed and unfocused. But after a few minutes of wonder and awe, I refocused, and they were back to normal; the only time I've ever had this sensation in my life! I was very present with my heightened awareness, especially noticing my digestive system, as I experienced sensations and perceptions at a level I had never felt before. Dan and I were lucky enough to have a pleasant high, while Herman was obviously having a bad trip, rarely talking, but when he did, it was usually about something disturbing, like having sex with animals. After a few of those uncomfortable outbursts, Dan and I decided to enjoy our experience elsewhere. So, we left the trailer, grabbed our bicycles, and hit the road.

There was a massive storm blowing in, evident by the dark gray clouds that were filling up the sky, so we raced along toward the storm, hurrying to get into the last sunbeams as the clouds swallowed up the breathtaking blue above. I have an incredibly fond memory of Dan racing off in front of me, as he was a far stronger rider, and standing up on his pedals in the middle of the road, basking in the last strong ray of warmth before the clouds consumed it too. We stopped along a fence and laughed before gazing off into the storm; getting drenched to the bone all the while.

After the torrential downpour turned into a mild drizzle, still tripping, we returned to Vlierhof and *separately* took gloriously long, hot showers to aid our shivering bodies. After I got out, I noticed a stunning and breathtaking sunset was beginning, and since I still had so much energy, I could not resist going out again into the majestic natural beauty. But first, I went to find Dan to see if he would go on a run with me. I found him back in the tent, resting in his sleeping bag, as he hadn't eaten for seven days prior, and his whisper response was superb. "Run twice as hard for me." So, off I went, across the opposite field, onto the familiar dyke where I began running like the wind, feeling as though my body could hardly keep up with the furious pace of my legs and feet. Five miles in, I found a bench, sat down, calmed my breathing, and enjoyed one of the best sunsets of my entire life.

The lower-level rain clouds had thinned out and moved on, providing a view of some cumulonimbus clouds catching the sun and turning to magnificent warm colors, from bright yellow through orange and red to deep purple in a gradient that deepened over time, enhanced by the contrast of the deep blue hues of the background. I had never seen a sunset so beautiful before in my life. It made me feel connected to God/Source/Creator and blessed by its connective presence, with no thoughts, only feelings. Feelings of gratitude, abundance, awe, amazement, and a sort of worship for the present moment, as it felt more holy than attending church ever had; a true spiritual experience. My attention was only pulled away from this presence when I realized that it was getting dark and colder. I had run off without a shirt on, so I needed to run back just to keep warm.

I took another shower when I returned, the sheer indulgence of it helping me to shrug off the cold, and afterward, I put on warm and comfortable clothes and headed to the library for the night. I reflected on and wrote about the serene journey I had just undertaken. The following day, my legs were certainly sore, and I had a voracious appetite as I had eaten nothing during the psychedelic journey. Yet, I had a newfound feeling, a connection with divinity, which has helped invigorate me for many, many years.

By that time, the familiarity of routine caused my deeply ingrained habits of distracting myself with computer games to pass time idly to return. The proof I had become too comfortable alarmed me, and the urge to move on to our next location returned. DJ and Dan felt the same. Summer was just starting, so we often took long, slow walks through the labyrinth, planning our next steps. We had heard about Rainbow Gatherings: temporary community encampments with the stated intention of living a shared ideology of peace, harmony, freedom, and respect. A congregation of various people made up this community, which took place in remote areas, all over the world, and existed for weeks at a time. These microcosms of a utopian culture sounded idyllic to us, and when we learned that they would hold one just across the border inside the Netherlands, we were eager to experience it, and decided to stay another week at Vlierhof to attend before departing.

Before the gathering, Dan once again surprised both DJ and me with our first ninja training mission; like something out of a video game brought into real life. At nine in the morning, he proposed we go biking together, as he had something pre-planned, a sort of trial. It was a warm day, mostly cloudy, and he told us to wait by a river embankment as he set up our task. DJ and I reflected on our time thus far, and a philosophical point we had been mulling around; namely that anything we do or learn in this lifetime, the purpose of doing it is to become more of who we are. Getting better at individual things causes us to be better at being ourselves, more whole, and complete as a being.

When Dan returned to our location, he explained we would enter a compound inside of which there were two 'bombs' that needed to be diffused, and that there was also an envelope with nine 'keys' with which to defuse them, and that we could not 'drink' them, but instead, were to retrieve them. After ten minutes, an enemy horde would appear and the mission would be over, unless we found a 'weapons cache' to fight them off, buying us another five minutes. However, one of us would have to exit the game at that time. After asking a few clarifying questions, we biked on to where he had found an old, lofty abandoned building, towering around eighty feet tall, made up of four double-height stories, built out of concrete and appearing like a hospital, two elevator shafts and stairways evenly placed on either side.

When the timer started, DJ and I ran over to inspect the building, finding all ground-floor entrances locked, so we climbed up an unfinished metal infrastructure to the second floor. The immensity of the building left us pondering where to go, so we split up, running around, checking each level individually. Bolted doors blocked off all the stairways, and broken glass was scattered around the floors inside the building, so we had to think outside of the box as we searched. About half way through our time, we finally found the weapons cache, and DJ found the keys, a.k.a. chocolate kisses, but before we knew it, the enemy horde arrived, evicting me from the game and leaving my teammate alone. On the top level, an entrance to the stairwells was unlocked, and descending into them, DJ found the basement flooded with water, and right above the water level was one of the 'bombs'—a bottle of wine. Checking the other stairwell, he found the other objective: a six-pack of Grolsch Kanon beer. We celebrated our achievement, brought our booze and chocolate to the top floor, and climbed up onto the roof to enjoy the spoils of our victory!

While sitting on the roof, basking in the sunlight, I had the feeling as though I was being rewarded for my choices and actions, as if the sun had come out because we were successful. The beer was eleven-point-six percent alcohol content, so it didn't take long for us to get buzzed, just as it didn't take long for our buzz to get killed when some locals spotted us on top of the roof and yelled at us until we scaled our way back to the ground floor. Instead of answering their incomprehensible German questioning, which seemed to interrogate us as to why we were up there, we gave a brief apology, got back on our bikes, and had a lovely inebriated afternoon ride.

We bantered about how the well-thought-out level required teamwork, planning, communication, stamina, climbing skills, and quick-thinking. We commended Dan for providing us with this incredible experience and agreed to continue creating similar levels for each other when possible, increasing the difficulty each time. After riding for another thirty minutes, we found a spot along the river to finish the wine and smoke a few cigarettes, one of the first times I would join them in this, which began a new habit for several months. We were giddy and in a playful mood, so as we biked back toward Vlierhof, we found a small hill and rolled down it. After continuing on, I was weaving through a bicycle intersection and collided with some trash bags; more tumbling ensued.

We ended at a lake surrounded by spearmint plants, so after our swim, we came out smelling great. We even found a perfect climbing tree to jump into the water from, and a short platform which I ran down to do a flip off of, but broke the board right as I was launching myself into the sweet-smelling lake. Although I was grateful that I didn't hurt myself then, I didn't walk away from that day without harm, as on our way back to Vlierhof, DJ attempted a bike trick while still drunk, and failing, he crashed into me, ripping off a part of my big toenail. Once back at the community, I cleaned my foot up and passed out early, napping for five hours until eleven at night. When I awoke, I still felt the energy of the day and wanted to be as productive as possible. I read, wrote, and trained in all ways until I fell back asleep.

Many community members were preparing for the two-week long Rainbow Gathering, so we packed up and rode to one of the few hilly, forested areas in the Netherlands near a serene lake, where they were holding the gathering at a private property next to the water. This new cultural environment was unlike anything we had experienced. The central gathering point was a massive teepee tent, surrounded by a large circle for seating around an outdoor fire and several smaller themed hubs. Participants came from Greece, Italy, Switzerland, Belgium, Israel, Germany, and the Netherlands, expanding our network with more offers of places to stay as we socialized.

The property was owned by a few of the members, sympathetic to the ethos of the gathering. They had offered their land for our use and maintained a home that was off-limits to everyone else. The Hare Krishnas, a religious group, brought a unique mobile home where they chanted, "Kirtan," outside of, held drum circles, and sang late into the night. The gathering site had a Zen space, an open-air activity area, a variety of private tents and yurts, several primitive long troughs for human waste, and a communal outdoor kitchen. Pretty tapestries separated spaces and incense was constantly burning. About a hundred

Willing Workers on Organic Farms (WWOOF)

people dressed plainly or in flowing, psychedelic clothes attended this assembly, culminating on the full moon in early June. There were no DJs, speakers, or power—just natural instruments and human voices. It was a beautiful hippie-filled gathering with consciously connective individuals.

The entire economy was based on gifting and donations; no bartering or trade. After each meal, we sang "The Magic Hat" song and passed said hat to collect donations, which always gathered enough for bulk vegetables, grains, nuts, and other essentials for camp meals. Chocolate was a delicacy, and was highly esteemed when gifted. Daily skill-sharing workshops included basket weaving, meditating, sustainable harvesting, seed saving, drumming, guitar playing, and juggling. I met a captivating young woman named Mel, with blond hair and brilliant blue eyes. As it was my first romantic interest on this adventure, and a hopeful reprieve from my lack of sexual interaction for months, I tried to spend time with her daily, but I eventually learned she had conceived a child with another man during the full moon. We kept in touch as friends, closely for months and more infrequently for years; I wondered how completely my life would have changed if I had been the one she was having a child with and how the rest of these stories would have never occurred. It may have changed my gaining the ethos of the cycle of kindness altogether.

Experienced jugglers showed us advanced tricks like four clubs, five balls, and complex passing patterns. I also attempted to learn the guitar and fell in love with the accordion, masterfully played by a nomadic Gypsy. Smoking was common, with tobacco, marijuana, and hashish shared freely. We spent most days high, wearing only shorts, barefoot, and connected to nature. The sense of community was profound, encouraging, and supportive. Everyone was mindful of our impact on the Earth, our carbon footprints, and specifically the land we gathered on. No one carelessly discarded anything and performed all tasks with presence and awareness.

The belief system was a blend of paganism and Hinduism, emphasizing a primal belief in God and the divine within ourselves. This aligned with my journey and evolving self-identity. Everyone's kind and connective demeanor, as well as the warm embraces and familial atmosphere, made it feel like home, a grounding and uplifting experience that deeply resonated with me. I remarked in my blog:

All the people feel like family, and they all treat me like it. There is no hatred, anger, animosity, childishness, greed, or desire. Everyone is happy, and we all get along. If someone needs something, you just ask for a connection, like, "Coffee connection," and someone will hand you a cup of coffee or tell you there is none, and then someone will make some and offer it to everyone. There is a lot of music at the Rainbow Gathering, some well-known songs, a bit of reggae and other peace-focused music, and also Mantras, which are like chants that can induce trances.

Because of Dan claiming to be a mute and members of Vlierhof being present, he mostly remained silent the entire festival, but skepticism had grown and the ruse was up. People still liked him very much, but they didn't like being lied to. My travel companions and I would often go to swim at a nearby lake or sunbathe on its small but sandy shores. The highest point in the Netherlands at five-hundred and forty-five feet was nearby, so we certainly climbed that hill one day and had a glorious view.

Several days into the gathering, I left the grounds to have some alone time. I found a defunct building with a fallen-in roof, but the walls were still intact. It was the perfect place for my ninja training mission. So, the next morning, I told Dan and DJ that it was their turn to be a team and that they would have to collect all nine of our juggling balls from my chosen location. I gave them a couple of hours to mentally prepare while I set the balls back at the building in precarious and hard to reach locations. I climbed as high as I could in a tree and perched one high on a branch. I placed another at the highest point of the brick structure next to the chimney, and others hidden lower, but most of them required climbing. The rules were simple—I gave them fifteen minutes to collect all nine, without other stipulations or parameters.

They quickly saw and collected a few, but the balls higher up baffled them, and they wondered how I had managed to place them there. DJ stood on Dan's shoulders to reach these ones, often throwing another juggling ball, trying to knock one down or using a stick to hit it since they were still out of reach. When time was up, two balls were remaining out of their collection, and I showed my climbing ability, balance, and surefootedness to retrieve them. This amazed them, but they also felt slightly disappointed since this training defeated them and they hadn't conquered my level. Therefore, they wouldn't receive a reward. Sadly, this was the last ninja training level we ever did.

The next day, DJ and Dan cycled an hour each way to check email at a local library and returned with somber faces and bad news. DJ's mother sent him an email saying she was dying, so he needed to go home. He agreed, and she bought a plane ticket for a week later, with his promise to repay her for it after finding work in North Dakota. Before DJ departed, we threw him a farewell party. DJ and Dan bought a bottle of hard alcohol and some beers, and the three of us headed to the lake, reminiscing about the last two and a half months—our incredible experiences, good times, and DJ's numerous accidents.

A little while later, I stumbled back to camp alone and drunk, only to face disapproval from nearly every community member I encountered, as Rainbow Gatherings were alcohol-free. I learned, for the first time, that while the community tolerated smoking, they considered alcohol toxic. I promised not to drink again and was allowed to stay. When Dan and DJ returned, looking roughed up, they received the same lecture while being treated for their injuries. Unsurprisingly, DJ had fallen into the shallow lake, and Dan, trying to help him out, got pulled in also; at least, that was the story they told us. DJ initially lost his glasses but miraculously found them in the lake and bent them back into shape, proving their supposed unbreakable-ability. Between DJ leaving and the three of us getting lectured, we weren't in the mood for singing and dancing that night. I reflected on how the imminent departure and loss weighed heavily on us, marking a somber end to our time together in my journal:

On a sad note, DJ is departing. I've only just begun to know what kind of person he is. I'm going to miss him, like I would miss a limb if you hacked it off with a machete. I truly don't want him to go. My apologies to his sick mother who needs him, but it's just unfair to take him away from his life... Why him? He's in the prime of his life, doing exactly what he wants to be doing. It's quite a sacrifice that shows a great sense of honor within him. I don't know if I could bring myself to go back if I were in a similar situation. It would take a hell of a lot more contemplation.

The last night of the Rainbow Gathering culminated in a full moon ritual and ceremony, and we stayed up all night dancing to the beat of the drum circle until our feet hurt and the sky grew light with the first shades of morning. After a brief rest, we packed up our things, filled our journals with what contact information we could acquire from our new friends, said our goodbyes, and vowed that Dan and I would go to an even larger Rainbow Gathering in Belgium in a month. We then cycled back to Vlierhof to crash into a deep slumber from exhaustion.

We informed Vlierhof members of our intention to leave the community in a few days after we returned. We filled our last days with our usual routine of working and eating. Community members held a small farewell ceremony for the three of us. They praised our hard work and the abundance of crops we planted, one member even expressing gratitude that our efforts would sustain them through the winter. We received gifts of food, dried goods, a dry-seal bag for valuables, and fifty-six euros to help us on our way. Their gratitude and kind words brought me to tears; no one had ever lifted us up like that before. It differed significantly from being called angels or saints after the Ayahuasca ceremony.

The morning after the goodbye gathering, we disassembled the red mountain bike, Fear, and packed it in the cart, ready for the thousands of miles ahead. The only reason we kept the bike was because of Red's, my college girlfriend, expressed intention to join us, who continued to keep in contact. Dan continued his mute act, not wanting to prove the suspicious community members correct. He used his eyelashes for a nonverbal goodbye to Elizabeth and wrote thank you cards to the community members. Afterward, Dan and I hit the road; it was easier for us to leave DJ than for him to leave us. We exchanged heartfelt hugs and farewells with a mixture of emotions. As we parted ways, I wondered if I would ever see him again.

It wouldn't be until after DJ returned home that he would find out his mother wasn't dying; she was just worried about him and wanted him back home where she could keep an eye on him. The deception that cost us our companion and team member outraged us when we found out. The impermanence of our adventure hit Dan and me hard, making us question what might cause us to return home.

Chapter 7
Becoming Brothers

A team of two is a stark contrast to our previous team of three. Nonetheless, spending nearly every waking moment with another man for the next three and a half months created a kinship and a brotherly bond that lasted twenty-four years and felt much longer than that. I am thankful for Dan, and tell people he saved my life in a variety of ways. If it weren't for him, I likely would have continued playing video games, neglecting my health, and eventually, paying the highest of costs. If I hadn't gone to Europe with him, I likely would have disconnected socially from my friends, classmates, and family, losing touch with everyone in my life who wasn't gaming with me. I also would have never met the incredible people on this cycling adventure or accomplished so many unbelievable feats that prompted this book. Last, I likely wouldn't have recovered my ability to trust and have close bonds with other men.

I'm sure Dan appreciated having me along as his sidekick, as he was initially prepared to go without anyone. With DJ gone, Dan would have faced the daunting choice of continuing alone or returning home. But there we were, just the two of us, pedaling into the great unknown. We had navigated foreign countries with unfamiliar landscapes, armed only with a few vague paper maps, a trusty compass, and sheer determination. We intended to cross Germany from west to east in the same fashion.

We started out that first day by pedaling quickly, wanting to cover at least a hundred miles a day, but our pace slowed as we felt the loss of DJ, our reliable third companion and the jester whose every mishap made us laugh. No more hacky-sack games, push hands tournaments, or DJ's infectious humor. While I welcomed the thought of needing to take fewer smoke breaks, Dan and I still took breaks to light up a cigarette or spliff in DJ's honor. I commented in my blog:

We left Vlierhof and said goodbye to DJ. Both Dan and I teared up. It was very difficult to actually say goodbye to him. We've talked about him a bit since... Not only is he a nice, friendly guy who is usually smiling, but he provided such a different dynamic to our group. He is so amazingly random, interrupts himself mid-sentence, and brings an essence of truly proper debauchery to the group.

Our journey continued, but the mood had shifted, marked by a bittersweet resolve. We didn't have any maps of where we were going and could only estimate how long it would take to reach each destination. We decided to let the journey be the fun of it and recognized we would get there when we got there. Fortunately, Northern Germany is pretty flat, making our riding relatively easy, even in low spirits. Plus, we had longer days tanning our hides. The enjoyable riding weather was just right, without being too hot and often giving us a smooth tailwind. We were thankful there were more trees and forests than in the Netherlands, which offered us ample hidden sleeping spots. Occasionally, we would sleep on the inside of a turn on a country road, knowing that the headlights would never illuminate us, and that we could hide in the darkness.

The first day out quenched our wanderlust, with roads rarely going in the exact direction that we wanted. Sometimes, we would start out heading in our desired direction, northeast, but eventually, we'd be going northwest or southeast. This flustered us, and so, to boost morale, Dan came up with an agreement: at every intersection when it was unclear which was the best way to go, we would play rock paper scissors, and whoever won chose, whoever lost didn't complain. Those were the rules, and it served us well. It felt as though we were crookedly meandering across the farm-dotted countryside; our travel route looked rather zany when we attempted to draw it later, and occasionally, we went in circles, or at least, the furthest thing from a straight line as possible. This added many more miles every day, as we passed through Bedburg-Hau, Kalkar, Rees, and Isselburg, crossed back into the Netherlands without realizing it, until seeing more Doorgaand Verkeer signs and towns named Dinxperlo, Aalten, Lichtenvoorde, Groenlo, Eibergen, Haaksbergen, and

Enschede. We then crossed back into Germany and through Gronau, Bad Bentheim, Samern, Salzbergen, Lunne, Messingen, and Freren. My journal reiterated these points:

We were zig-zagging across the country. It ended up thoroughly frustrating me. I just wanted to go in the right direction. It is more difficult to bike in Germany than in the Netherlands... We got to see more scenery, some amazingly beautiful and fertile lands, tons of farmsteads and crops, several small villages, and other quaint little sights. I had to take a small nap in the middle of the day because I got so frustrated about not being able to go in the right direction. Dan helped me realize: we came here to be free, not to be obliged to arrive at a specific place at a specific time. I have begun to think a lot about freedom, what it precisely means, and how freedoms are constantly given up, and for what? "Those who would give up essential liberty, to purchase a little temporary safety, deserve neither liberty nor safety," Benjamin Franklin once said. He sounds like an anarchist to me!

Dan's advice and perspective were a constant help, as I continued to admire and look up to him. As our teamwork solidified, we got to where constant communication wasn't necessary. I could simply point at food, water, or a tool during maintenance, and he would hand it to me. We also improved our ability to identify bicycle maintenance needs and perform them in a timely manner without too much headache. This was a vast improvement from taking hours on our first repair job. Although, if it weren't for the complicated servicing tasks, we wouldn't have met such peculiar characters. My blog expounded:

While fixing the bikes, an older man walked out of his home and saw a small flaw that he could help fix. We were a little wary of the guy. He invited us to come back to his house, and we said, "Thanks," but then decided to bike off; he had a strange Nazi-ish tattoo, and his body had an odd, disfigured manner. A few minutes later, a car came down the road beeping his horn at us, so we pulled over, and he gave us a wrench, a couple screws, and nuts and said, "Here you go!"

Another time, we got lost on an increasingly smaller, less maintained road until we ended up on a single-lane path. Suddenly, tank tracks took over where the road used to be, concrete slabs with precise slat-openings.

Our bicycles fit perfectly, but we had only a two-inch-wide margin of error. Eventually, the cart's wheel fell into a rut, causing a couple of bicycle tube punctures. That's when we realized we didn't have a bike pump. This was a moment where I felt words were needed, nearly yelling at Dan, who was responsible for our repair kit. "How could you not bring a bike pump?!" Fortunately, after walking into the next village and knocking on doors to ask for help, an older man in a nearby town gave us his.

We became a great team, splitting the responsibilities to increase our cohesion and comfortability. When we stopped for lunch, one of us would busk while the other roamed the town to dumpster dive or beg. Our translated Magic Note helped significantly in Western Germany but less so in the East, leaving most of the work up to us. Sometimes, we'd have no other option but to glean produce from fields. Once, Dan found a strawberry farm while wandering around as I napped in a grassy clearing. Upon returning, he shared his plan to sneak into the opposite side of the farm, where the workers were picking the fruit further away. He expressed concern as one major risk was one man on horseback. His plan involved army crawling in, filling our Nalgene water bottles with strawberries, and sneaking out again undetected, eating as many as he could along the way, of course.

I was nervous, but didn't want to shy away from this risky endeavor, as his excitement and eagerness seemed insatiable. He was not to be dissuaded. So, I stayed with the bikes somewhat hidden by trees, facing away from the plantation, ready for a getaway. I watched as he snuck through the trees, army crawled to the ripe strawberries, and started stuffing our bottles and himself. As he was getting ready to crawl back, the man on the horse spotted him, and was galloping over to catch my friend, the thief. Dan immediately stood up and sprinted to my location. I couldn't peel my eyes away as the horse drew closer, quickly covering the small distance between my sprinting compatriot.

It seemed as if he had caught Dan as they reached the end of the field, but just before being captured, Dan managed a massive leap over the deep trough that was used instead of a fence. The horse reared up, nearly throwing the rider to the ground, not wanting to hurt itself over such a crevasse. Dan hit the far embankment, scrambled up it, while the horseback rider steadied himself and charged toward the nearest road opening where there was no ditch. I unhitched our bicycles, mounted Junior and steadied Lord Pancake, who was carrying Hangar, ready for Dan to begin our getaway. Once in the saddle, we immediately sprinted down the road and heard a truck engine starting behind us, creating a sense of urgency.

We turned down the first road we came to and continued sprinting, choosing whichever passage had less visibility. We dodged down small roads and took nearly every turn we came across, knowing all we had to do was get out of eyesight, and then far enough away that it was no longer worth their time continuing to pursue us. An hour of fast cycling later, we crossed a county line, and upon confirming no one was following us, we looked at each other and burst into laughter. Once we collected ourselves, we found a cement picnic table alongside the road, and sat down to eat the most delicious strawberries of my life, amidst snickers and jests and the regaling of the entire experience from his perspective. I appreciated his gusto and courage. He did things that most humans don't dare to do.

With the longer days approaching summer solstice, we consistently met our goal of riding around one hundred miles per day. However, we were still rarely traveling in direct lines toward our destination. I'd often pull out the compass after miles down a road to realize how far off course we were going. Days passed leisurely, as we wandered in the general direction we needed to go, enthusiastically debating video games, comics, philosophy, and the meaning of life.

We loved hypothetical questions, such as, "If you could create a hybrid animal out of any two creatures that would become a lifelong companion, what would you choose? Which traits from each would it have, and how would this mythical beast benefit you?" Often, debates arose around which superhero would win in a hypothetical battle. Discussion consistently focused on the difference between anarcho-syndicalism, anarcho-communism, anarcho-individualism, socialism, and other viable systems, as we weighed their strengths and weaknesses, comparing and contrasting their up and downsides. We designed our ideal community by formulating concepts, structures, and guidelines. Each of us concocted our own perfect design, including who would be in it, where it would be, and how we would organize it. We created visions for our lives, dreamed about a world free of war, where humanity was united as a species and no longer quarreled amongst ourselves.

The Cycle of Kindness

One afternoon, we were cycling alongside a forest when a massive cloud of insects suddenly came out from the trees, apparently lured by my pheromones. The little flying beasts would dive bomb me, slapping into my skin by the dozens, while Dan had only a few gently buzzing around him. He cackled like a hyena at my misfortune. I was thankful to be wearing glasses and had learned by then not to ride with my mouth open. I grew increasingly frustrated by his mocking and teasing and began sprinting, hoping to outpace the insects, which finally worked after about a mile. I temporarily harbored some bitter emotions against Dan for his playful jokes, which I took to heart more than I normally would have because of the harassing bugs. Later, Dan recommended I sit in a swampy marsh somewhere, atoning with the insects, becoming one with them, like a superhero comic book character who could control the insect world. I refused to play along, though, thinking the whole idea stupid. As we cycled past Furstenau, Bersenbruck, Badbergen, Quakenbrück, Essen, Cloppenburg, we found ourselves in the Zweckverband Naturpark Wildeshauser Geest, the largest nature park in Lower Saxony, a unique landscape of woodland, fields, moor, and heathland. Little did we realize this was a well-known area for its serene cycling.

It took two and a half days of riding and adding nearly three hundred miles to our tally to reach Bremen, a funky city, with a lot of old walls and architecture. We felt highly accomplished when we arrived. Cycling across a foreign country was no easy feat, let alone within the approximate number of days we estimated it would take us, and without maps. From Vlierhof, a few weeks prior, I reached out to two of my pro gaming buddies, a couple, Becky and Cam, who lived there and agreed to put us up for a couple of nights. After hundreds of hours spent online together, it was the first time we ever met in person, the four of us hanging out in the evening, eating junk food and drinking beer. All the while, they played the game we met within, my old addiction, while I laughed and reminisced about those times, staying up late into the night on unceasing virtual raids for epic loot and glory.

Beguiling old stone buildings, as well as elaborate and magnificent fountains that were a staple of old European city centers, the town hall was picturesque, even holding a famous statue of Roland nearby. It was here that we wandered onto the Schnoor without realizing it, acclaimed as one of the coolest streets in the world. We avoided the bars and pubs as we didn't have spare money to spend, and our busking attempts weren't very lucrative. Dan was devotedly Catholic, so whenever possible, we would also enjoy the ornate decorations within churches, the cathedral in Bremen being extraordinarily beautiful. Even though my parents had also raised me Catholic, going through all the rites of passage like baptism, first communion, and even being an altar boy in high school, I lost the faith shortly thereafter and have been studying world religions ever since. It's amazing to me how many of them tell nearly the same stories with only slightly different names of characters and details.

As we passed through new cities and towns, we would seek out a local library to check email and update our blogs once a week or so. Our families had no other way of hearing from us, and I'm certain they were relieved every time they got an update, knew we were alright, and had a vague idea of where we were and would be going next. We aimed to calm their fears by assuring our families that the local culture and residents here were accepting of us and were frequently helping us. As I recalled in my journal:

We always find that people are generous when we need it the most, or at least, when they think we do. We got to Bremen on Wednesday and found a little gathering in the center around a small stage, with blow up jumping apparatuses, toy cars to play on, the longest foosball table in the world and more... Dan started juggling and made a little money. We also checked the trash cans in the area as there were plenty of restaurants nearby and had a downright feast. We both got full and even had a little bit of food to save for later. We also found some candy in one of the bins! One angel of a stranger bought us food after seeing we were eating out of the trash cans. Sometimes, people can be so nice. She didn't even want to say hi or for us to see her face. She just held out the food. We could feel her say, here, you need this, although she said nothing.

This consistent generosity and kindness had eroded my belief that humans were evil, selfish, and corrupt. As I stopped focusing on the realm of politics and had many encounters with strangers, mankind was winning me over. This newfound faith brought optimism and altruism out of me, and I interacted with locals in a noticeably more pleasant and trusting manner. As I noticed how my positivity influenced whoever I interacted with, they responded in kind, and the cycle of kindness grew and perpetuated itself.

As adventures in Bremen continued, we frequently wandered through downtown areas, relishing the World Cup viewing centers, cultural hubs, and the atmospheres they created. The 2006 World Cup in Germany was my prime motivation for touring the country. I hoped to catch games in Hamburg and Berlin, even dreaming of snagging a free ticket to the finals, although I knew it was highly unlikely. As Germany's wins fueled celebrations across the nation, villages erupted in song and dance. People drove around waving flags, marking a resurgence of national pride unseen since World War II. While Germany didn't play every day, the entire country, and Europe at large, glued themselves to their televisions during matches. Spontaneously, we joined in celebrations as we came upon them, enjoying the cheer and camaraderie, as well as a sense of community and belonging.

After Bremen, we cycled through Lilienthal, Grasberg, Wilstedtermoor, Tarmstedt, Westertimke, Kirchtinke, Badenstedt, Zeven, and Heeslingen, and we found a public park to camp in. As darkness fell, mosquitoes attacked in waves. The only good part about this was that, unlike earlier, they didn't single me out. They were relentless, biting both of us through our clothes. We swatted and clapped at them, killing many, and Dan decorated his pants with a mosquito graveyard, like dog tags displaying his confirmed kills. Finally, we gave in, allowing them to feed on us so we could set up the tent. Afterward, we dove inside, killing the few that got in with us. It was an ordeal unlike anything I'd ever experienced, and I felt no remorse for the pesky bugs I'd killed. Later on this adventure, I learned the poignant joke; if you think you're too small to make a difference, try sleeping in a tent with a mosquito!

We continued pedaling northeast across the country, through Wangersen, Ahlerstedt, Hollenbeck, Harsfeld, Grundoldendorf, Neukloster, Buxtehude, Neu Wulmstorf, Neugraben, and Brakenburg before struggling to find a bridge crossing into Hamburg. Our journey was also being driven by a desire to experience Berlin, underground raves, and the Love Parade.

Nonetheless, the excitement of the World Cup, summer extroversion, and our growing bond made these weeks unforgettable. Navigating into Hamburg posed a major challenge because of bike restrictions on major bridges. After being directed to wait at a bus stop immediately prior to one such bridge, we did so as we prepared to explain our situation to the first bus driver that arrived. We fortunately met a sympathetic public transportation operator who helped us cross for free, although we comically struggled to lift Hangar onto the bus and mount our metal chariots to the front. Arriving in the large port city amidst another victory celebration, we scavenged for food and did some busking. By the end of that day, we reached our next community destination within the city: Brut N Rosen (Bread and Roses). We were exhausted and ready for rest. Before beginning our trip, Dan had found this organization, run by nuns, that aimed to feed the homeless and bring them to their Lord and savior: Jesus Christ.

After a few days of chores and menial labor tasks, excursions into the city center and simple meals in contemplative silence, I felt ready to depart. During this time, Dan gave me a journal he found on the religious bookshelves, marking a shift in how we recorded our journey. As our time away from technology grew, he wanted to ensure I kept recording my experience. It became a tool for self-reflection and improvement, strengthening our bond as brothers on this adventurous odyssey. I was and am so thankful that he invited me along with him, as I stated in my first handwritten entry:

I've been using the word 'perfect' a lot on this trip, yet appropriately. The perfect day, sunrise, temperature, camping spot, or resting spot. They do feel perfect. They are exactly what we need. I call this trip the best decision of my life. Dan and I talk in the plural, think the same things at the same time, and are more conscious of what is best for us both. It's like women synchronizing their lunar cycle after living together for a while. He never ceases to amaze me. I'm always learning new things about him, how he lives and treats others. It honors me to keep the company of such a great man. I have promised to never be his foe. We've recommitted to our vow of remaining together on this journey until after Greece.

Our stay at Brut N Rosen marked a departure from our previous community experiences. It stood in an urban environment and the nuns ran the place with strict order and organization. As usual, however, we volunteered for room and board, receiving a small room with bunk beds to stay in while undertaking tasks like scrubbing bathrooms and tidying their small church. In line with my loss of faith in the church, I was relieved that our five-night stay prevented us from being there during Sunday mass. Yet, these sisters offered charity, grace, and humility; lessons worth learning.

Outside our volunteer hours, we explored Hamburg, marveling at its architecture and bustling port. The city's intricate network of waterways brought Venice to mind. Despite our tight budget, we soaked in the metropolis atmosphere, occasionally busking for extra cash. During our stay, we stumbled into a protest against deporting illegal immigrants, and ironically, on the same day, we realized our own visas had expired. Yet, the main draw for me in Hamburg was the World Cup village. Every game drew massive crowds, with even the group stages capturing the city's undivided attention, especially when Germany played. It was a time of camaraderie and celebration, where even the pouring of beer paused for the love of the game. My journal was accurate about our initial experience of Hamburg, getting lost finding our host, and two rather bizarre occurrences:

Germany has just defeated Sweden, and there was a giant party of people driving around in cars, singing, honking, and waving flags; general revelry was everywhere. It's legal to drink in public in Germany. They produce so many types of beer it's astounding. We used the Magic Note, and Dan said that the chick working seemed like she'd rather be out celebrating but got stuck with the shift, so she was happy to stick it to her boss and gave us about twenty Euros worth of sandwiches, good bread, and lots of desserts. A little later, we found a huge waterfront festival with an illuminated foundation show, which later proved to be a good place to juggle and relax... I cut out a newspaper clipping of the fanfest area, filled with over one hundred thousand people, all affixed on one screen watching the game. This zone was right next to a famous area of Hamburg, Saint Pauli, which is most notorious for its history with prostitution, live sex shows, and other various XXX paraphernalia. It's famous now for the big part of it containing bars, taverns, clubs, and discotheques!

Later, we got lost trying to return to Brut N Rosen. We biked around Hamburg for about three hours trying to find it, asked for directions twice in the process, and finally located it around ten at night... The other crazy circumstance in Hamburg came when Dan was juggling, and I was watching our stuff. A man with a completely shaven head, button-up shirt, nice slacks, shoes, and a big wooden cross came to the market-area where we were and started preaching in German. At first, he was doing it to a compact disc on a stereo and then later, on his own. He also had a bible, a bottle of water, pamphlets, and a towel to wipe the feverous zeal-filled sweat from his head. This completely ruined our busking attempt. It was amazing to me how many people came by and shouted back, "Amen!" to him. Although, plenty of people gave him scoffed looks of disdain, as if they were embarrassed for all of Germany. It was hard to decipher, only learning German for four weeks and practicing for a mere five days, but I caught him preaching against false idols like Harry Potter and Mickey Mouse. I assume most of the rest was as extreme based on audience expressions and gestures. I was so surprised to see religious extremism still present. It was North Germany, which was described to me as 'cold and distant' compared to the warm hospitality of the southern areas like Bavaria...

While busking, a pane of glass broke several stories above Dan's head, shattering after falling on the ground nearby him and crashing in all directions. Because of juggling and other reflex practices, he dodged the pieces of glass in a split second. People came up to him, made sure he was okay, and then proceeded to give him food and money, basically for being unbelievable. We are on our way to becoming super heroes!

In contrast to Dan's mild interest in soccer, my passion for the sport ran deep, rooted in childhood dreams of scoring goals on a professional level. Standing amidst cheering crowds during the World Cup games, I felt a sense of belonging, reliving my earlier days playing the sport and memories of watching pivotal international matches with my father. After each game, I'd bike back to our community, replaying the highlights in my mind.

Our time at Brut N Rosen passed quickly. With our sights set on the Rainbow Gathering in Belgium, which was at least a full week's ride away, we departed Hamburg on the fourth morning and raced toward Berlin. We passed through the countryside towns of Volksdorf, Lutjensee, Trittau, Schwarzenbek, Lauenburg, Boizenburg, Amt Neuhaus, and the Elbetal Nature Park, hugging the Elbe River for some time, then Friesack, Nauen, and into the immense urban sprawl of the biggest city in Germany while relishing the relatively flat terrain.

We covered another two hundred miles in three days, bringing our total to over eighteen hundred miles in our first three months, with only four weeks of real riding. The rest of the time we had spent in Amsterdam, Het Carre, and then Vlierhof. The long days of June afforded us about fourteen hours of daylight, which we took full advantage of to cover over one hundred miles every day, despite rarely traveling the most efficient route and having started out riding only thirty-five miles per day. Our joy grew with our confidence. We were truly accomplishing our goals and improving our abilities, everything becoming easier as we did. Our trust in the cycle of kindness increased into a solidified confidence as we began to believe nothing awful would befall us.

This far into our journey, our biking skills had also improved tremendously, allowing us to perform tricks, such as riding without our hands touching the handlebars, which eventually turned into juggling while cycling. A picture from this period shows me relaxing, feet up on the handlebars, cruising alongside a field. Dan would stand on his seat on long stretches of slight downhills, not needing to pedal to keep momentum, or he would lie flat with the seat against his lower abdomen, flying like Superman. Occasionally, an error during our tricks would send us hurtling into the ditch nearby, amidst cries of pain and shrieks of laughter.

Traveling through ancient towns evoked a sense of nostalgia, imagining the lives of past generations amidst cobblestone streets and historic bridges. Many of the forests reminded me of my native Oregon, with large lush firs and pines surrounded by the underbrush of ferns, wild grasses, bushy plants, and a thick ground cover. Entering East Germany brought subtle changes in the atmosphere, with people appearing less friendly as our resources dwindled. I later calculated we were burning over twelve thousand calories every day of riding, and despite consuming as much as my stomach could hold as frequently as I could, especially when we were in communities, it rarely felt like I was getting adequate nutrition.

Nearly all of my body fat had fallen off me. I was mostly muscle, skin, and bone. One night, we slept in an orchard just off the side of a road so we could see the night stars; I struggled to sleep because of the incredibly bumpy ground. I awoke the next morning frustrated and in pain, and vented my bereavement to Dan, to which he replied he slept like a baby and that his spot was comfortable. After he got up to urinate, I rolled over into his spot and found it was even bumpier and more uneven than mine. I had to laugh at his positive perspective, but struggled to maintain pace that day. Despite the challenges, our journey continued, fueled by determination and the thrill of adventure. Aside from occasional frustrations, I heralded Dan's amazing abilities:

After leaving Hamburg, we had one day of some pretty rough problems: getting lost off roads onto dirt paths, abandoned roads, or worst of all, more tank tracks... After four flat tires from going down an old, steep, bike path with sunken ruts and large jagged stones, a piece of copper stuck in and slashed our tire on Hangar, which came detached from Lord Pancake. Amazingly, Dan was able to catch and hold it with the back of his foot for the rest of the descent. His feats of magnificence just keep on coming.

The following day, we decided to have Dan head into the next big town and buy a new tube. Unfortunately, on the way back, he went eight miles in the wrong direction and got completely lost; I became worried while idly hanging out in a park for four hours, having no clue where he was. After lunch, we realized we had another flat and had to walk around a fairly nice, ritzy area trying to find a replacement. The only woman I could find ended up giving us another full lunch of yogurt, bananas, meat, cheese, and veggie sandwiches, as well as sparkling apple juice; all of which would've gone bad had we waited to eat them, so we sat back down and had a second lunch. Afterwards, we were full to the brim, laughing at our luck at the things people give us when we simply ask for help.

One of my favorite nights came as we closed in on Berlin, cycling through a small town called Barenthin that appeared empty, except for one long house on the outskirts that seemingly held all the residents of the village. After passing it, my intuition spoke to me saying to go back. I fabricated the excuse of asking for water, hoping the person who answered the door would want to give me more than my humble request. As we approached, a small dog ran up to me barking, with the owner following shortly behind. As I cordially leaned over to pet him, the owner said something to me in German. I responded I didn't speak much

German, but fortunately, she spoke English. She asked the usual questions, such as where we were from and where we were going. Then, before I could ask for water, she offered some and asked for Dan and me to meet the others. There was such an air of celebration inside that the people, curious about who these two bicycle travelers from America were, as well as what we were doing in their town, immediately invited us in, got us drunk, and fed us until we were stuffed.

It turned out that two young members of the village had just consummated their courtship with a wedding reception and promptly left for their honeymoon. This party showed how happy everyone was for them. Even though we were eager to get to Berlin, the hosts were too inviting to object, as the whole merry bunch had a demeanor that was so festive and generous that the offer was undeniable. People even wanted to take pictures with us because we looked so different from them, myself being a deep shade of brown by this point, and Dan being unusually tall with uniquely identifying tattoos. One resident offered their backyard as a camping spot, which we graciously accepted despite the difficulty of erecting a tent while inebriated. Before passing out, we ate some sausages they had given us—not because we were hungry, but because we were afraid that they would spoil and rot; both in calorie intake and supplies, we couldn't afford to waste a thing.

The next morning, I slept in while Dan was up early, exploring our host's garden. He came across some of the biggest bunny rabbits he had ever seen. He took one out of its cage and played with it as the giant hare frolicked with a few others already outside. My hangover was a force to be reckoned with, keeping me from enjoying the same moment, but fortunately, our hosts had cooked us a whole breakfast and laid out a delightful spread of eggs, rich cured meats, which I'd never tasted before, bread and marmalade, pickled items, coffee, tea, juice, and scones; a truly delicious meal!

We conversed with the older couple while eating, and informed them where we had been and intended to go, which astounded them. By the time we were ready to go, it was already nine in the morning. The sun was hot and high in the sky, and we didn't want to put off our progress any longer. When we said our goodbyes to our gracious spontaneous hosts, they gave us even more gifts, including maps of Germany and nearby countries, as we didn't have any, an entire loaf of bread, and a massive meat log that must have been at least two pounds, and while we were unsure what kind of meat it was, we didn't care as it was free food.

We cycled for nearly six hours before getting hungry again. In the middle of a long summer afternoon, we stopped in the shade of a church alongside a graveyard to rest and eat. We had no idea how long the meat would stay good for, and as I knew nothing lasted long unrefrigerated, we devoured the entire thing and most of the bread. Whilst sitting and talking, speculating about how long it would take to get to Berlin and ruminating on what we wanted to do while there, we remained puzzled about what kind of meat we had just eaten. Because of the appearance, texture, and taste, I knew it wasn't pork, beef, chicken, turkey, or lamb. Suddenly, Dan realized that it was rabbit... None other than the cute, adorable deceased relatives of the friends he had made that morning and frolicked with in the yard. He felt emotionally ill, so much so that he eventually became sick to his stomach and went around the corner of the church to vomit in private.

Once he could finally continue, he remained silent for the rest of the day. By nightfall, he told me he didn't want to eat meat anymore, and that anything we received from that point on would be mine. He was going vegetarian. As he was already thin and possessed a lanky and wiry build, I worried about him getting proper nutrition and enough protein. His ability to fast for days on end and maintain energy levels reassured me, and I was more mindful to give him greater portions of all meat-free foods from then on. This became a pivotal turning point in his life; he would eventually go vegan and gluten-free, leaving our diets to be stark contrasts of one another, myself eating anything I could get my hands on; him sticking to what people harvested from the soil. Around this time, he had also started alternate-day fasting. When he was carrying the heavier weight of Lord Pancake and Hangar, he would eat, and when he was on the lighter-weight-bearing Dutch cruiser, he would fast, still keeping up with me going one hundred miles a day. His willpower and determination never ceased to astonish me. I was traveling with a living legend.

Chapter 8
Berlin

We made it into Berlin the following afternoon, after an epic moment that morning when we came across a giant watchtower, nearly seven stories tall at an intersection where we didn't know which way to go. Despite having recently gained maps, I was not yet used to reading them and was uncertain of where we were. We yelled up to the men in the tower, and a man poked his head out, but they couldn't understand our question because of the language barrier. So, we simultaneously yelled, "Berlin!" at the top of our lungs. He pointed us in the right direction.

As we entered the city some forty miles and five hours later, we found it surprising how long it took us to cycle from the outskirts to our destination near the center. It reminded me of our very first day getting into the heart of Amsterdam, and that, somehow, what we were doing had a sort of cyclical nature. While each was different, the similarity of cities blended together, and I grew to prefer the open countryside over the chaos of crowded urban streets.

I recorded my journal entries almost entirely in my new paper diary during this period, as we would get up at the crack of dawn, pack up, and leave our ninja camping spot before anyone saw us, and be on the road and moving nearly all day, minus breaks, until nightfall, where we would find another hidden sleeping location. At one point, I didn't post anything online for over a month; only hindsight shows me I could have left my parents, relatives, and close friends in a state of worry, unsure of my whereabouts and whether I was alright.

In Berlin, amidst the World Cup frenzy and the entire city having no vacancy, as well as police being on the watch for loiterers and vagabonds like ourselves, we desperately needed a place to stay. Through our network of intentional community connections, we discovered there was an organization in the area called BUNDjugend, akin to Greenpeace for young people, dedicated to environmental stewardship. Their mission resonated with us, making it the perfect refuge. Naturally, we headed there. Upon arrival, we explained our predicament and offered to work for accommodation. They agreed to host us for six days, and immediately put us to work loading a truck with old furniture and trash, which we gratefully did. The community complex buildings were eleven stories tall, and they gave us a rooftop with a magnificent view. Its small gardens and yoga space made it feel like a home, something we were devoid of for a long time.

We made connections within the community that same night, offering our services wherever we could to make a positive impression quickly. The following morning, we teamed up with two young German women, Julie and Zola, as the same truck needed to be reloaded and emptied at a dump station. Showing off our strength, we performed the task topless. When space ran out, we disassembled the remaining furniture and repacked it efficiently, thanks to my Tetris skills. Dan noticed some of the chair legs were perfect for juggling and delighted onlookers, including our new friends, with his flashy skills.

On the Fourth of July, lacking any familiar American traditions, we embraced the warmth and hospitality of our new environment. While we craved the comforts of familiar things, we felt welcomed by the kindness of this organization and our two lady friends, which turned a potentially difficult situation into a memorable and enriching experience. Our handcrafted juggling clubs, which aided us in busking as we refined our skills with them over time, remain a testament to that chapter and are still in Dan's possession today. That first night, after settling in, I finally posted a blog entry after an entire month, reflecting thoughts about my future and my idealism:

I have one dollar in a bank account and over fifty thousand dollars in debt, no car, no possessions, nothing. It's hard to know if I will ever go back to the States. I already have places here I could live in for years and enjoy greatly. I can't wait to go to France, Spain, Italy, and Greece and see what the places there are like. I love seeing and working with communities to learn new trade skills, ideas, and ideals. But right now, I'm living a dream life, I'm at the world cup...

The following day, my mind reflected upon the social interactions and added to the blog post:

The German strictness of government still exists in many social services. Rules are rules, strict, unforgiving, immobile, and no longer associated with negative groups like Nazis. While they are described as cold, uncaring people, it fades away with the generations. The older people in the area immediately see us as foreigners. A smile or greeting does not lighten their demeanor. I have always enjoyed smiling at complete strangers and seeing them smile back. But to see them maintain a frown or bitter face nearly breaks my heart. Why can people not be warm, caring, and loving to others? I have so much love; it feels limitless. I want to share it with the whole world. I want to give them peace, equality, and happiness. I want everyone to have great lives. I want the potential of mankind to expand. I want to unleash the great, and hopefully positive, capabilities of humanity. No more fear or hatred as enemies against each other. Instead, one world working together.

After driving to a landfill and dumping piece after piece of the debris until the truck was empty, we asked our new friends, Julie and Zola, to have dinner with us. I found Julie stunning and dreamy, and although I had no idea how she felt about me, she captivated me. As I practiced juggling shirtless in the courtyard, following Dan's example, I tried to catch her eye. As our friendship grew, we continued to be paired up for tasks, like handing out leaflets, and I cherished every moment with her, making eye contact and asking for hugs when we parted.

It was clear that Julie and Zola enjoyed Dan and my company as well, and we spent each day getting to know each other, laughing and having fun. Julie accomplished whatever tasks the organization gave her during volunteer shifts at BUNDjugend and commuted there by bicycle. After all of us completed our daily assignments, she and Zola would show us around Berlin. One night, a breathtaking thunderstorm hit, with over a hundred lightning strikes per minute. I was awestruck, sharing this incredible experience on the community rooftop with my new crush and joyously getting soaked in the rain.

I did my best to make Julie laugh and appreciate our time together, despite having little to offer beyond good company. Her English was much better than my German, and I adored her accent. The four of us explored the city nightly, cycling through the World Cup fan center with its massive TV screens and quirky sculptures. Berlin's mix of modern and ancient architecture captivated me, especially the Hauptbahnhof, or central train station, a landmark that helped me navigate the city. We'd never had tour guides until this point, and this newfound treat we received in Berlin forged unforgettable experiences, highlighting the beauty of human connection and reciprocity.

One afternoon, Julie took Dan and me to the Berlin Wall. Overwhelmed with sadness at the atrocities committed, the division of families, and the slaughter of so many humans, I shed many tears in grief, sorrow, and disbelief. This act seemed to earn her affection as she hugged me without prompting. I also visited the Berlin Historical Museum alone, where I immersed myself in rich exhibits until closing time. The historical significance of our destinations deeply moved me, reinforcing my love for history and the importance of learning from it. My journal reflected on experiencing aspects of the past:

We've biked through some towns that are over eight, nine, or even twelve hundred years old. The Berlin Historical Museum had over eight thousand items and spoke of the history of many places we have already been to and others we hope to visit. I love learning this stuff; it fulfills me more than any course at college ever did. It went chronologically, and I started out reading everything, my mind filled with information about early European domination, new religious thoughts and thinkers, Charlemagne, and inventions; by the time I got to the seventeen-hundreds, my brain was already exhausted. I started skipping most of the paintings, portraits, and miscellaneous display cases, even though I wanted to know more. There was also so much about the two World Wars, especially posters, propaganda, and the like... It's amazing what we don't learn in school.

By the fourth day, our time at the community was nearing the end of our agreement, and it was time to move on. After Julie's shift, we shared beers and smokes with her and Zola. Finally, I mustered the courage to express my attraction to Julie, which likely came off as me divulging undying love and everlasting loyalty. She felt flattered, although days later, she confessed that she simply wished I had told her about my attraction to her and my desire to have sex with her. Nevertheless, we made love later that night on the roof, on top of my sleeping bag. I was thankful I had saved condoms for months and had one readily available, as I hoped this would happen. Afterwards, we kissed and cuddled as the sky went from lighter blue through the deeper shades and hues of purple and black. Finally, Julie said she needed to go home, so we embraced for what I hoped wasn't the last time, and I bid her farewell.

The next day, Dan and I had concerns about our lodging. With the World Cup filling all accommodations, we wouldn't have a place to stay. I desperately wanted to experience Berlin's biggest weekend, which included the World Cup semi-finals and final matches, as well as the notorious Love Parade, the largest rave in the world, but we could no longer keep our spot on the roof. I told Julie our worries when I saw her later that morning and she generously offered her flat, where she, Zola, and three other flatmates lived. I was ecstatic and kissed her openly in appreciation. This freed us from working for lodging, allowing us to fully enjoy the city. I calculated that we were now going to miss most of the Belgium Rainbow gathering, if not the whole thing, since it had already begun. Nonetheless, we loved our experiences so much that we wanted to stay. Julie took time off to spend with us, facilitating a full immersion into the vibrant atmosphere.

Germany's semi-final match against Italy was a tense experience. The extremely close contest led to an unbelievably profound despair when Italy won after being tied for nearly the entire game. Many manly men wept openly, yet, despite the sorrow, a lone Italian fan's defiant celebration stood out. Even though Germany wasn't in the World Cup final, we joined the festivities, witnessing Italy's victory over France. The match was thrilling, though marred by Zidane's infamous headbutt. Exhausted but exhilarated, we skipped the all-night revelry to rest. That night, I slept in a loft next to Dan, and reflected on the intense emotions and experiences. We longed to be a part of something that mattered to us and still felt disenfranchised by culture as a whole.

On the sixth day, we explored various iconic landmarks, cultural icons, and local favorite hotspots thanks to Julie and Zola, who enjoyed being our tour guides. After a full day, we stopped by their flat to change clothes, freshen up, and went back out to discover Berlin's infamous underground nightclubs. We danced and drank, enjoying the freedom and connection we felt. We emerged from our sixth club into the Aurora, or first breaking light of dawn. As neither Dan nor I knew how to get back to the flat, Zola simply pointed in a direction. We hopped on our bikes and let them sit on the seat as we pedaled, standing. Before long, we found a familiar landmark and made our way back to their flat. The sunrise kisses at traffic intersections made it unforgettable. We felt truly alive, embodying freedom and love. Dan and Zola's romantic interest for each other blossomed within the shared positive experiences, creating deepening connections, which further grounded us and shifted our motivation to stay longer, soaking up every moment of this incredible journey.

Dan had introduced me to the underground rave scene five years before, when he got us both into a basement party on a weekend between Christmas and New Year's Eve in Portland, Oregon. I picked him up and drove us to an address he'd acquired online with very specific directions. Upon arriving in a quiet industrial zone, we parked and changed clothes into outfits unlike anything I'd worn up until that time: skin tight artistic black and white shirt with black pants with straps and buckles. We exited the vehicle, walked to the corner of a building, descended some stairs, and opened a door with a black light over it. That door was a portal to another world. We could faintly hear the bass pumping as he turned the handle, finding it unlocked. Inside, a man stood guard and motioned us to enter, quickly closing the door behind us.

As I followed Dan down another flight of stairs, I didn't make eye contact with the man. With every step down, the music got louder until we stepped onto the ground floor level. We couldn't hear each other speak by that point, not that either of us was talking, anyway. We could now see strobe lights and lasers, accompanied by the overpowering smell of sweat. Inside was an orgiastic crowd of energetic ravers bouncing, thrashing, and flailing to music, the likes of which I'd never heard before. I caught the rhythm and didn't stop dancing for hours. By the time we left, sweat drenched my body and my ears were ringing. We changed back into our other clothes, hiding the sweaty apparel from our parents, then I dropped Dan off at his house at three in the morning. After sneaking into my bedroom as silently as possible to avoid my father's detection, I laid down in bed and felt as if I were still catching my breath. I replayed the night in my head; I felt alive that night like I never had before, as if something inside me woke up. That singular experience turned me onto electronic music and changed my life for the rest of it.

The electronic music scene has transformed significantly over the years, with the meteoric rise of events like the Electric Daisy Carnival (EDC) and, in a parallel vein, Burning Man, which is a counterculture art festival just as much as it is a music festival. Now, there are regional 'Burns' in around eighty countries, with other big ticket music festivals happening around the world. Much of it started in America and Europe with synthesizers and beat machines, artists recording noise onto records, and scratching them on turntables. Some of it started in Berlin, and it felt like we were about to touch the heart that sourced this culture to the world. In the beginning, there was only one massive rave, worldwide, and we were about to be a part of it: the Love Parade. Started in nineteen eighty-nine, this rave had grown to truly epic proportions, just over one and a half million people in attendance, from infants to octogenarians, truly representing all walks of life and regions of the world, but especially all lovers of electronic music. For perspective, Burning Man that year drew around thirty-nine thousand participants.

I awoke next to my best friend after our sleepless excursion through underground Berlin night clubs and reflected on our first experience of that culture together. This rave scene was truly transformational, and it had opened me up to the world of digital sound. I changed a lot in those five years and was in the middle of one of the biggest periods of personal growth in my life. Our excitement had grown throughout our time in the city for one highly anticipated experience. After the World Cup concluded, the center of the largest roundabout in the city underwent an overnight transformation from the fan festival to the biggest party of the year.

The Love Parade organizers constructed a magnificent and elaborate tower inside the main circle, with a DJ booth at the top, reserved for the headliner, the big name that drew the crowds, none other than the almighty Paul Van Dyk himself. They installed all kinds of lighting and visual projects on the monument, as well as the biggest speaker towers I had yet to see in my life. Throughout the day, around one hundred and fifty double-decker buses paraded the event grounds, pumping out the widest variety of electronic music I had ever heard. At the beginning of the day, we got dressed up in our fanciest festival costumes, which wasn't much for Dan and I. Before departing for the event, one of the roommates, a Swiss guy, in his best English, offered us some speed. I had never taken speed before but understood that it was an amphetamine that boosted energy levels while decreasing appetite and increasing bodily sensations, creating a pleasant high. It certainly did not disappoint. By the time it kicked in, our entire group was inside the festival, dancing and having a grand ole time, as my blog later regaled:

It's just so unbelievable to me to go to a rave with a million people. I couldn't see the end of the sea of people strewn out over the four-mile grounds. My group started out with eleven people and over nine hours of dancing dwindled it down to the hardcore three: Dan, Zola, and me. Everyone else left or got separated. There were large semi-trucks with big platforms attached to the rear where the DJ played that carried thirty to fifty people dancing on each one; they also had all of the speakers hooked up to each truck. There were people selling stuff all over the place and others climbing anything in sight to party on top of. People described me as an aggressive dancer. Tons of people took photos of Dan's tattoos.

When we loved the music, we would follow a bus until the DJs transitioned. If not, we could head in the opposite direction toward the next oncoming bus or divert to a different spoke of the roundabout. We had an epic time, Dan and I vowing to stick together the whole day, and all eleven of us agreed to meetup back at our entry point at the end of the event. I have no idea how security maintained a perimeter or controlled access in and out of the massive space.

The sun was out, and people were colorful, festive, positive, enjoyable, friendly, and often had artificially enlarged retinas. There was a unity to the community. The smell of marijuana wafted through the air, while children were being rolled around in wagons by their parents. Some folks looked distinctly like hippies, others like party boys, and yet most individuals looked pretty average, enjoying the music and an excuse to get outside on a glorious summer day.

By the time dusk came, most people had gone back to their homes, but the remaining throng gravitated together around the central DJ tower, like moths drawn to a flame. The sheer energy and excitement of the crowd climaxed at the first sight of our musical hero. When the first beat dropped, it felt like salvation for sinners. For the next ninety minutes, I wasn't a single individual, but a single cell in a body, a part of something greater, sharing in the bliss and collective high, like the ancient Dionysian or Bacchanalian festivals.

Paul Van Dyk played his best hits and some of my absolute favorites, all of which came to an apex during the encore; he saved his number one single, the best, for last. Despite my sheer exhaustion from eleven hours of dancing, roaming around, and the beginning of my comedown, I danced harder than ever, and I knew all the notes, sounds, bass drops, and could sing along to it. Afterwards, the crowd breathed a collective sigh, full of gratitude and bliss, and then slowly dispersed. The three of us walked back to the rendezvous point, elated and completely spent. While waiting for Julie and the other flatmates, who never showed up, I realized how famished I was, and asked Dan for some money. He agreed we needed to eat, so we found a cheap Mediterranean food truck that served us some hot kebabs, which we devoured while walking home to Zola's and Julie's flat on wobbly legs. I climbed up into the loft after a hot shower and fell into a deep slumber. Babies don't sleep as well as I did that night.

I could tell a distance had grown between my lover and me that day, as we didn't stick together at the festival as I had hoped, and she'd become colder, distant, and aloof since. The following day, we had a small confrontation, where she told me she wished there hadn't been the emotional attachment in our connection and expressed a little regret that it hadn't remained purely physical. My feelings for her had grown, and while we both knew I would depart, it was still a bruise to my ego.

I continued to share how grateful I was and how much I enjoyed our connection, which only made me feel worse when my doting was unrequited. On top of that, she expressed she liked Dan more than me and that she would have rather connected with him instead—this outright hurt. Meanwhile, he had connected with her friend, to what level, I will never know, as he was very private about such matters. Needless to say, it was time to move on. Dan and I spent that day doing laundry and preparing to get back on the road and cooked our hosts a magnificent feast from food we had dumpster'd as a way of sharing our gratitude and saying thank you for the amazing days and nights that we would not have been able to have without them.

During our time in Berlin, Julie and Zola expanded our awareness about food banks and soup kitchens, which were great alternatives to dumpster diving, an option we taught them how to do. The reciprocal exchange differed from anything I'd experienced because of the intimacy, it having such depth that it caused us to stay longer than expected. I felt love and attachment to that kind of acceptance and entanglement. The qualities of this experience were in marked contrast to the kindness we received in brief interactions whilst on the road. This awakened something in me, a new way of being, and brought up a wellspring of emotions, causing me to feel more secure in my self-worth.

After ten incredible days in the city, Dan and I were up with the sun, said some emotional goodbyes, and wandered out of our favorite megalopolis. Berlin held incredible times, some so uniquely dreamlike that they hardly felt real, as if our minds had conjured them up as memories that were better than the actual events. We had seen churches and cathedrals, historical sites and ancient architecture, underground nightclubs and significant landmarks. We took pictures, cycled, busked, danced, made love, and so much more. In the brief time we were there, we'd gained a deeper rooting and greater understanding of anywhere we'd been yet. Thus, our departure was more emotionally draining and difficult than anything so far. If our trip kept trending in this direction, we wondered what was next. We had no idea we were about to be in for a fall.

Chapter 9
Mechanical and Energetic Breakdown

Our departure held an odd mixture of emotions, with sadness mingling with relief, anticipation intertwined with liberation, and connection entangled with love. The hugs and goodbyes were profound and simultaneously shallow as we bid farewell to our lovers. We cycled for more than half of the day just to get out of the suburbs of Berlin. We decided on a more direct route, west across the country, planning to beeline it through Hannover, back to the Netherlands, and into Belgium; giving up on our dreams of visiting Zegg and other communities in the south of Germany. For the first time in the entire trip, we were in a hurry, as we prayed that we might catch the last few days of the Rainbow Gathering. Alas, that was not to be. What was about to happen to us crippled our ability to cover distance. My journal stated a premonition:

I think we can make it back across Germany in five to seven days. It's about five hundred miles. I'm noticing some wear and tear on the bikes. We've put about one thousand seven hundred and fifty miles on them so far, and probably around another thousand joyriding. It worries me, as we are short on funds. Berlin has not been a good place to juggle for money; all the tourists were giving to the World Cup and not us. It's been great getting back on the road. I wouldn't want bike failures to keep that from happening. It was nearly miserable the day we had four flats. Anything permanent or more difficult would completely suck.

We stuck to main roads—no more wandering. Beyond that destination, we received a message from Dan's lady friend from Olympia named Hanna, confirming that she had purchased tickets to fly into London, as it was on our route to the international Rainbow Gathering. Her intent to travel with us created urgency and excitement. We traveled quickly through places with names like Dorf Schonenberg, Steglitz, Zehlendorf, Kleinmachnow, and on to Potsdam, Werderhavel, Brandenbeurg, Genthin, Burg, Magdeburg, Helmstedt, Konigslutter, Cremlingen, Braunschweig, Vechelde, Peine, and Sehnde. Using all our skills, dumpster diving, the Magic Note for food, and ninja camping, we aimed to travel efficiently. The following morning, we woke up sore from the first uphill climbs we'd experienced, but had no choice but to make haste onward. Covering one hundred and eighty miles in two days, we made it to Hannover. There, we noticed a cathedral with an upside-down pentagram and wondered about its origins.

When we were seeking a place to sleep, we came across a large event in a central park, where we met some street kids. Enjoying each other's company, we stealthily acquired several bottles of wine from the catering tent and shared them with our new friends. One of them brazenly brought back an entire case after witnessing our demonstration, and we spent the night drinking and exchanging stories. I got belligerently drunk and struggled to walk straight and maintain any composure. Luckily, Dan somehow found us a safe sleeping spot.

I woke up in a delightful park by a lake, feeling hungover and realizing I had blacked out the night before. Upon inquiring about what happened, he reassured me I hadn't done anything stupid, and he'd led us to safety. Dan was giddy, playing with hedgehogs despite them pricking his hands. This reminded me of our night in Barenthin, and his experience with the bunnies. We shrugged off our aches and searched for dumpsters. We met our new friends again at midday, who teased me about my drunkenness. They offered beers to help my hangover, which worked. When we felt better a few hours later, Dan and I left town before it got too late. None of our new companions could offer us a place to sleep, as they were mostly young and were also homeless or living with their parents. Leaving Hannover was a relief; the fresh air calmed my nerves and steadied my stomach, which had been in knots all day.

It was on the second day out of Hannover that disaster struck. Dan was riding Lord Pancake as we heard a sudden, loud *bang*. The cart's front dropped, hurling him over the handlebars. The main arm connecting

Mechanical and Energetic Breakdown

the cart to the bike had fractured, the metal a mess of bent shards. We guessed the hills and the cart's heavy load caused the damage. Lacking welding skills or tools, we were stuck miles from the nearest town with minimal supplies in the middle of the German countryside. Returning to Hannover wasn't an option due to how far we would've had to backtrack in this condition. We had no idea how sparse supplies would be in the small town ahead of us. We'd hoped to reach the Rainbow Gathering in Belgium and had been making good progress so far, but our goal seemed impossible now. It was over five hundred miles away, which felt unfathomable in our current state, our speed cut in half, and the change in topography ahead that we were sorely under prepared for. To add even more pressure, Hanna was arriving in London in one week.

We improvised a temporary solution with duct tape and zip ties we had on hand, trying to fix the cart. It barely worked for the moment, as we continued on our journey at a painstakingly slow pace, and we limped into the next town at dusk. The zip ties had warped, causing further damage. Without perfectly even riding, Hangar's arm would sag and grind against the ground, the friction slowing us down and causing an awful sound. All the shops were closed and there was no bike store in town; we felt defeated. We spent the night in a nearby forest, seeking tranquility and avoiding the incessant insects that had plagued us in the farmland areas. Silently, we pushed our bikes uphill and pitched our tent. We ate emergency provisions and drank wine Dan had saved from Hannover. Exhausted and frustrated, we fell asleep without saying goodnight. I woke up in the middle of the night, thirsty and desperate, my water bottle empty. I felt the weight of our predicament and poor planning.

This was the first time in our travels we had been without water. In the midst of feeling the stress about not being able to get supplies to fix our gear, we had forgotten to fill up this ever-so-necessary resource in town. I tried to go back to sleep with a parched mouth and yearning stomach, but with great difficulty. But by early morning, around first light, clouds had rolled in. I woke up at the first sounds of raindrops on our tent and hastily put up our rain fly, then strategically positioned our few pots, pans, open-lidded water bottles, and anything else that could hold fluids under the flaps to collect rainwater. I also held my head out of the tent against a flap with an open mouth, funneling the sweet nectar from the skies into my open lips, filtering out the tree debris and whatever else the rain brought down with it through my teeth. No longer feeling so dry, I could pass out once again, needing more sleep than I had gotten.

When I woke up for the last time shortly thereafter, Dan had already arisen and was examining our cart. I collected the water from the pots into our canteens and bottles and filtered out whatever I could through the only clean tee shirt I had. He applauded me, praising my ingenuity for the water collection. As the clouds cleared, the evaporating dew from the forest, combined with the brilliant sun rays, created some of the most stunning visuals of the entire trip. Misty sun bursts shone through the tree branches in a beautiful, luminescent, and ethereal manner, my best photo not coming close to their magnificence.

We packed up and walked into town, still pushing our bikes, and we split up to handle our tasks. Dan went to the only car shop, where two non-English-speaking mechanics agreed to help after he mimed our need to fix the broken cart piece. Meanwhile, I scoured the town for resources. The Magic Note failed, and there were no dumpsters to scavenge within, but I could at least fill our water bottles with fresh water. Juggling also produced no tips, but I found a donation box with enough coins to help pay for the repair. I broke into it and stole the meager sum, feeling guilty, ashamed, and desperate. When the mechanic finished the repair, they asked for eighty Euros; we had less than forty. After some negotiation and taking their photo with Dan, they let us go, thankful their boss wasn't around.

We continued on through Ronnenberg, Stadthagen, Buckeburg, Minden, Lubbeck, Ostercappeln, Osnabruck, Ibbenburen, Rheine, Neuenkirchen, Ochtrup, Gronau, and across the Dutch border to Enschede, Haaksbergen, and beyond. Amazingly, we crossed over our earlier route, and a particular intersection felt familiar, as if I'd had déjà vu.

As we slowly pedaled on, our repaired cart still required smooth and steady riding, slowing us down. No more racing or tricks; we had to be cautious. A steep hill tested our resolve, and within a day and a half, the weld broke again, shattering our spirits completely. With no money or way to repair it, we pinned our hopes on a distant community with a bike shop outside Rotterdam, hundreds of miles away. We used the last of our zip ties and duct tape, vowing to ride even smoother. Our seven-day goal turned into ten, and we missed the Rainbow Gathering in Belgium. Our nerves frayed and our resources dwindled. If it wasn't for West Germany, where the Magic Note worked better and we managed to busk for some funds, I'm not sure how we would have lasted much longer.

Crossing a bridge over a dyke, I suggested we jump off of it into the canal to lift our spirits. Despite Dan's initial hesitation, we both plunged into the murky waters, laughing amidst the adrenaline rush. This brief joy was a highlight, regardless of our struggles. It was a shared moment of exuberance and triumph, further cementing our brotherhood, and we took a picture afterwards to capture the moment. However, this did not last long, as tensions soon rose again. Eighty miles from the Dutch border, Dan and I had our first big fight over the failing cart.

Our usual camaraderie slowly devolved into anger and blame through our frustration at the situation. The cart continued to bump and drag on the ground with any uneven riding, requiring consistently smooth pedaling, which was increasingly demanding of our focus and attention. While discussing potential solutions around remedying our situation, Dan said something, I don't remember precisely what, that thoroughly pissed me off, and when he asked why I was so mad and if it was something that he said, I replied, "It wasn't what you said, but how you said it." He responded with, "Woah, woah, woah. Now we sound like a married couple!" and encouraged me to stop at the next good place so we could pause and regroup.

We pulled over at the next bus stop, parked our metal steeds, sat down on the bench, and calmed ourselves by focusing on our breathing, while Dan quietly rolled a joint. It never ceased to amaze me how he would conceal these treats from my knowledge and awareness, revealing them at the most opportune moments. Smoking together, we apologized, and I commended his ability to stay level-headed and solution-oriented— although neither of us thought of cannibalizing tires from Fear to replace the worn-out rear wheel of Lord Pancake. I kept the rest of my complaining about my agitation and bothersome mood for my blog:

Being dirty doesn't bother me, sleeping on bumpy ground does, though! I'm fine as long as it is flat, but there are some nights when we just have some shitty spot, and I lay awake for most of the night. Fortunately, the stars and the moon have been so magnificent to gaze at. It's serene to be out in the country and be able to see things clearly, but it never ceases to amaze me how polluted our atmosphere has gotten... It's comical to see what has become life's little pleasures, like cold water, a mattress to sleep on, someone you care about to cuddle with, a shower, snack food, ice cream, pizza. I have plenty of time walking around barefoot, warm weather, good companionship/friendship. There are so many things that are luxuries to me now that I highly appreciate and used to take for granted. The cart has its connecting arm extremely bent down and to the left, and the metal spring at the front is thoroughly warped, indicating other problems; the cart has started to sway and wobble constantly, which makes it more difficult to pull. Also, the left tire wore completely through... We've recently had to replace two tubes, one on Hangar and one on Lord Pancake. We also switched the front tire with the back one, as it seemed to have more wear from the cart.

That afternoon, we passed by a massive encampment of gypsies along a river that caught my eye. Their lively community with guards, children playing, music, and food made me curious, but we didn't dare approach as we wanted nothing to deviate us from our course. As much as I longed to learn about their culture, we continued on. Thoughts drifted to Red and the soon-to-arrive Hanna, and I wondered how our group dynamic would change. It amazed me we had crossed the entire country in five days of riding, covering four hundred miles despite the catastrophe that had crippled Hangar.

As we slowly pressed forward, we reached the Dutch border and limped through the Netherlands under constant rain. Our clothes were perpetually damp, adding to our misery. We rode over a hundred and fifty muggy miles past Haaksbergen, Neede, Borculo, Zutphen, Eerbeek, Loenen, Woeste Hoeve, Hoenderloo, Otterlo, Barneveld, and South of Amersfoort, where we had our previous epic day on 2CI and MDMA. We continued on through Utrecht, Leidsche Rijn, Kromwijk, Bodegraven, Waddinxveen, and Moordrecht before the cart broke again just outside Rotterdam, but luckily, it was a minor issue with the spokes.

When we arrived at our host community, what greeted us was a disarray of unfinished projects and a hidden marijuana farm, not the co-op we had imagined from the description online. The hosts were wary and made us pay for our food, increasing our financial tension and overall distrust for them. The bike mechanic fixed our cart for us but failed to mention beforehand that we would need to pay for the repairs and became angry when we couldn't pay him adequately. Tensions ran too high amongst this group, adding to our desire to leave as soon as possible. The day after the mechanic fixed Hangar, we left hastily, relieved to be on the road again despite our continuing struggles.

To alleviate weight from our cart, we reassembled Fear and ghosted her alongside us for the next month, an arduous task that made every mile harder. Hanna had already arrived in London, elevating our stress and anxiety, as it was still a three day's ride away. We cycled out of the suburb of Rhoon through Barendrecht, Puttershoek, 's-Gravendeel, Moerdijk, Standdaarbuiton, Bosschenhoofd, Schijf, Achterbroek, Kalmthout, and Kapellen before arriving in Antwerp. Regardless of our dwindled food supplies and low funds, we skipped the city, prioritizing getting to Hanna as soon as possible. We managed eighty miles on the first day, stealthily camping near the Belgian border. The weather improved the next day, making our journey slightly easier. We continued through Zwijndrecht, Sint-Niklaas, the name of which caused us to laugh for the first time since jumping off the bridge, Lokeren, Zeveneken, and Lochristi before arriving in Ghent, where we admired the medieval architecture, feeling like we had stepped back in time. Determined to make up lost time, we hurried west. In Evergem, I insisted on stopping for a Belgian waffle with whipped cream and ice cream; it was such a rare treat that it significantly improved my mood. Dan busked and earned back the money we spent, providing a moment of lightheartedness.

Reaching Bruges by early afternoon, we were starving once again, but our lack of food supplies forced us to dumpster dive. The challenges ahead consumed my thoughts, and I wondered how traveling with Red and Hanna would be. Despite our hardships, we pushed on, motivated by the hope of better days and the adventures still to come. An entry on July eighth captured the travels at the time:

Bruges, Belgium, is one of the most unique and alluring places I've ever seen. Gorgeous architecture, a castle right in the middle, ancient buildings, all of it awe-inspiring. Who could ever bomb such a place? The Nazi's, that's who... There is still the old moat that runs along the outskirts of the oldest part of the town, complete with windmills and guard-gates. Blows my mind away. A place like this... We found multiple garbage bags full of one-day-too-old food, so we now have tons of tomatoes and other veggies and probably eight loaves of bread. We

The Cycle of Kindness

couldn't even carry it all, and I found a bag of chocolate covered malted milk balls just lying in the street.

We woke up in a beautiful forest this morning, biked off of our Netherlands map and onto our French one, although we are not over the border yet—tomorrow, France and maybe even England. This trip never ceases to amaze me. I cannot help but turn to everyone I see and give them the biggest, most sincere smile. I cannot believe that such a large amount of people seem unhappy when this life is so sensational. What is the difference between our two lives to make me considerably happier? I've gotten to meet people from around the world; global diversity! I am dumbfounded at how ethnocentric the U.S. seems. It's apparent in the outskirts of these old, historic towns that westernization is slowly creeping in. The world is a big place; I think days like this make it so I could travel my entire life. I also start to feel this way at Rainbow Gatherings. I feel like the presence of my aura just goes BOOM when this happens, and I can just absorb a great deal around me, seemingly slowing down time as I'm more present than ever before.

As my post suggested, after scoring a mother lode of free vegetables from a dumpster, our cart, Hangar, overflowed as we pedaled into the town center. Stuffed with food, a guard then stopped us, informing us that the city didn't allow cycling in the pedestrian area. Normally defiant, we walked without question, pushing our bikes and took in the city's beauty, feeling as if we'd stepped into the past. The city's restoration after World War II was impressive, and we examined its historical plaques and architecture.

As we walked, a friendly man approached us, fascinated by Dan's tattoos. He invited us to his home to photograph Dan and offered to pay for these photos. While Dan posed, I cooked tomato soup with our newfound bounty, and we enjoyed a lavish dinner with our host and his wife offered us wine. Tipsy and content, we spent the night in a nearby bus stop, capturing a blurry but joyful photo of the two of us celebrating our journey. The next morning, however, we faced more adversity. Another broken spoke on Junior, which required multiple shop visits to find the right part. Unable to afford professional help, we struggled to replace the spoke and true the wheel ourselves, making us anxious as we pedaled on toward Calais. We slowly hobbled through Rhoon, Smitshoek,

Puttershoek, 's-Gravendeel, Moerdijk, Zevenbergen, Grauwe Polde, Schijf, Kruisstraat, Brasschaat before finally reaching the picturesque Bray Dunes by sunset. A stunning view of the North Sea and a brilliant sunset captivated us with a sense of awe, all-connectedness, and majestic natural beauty. Despite an accidental camera drop, we captured the moment and slept on an embankment, content but wary of the weather.

Awakening the next morning in a wet sleeping bag, we laid out our gear over our bicycles to dry in the morning sun as we feasted on our food supply to reduce our weight. With our cart intact and plenty to eat, we felt the tides had turned. We savored the moment, aware of the fleeting nature of our duo during this leg of the journey. Our group would shift back to three members, and maybe four, and an unknown new social dynamic left me feeling uneasy. We passed through Dunkirk, Grand Synthe, Loon-Plage, Gravelines, Oye-Plage, and Fort Vert that morning. Despite no longer being amateurs, my wayfinding wasn't perfect, and we still occasionally got lost, and rarely went on the most efficient route. I estimate that, throughout our journey, one third of our total miles were due to us misunderstanding signs, not knowing the lay of the land, and earlier, not having maps at all.

I had come to terms with Hanna joining us and welcomed the thought of a new member, even though I was quite attached to the current dynamic, and the strength of the brotherhood Dan and I had formed. Arriving in Calais by noon, I busked in front of the line of cars waiting to board the giant boat while Dan acquired ferry tickets to England, and he took over once he returned. Our busking efforts paid off, providing much-needed funds. Boarding the ferry with a sense of achievement, we looked forward to finally reuniting with Hanna in London and facing whatever challenges lie ahead. We had covered over thirty-five hundred miles, were stronger than ever, and had accomplished our longest continual ride thus far.

As we set sail for England, we locked up our possessions and moved toward the front, where we awaited the view of the infamous white cliffs of Dover, enjoying the salty sea air and the camaraderie we had built. Our foundation of trust, loyalty, and teamwork created a heartfelt and long-lasting friendship. We both felt that this chapter was coming to a close, and we were aware that our shared closeness for nearly two months would soon change.

I have said over the years that Dan saved my life in more ways than one; he helped me get out of an unhealthy lifestyle and brought me on this journey where the experiences have defined me as a person. This best friend also aided me in getting to a place where I could heal my childhood trauma from my brother and father and helped me to have deep platonic relationships with other men. I wondered what lie ahead as we crossed the English Channel and forayed into Great Britain. I truly relished in these final days with just the two of us together, our brotherhood formed, forged, and hammered, shaped and sharpened to a fine point, honed to perfection, constructed out of such hardened and durable materials as to be triumphantly everlasting. The strength we both felt in our teamwork continually reinforced it, and we became more than the sum of our parts. On top of all this, we continued to receive aid from strangers, and the cycle of kindness perpetuated itself, further reflecting the positivity, generosity, and charity that we received, gave right back, and returned to us over and over again.

Chapter 10
Great Britain

I had been to England one time before when I was seventeen, during a summer soccer tournament in Newcastle. That brief experience gave me a rare sense of confidence and familiarity as we approached London, our fourth country on this journey. It felt like a fresh start as we approached Great Britain, a place where they spoke English as the first language. This eased the communication barriers we had faced throughout the entire adventure thus far. However, the local slang and accents still baffled us at times, often leaving us scratching our heads in confusion.

Arriving at the White Cliffs of Dover an hour and a half after the ship got underway, their beauty left us speechless; regardless of which, we quickly pedaled off the ferry, eager to reach our destination. We immediately turned in the wrong direction, adding a full half day's worth of riding as we detoured through Shepherdswell, Aylesham, Canterbury, Chartham, Chilham, Challock, Charing, Lenham, and Harrietsham. England's hilly terrain and infamous wet weather quickly tempered our excitement, slowed our progress, and dampened our spirits. Just when we would recover mentally, it seemed as if there was always another challenging element waiting around the corner that tested our resolve. Navigating roundabouts and riding on the opposite side of the road added to the difficulties. We stuck to back roads, avoiding the busy freeway and making our way northwest as it became evening.

On our route, we discovered Leeds Castle, which was closed for the day. Dan wanted to go inside anyway, compelled by his adventurous spirit, leaving me to guard our bikes. We circled the area before Dan spotted a location in the outside barrier wall where he could climb a tree and scale up and over the wall from it. What a classic ninja he was, taking our camera to document the grounds to share with me later. After being gone for well over an hour, I tried to distract myself from the worry of the guards apprehending him by eating, stretching, and practicing my juggling. When he finally came back, he had the giddiest expression on his face, encouraging us to get moving quickly, and that he would divulge the tale once we had gotten back on the road.

Once safely further away, Dan regaled me with the story: after ascending the wall, he managed a higher drop on the other side before evading security guards, circumnavigating a moat, exploring and photo documenting until dusk. He witnessed a courting peacock and a peahen amongst a variety of stone structures that appeared ancient, well over one thousand years old. Upon relieving the itch of his curiosity, content and heading toward the perimeter, he realized he didn't exactly recall his entry point, so he didn't know where to exit or how. He searched around for nearly twenty minutes before finding a tree to assist his escape, and back over the wall he went. We both laughed about the whole experience. It reminded me of the time he stole the strawberries from the German field, the recollection of which put us both in a good mood and feeling ready to tackle the challenging terrain. Despite the new aches and pains from the relentless hills, we pressed on toward London. We found a good ninja camping spot and bedded down for the night.

After an early start to avoid detection and trouble, we cycled through Bearsted, Maidstone, Wateringbury, Kings Hill, West Malling, Snodland, Higham, Gravesend, Dartford, Bexley, Bexleyheath, and into Greenwich. The uphill battles left us exhausted and ravenous, quickly depleting our food reserves. By late afternoon, we finally reached the outskirts of London. As Dan and Hanna had been in consistent communication, we stopped at a library to receive the most recent update. Finally, we had the hostel's address where Hanna had been staying for the past week. Despite only traveling one hundred miles in two days, we climbed more elevation than in the rest of the trip combined. With a new kind of muscle fatigue, we found a corner of a tucked away park to sleep in, before getting deeper into the city. The following morning, we were underway even earlier, as we felt ready for the next chapter of our adventure, and maintained hope that morale would improve. It took us an entire day to cycle through the city:

Ah, in London, England again; it was nearly exactly five years ago since I've been here, and I can see many changes. I'm definitely getting to see different parts... London has about a twenty-mile diameter and is currently the most expensive place to live in the world. The Pound/Quid is worth almost double the U.S. dollar. We have over seven hundred pictures to go through that need to be uploaded. I need to email REI about getting new tent poles, and find out the date, time, and location of Red's incoming flight. We also desperately need to fix our bikes, but probably not in England, as they are toys here instead of serious modes of transportation. But damn, was it fun winding through downtown London traffic with the bikes. I accidentally hit the mud flap of a car halfway out in a lane while going fairly quickly and just kept going. The guy honked a whole bunch. Dan apologized and said there was no damage, but it was pretty unsettling. It was strange to see downtown again; I don't care to go sightseeing as I've done it already... The first night in England, we stayed in a park after meeting some fifteen-year-old kids who came over and chilled with us when we stopped for a rest at the top of a hill after I crashed and nicked-up my face. I had been taking the cart quite a lot and consequently, was worn out, so into late dusk, we put up the tent, and I promptly fell asleep.

After stopping a lot at intersections while pedaling through Peckham, Southwark, past the Tower of London, Westminster, Hyde Park, Notting Hill, Harlesden, and Wembley, and being perpetually delayed by traffic signals, confusing junctions, and pausing to check our map and compass, we finally found the hostel. When we arrived, we learned Hanna was no longer there. She had extended her reservation a full week after her arrival until they were fully booked and turned her away. We felt guilty for taking so long and worried about her safety. Unsure where to find her, we set up our tent in a nearby park and slept for the night, apathetic about the illegality of our decisions.

In an incredible stroke of luck, Hanna found us the next morning while strolling through the park, having had no communication with us for over a week, as she hadn't received Dan's email from the night before. Overjoyed, we embraced and listened as she recounted the story of her leaving the hostel, not knowing what to do, and while crying on a bench in the same park we camped in, a couple approached her, asking what was wrong, she told them her situation, and they offered her their backyard to sleep in. Dan went with her to gather her belongings, thanking the couple profusely.

We took a much-needed rest day, enjoying our reunion and reorganizing the tent to make room for Hanna. Dan headed to a library to update our families, while Hanna and I stayed in the park, sharing stories and getting to know one another. When Dan returned after a few hours, he revealed a mishap with Junior; he had lost the key to our bike lock, which prevented the rear wheel from moving, forcing him to carry it over his shoulder. As he returned to our location, officers stopped him, thinking he was stealing the bike. Unable to prove ownership, the policemen detained his bicycle. Now back at our camp, he found the spare key and departed to retrieve it, which left Hanna and me alone again.

What followed was one of the most traumatic experiences of the trip, casting a shadow over our fresh start in England. Despite the new outlook and initial sense of renewal, this incident left me with a lasting disdain for London:

So, yesterday was exciting. Some random kids asked to use our tent to roll a joint in because of the wind. Needless to say, many lessons learned— they tried to steal a bunch of our stuff and successfully made away with my sunglasses. Whatever, it is just stuff. There were about five of them in the tent, ten in total. Hanna and I ended up having to chase them down, attempting to get our stuff back. One kid got in my face, saying that he had a knife, threatening to shank me. I retreated to the tent for the juggling club. His friends got more involved, trying to provoke me to hit them and getting the clubs away from me. Scary. People just walked by, no one stopped to offer help. Fortunately, no one called the police, either. That would not have been fun to deal with.

After they left, threatening to return after nightfall and finish the job, we packed up quickly and got out of there. We hobbled all of our possessions, still locked together, back to the house where Hanna stayed the night before. Dan was absent for the entire conflict, returning in time to see us exiting the park. I wish he would've been there to back me up, but this brings me one step closer to being where I want to be, ready to fight and willing to take damage in the process if it comes down to it. Wounds heal, but ideals and principles cannot be broken unless I let them. I'm kind of glad it didn't come to violence, but it sure would've been fun, taking on six guys, but we would've probably spent a night in jail.

Dan unlocked our other chain, freeing us to depart the park much quicker. Once we had escaped to the backyard of Hanna's hosts from the night before, we ended up having tea, calmed down, and spent the night in their backyard. Dan realized I was shaking, so he sat me down, and I told him the full story. I could tell he wished he could have been there with us and wouldn't have hesitated to fight side by side. In a way, I am thankful he wasn't, as he was quicker to violence than I, increasing the likelihood of physical violence and a night in jail for all of us—on the very first day of our reunion, no less.

This experience rocked my newfound faith in humanity and created doubt and distrust all over again. The following morning, I still felt shaken and was eager to get far away from that ghastly city. I felt totally wrong about having a fresh start in a country where I spoke the language, and my doubt in my own judgment grew alongside my general distrust for groups of teenagers. While we continued to encounter similar packs of adolescents, we never had another incident like the previous one. As we cycled on, I realized we were now officially a trio, reminiscent of the days with DJ but with a different dynamic, as Hanna and Dan were a couple. Their closeness left me akin to a third wheel. Isolated, I felt distant from Dan, skeptical of their relationship because of how it could remove the closeness we shared before she arrived. Traveling with a woman for the first time made me yearn for Red's presence and a sense of balance in our group.

Heading north by northwest, through Wembley, Watford, Kings Langley, Berkhamsted, Aldbury, Ivinghoe, Leighton Buzzard, and into Bletchley, we aimed for the International Rainbow Gathering near Leeds. With a few hundred miles and lots of hills to go, we still had a chance to participate in the final ten days of the festival that lasted for an entire lunar cycle. Yet, fifty miles of picturesque rolling hills took us that entire day. I hoped to reconnect with friends from the Netherlands gathering, especially that woman named Mel I'd felt an attraction to. Despite only being a few months ago, it seemed as if ages had passed, and our email communication, which started out strong, had recently dwindled. My longing for companionship and love intensified, especially hearing my companions' intimacy at night. My long and expounding blog entries spoke of the new dynamic within the group:

Hanna is pretty cool, and it's fun to get to know her, as previously I had only spent a day and a half with her in Olympia on Saint Patrick's Day weekend... It must've been a leap of faith for her to come on this trip. She hardly knew either of us for long and decided to bike across multiple countries together. Her nice touring bike with full panniers causes me to question our idea of the cart even more. It seems easy for her to keep up with us after we've been going for four and a half months. So much time has passed already. It's kind of difficult seeing the interactions between Hanna and Dan. Trying to sleep or being awoken by them talking and laughing, wishing I had the same interactions myself. It's good to be three again, though, so two can walk around while one stays with the bikes. But when it comes to traveling on little money, always maintaining the best diet is not an option. Damn, it's cold, and it's only going to get colder. We're heading up to Scotland for early September and plan on making it back down to France in October. This country isn't so big to bike across, but the hills definitely slow us down. It gets to the point where they are just too steep for Lord Pancake's lowest functioning gear. We need to get the bikes fixed. We found a shop here in Bletchley that we will go to tomorrow, and hopefully, our seemingly minor repairs won't be too expensive. The little things just slowly build up over time, and I hate to see the bikes functioning at less than what they are capable of.

As we cycled on, we found solace in places like Saint Mary's church. Resting in a nearby park, we encountered two peculiar individuals eager for company. Despite their sketchy stories, we accepted their offer of marijuana and alcohol and enjoyed a drunken evening. A nearby fish and chips shop afforded us a feast that we split with our new acquaintances. I would have generally been distrustful of the ruffian and his convict friend, yet my intuition urged me to relax and trust. I'm glad I did, too, because the connection with these benevolent strangers helped me shake the previous trauma off. The next morning, amidst a hangover haze, we all marveled at swans in a nearby lake before continuing our journey. Battling through the hills, we made slow progress, and regardless of the challenges, we remained hopeful, aiming to reach the Peak District on our way to Leeds for the Rainbow Gathering.

The grueling hills tested our leg strength and perseverance like never before, and although dumpster diving provided consistent sustenance, cycling through farm country, our exhaustion grew overwhelming. Fortunately, we continued to find refuge in parks most nights, where locals were inquisitive, kind, and generous. My journal regales some sentiments from social interaction, as well as two specific dumpster diving extravaganzas:

I have already met people from the entire world over, compared to my small grove in the Willamette Valley. So many cultures, ethnicities, geographical backgrounds, skin tones, dress styles, languages, opinions, and personalities... Dan often refers to us as two out of seven billion, and it's completely unfathomable to me how big this world is, and how small we are. I further admire voyagers, adventures, and conquerors for venturing into vast, uncharted territory, toward the unknown. I've begun reading Herodotus' The Histories, which is filled with historical information. I went on a solo-ninja mission last night to a nearby grocery store for dumpster diving; I ended up literally jumping right in. I snuck up close and realized I would've had to cross a large, fully lit parking lot to enter, and as I had heard voices, I decided to double back and find a new route. After scaling a wall, which dropped me right near the bins, I began to rummage through as a motion sensor light came on. I sank to the shadows but kept going through the bins. At last, disparaged at finding nothing thus far, I saw two bags of baguettes and rolls.

About the time I finished, a car had pulled into the street. I peeked out for a glimpse and saw it was the cops! Maybe on a routine check or maybe some alarm was triggered by the motion sensor, but either way, I huddled down in the bin. They pulled in next to the bins, parked, and examined the area before leaving. I was free to escape secretly with my prize. Life is such a game. So, it's like we are awesome heroes that go on missions and find little quests to accomplish and levels to beat on the side. Too fun, we have begun to say, as well as too easy! Ah, the famous Nottingham, home of Robin Hood and his merry men. The nearby rolling hills are picturesque. I don't think the camera even fully captures the vast landscapes and territory that are magnificently viewed from the tops of the hills. And oh, do we climb the hills! It makes my legs so much stronger to the point where I am almost always comfortable in the highest gear on a good, flat road. We also went through Leicester yesterday and had a feast of three different containers of fries, four sandwiches, an English pie, two sodas, a spicy chicken wrap, and delectable Indian food to top it all off. We were so full; we weren't able to bike for a good hour afterwards. The cities are getting progressively more magnificent and fun to visit the further north we go. The architecture is a mix of old and new; chimneys that remind me of Mary Poppins, and new sheik department stores and restaurants. The new buildings are efficient and boring—there is no decoration and excess. It seems built with cost-effectiveness as the top priority.

We continued nearly due North, through Wolverton, Northampton, Brixworth, Market Harborough, Fleckney, Leicester, Loughborough, Ruddington, and West Bridgford before arriving in Nottingham, where we explored the elegant old castle, marveling at its architecture and reflecting on the centuries it took to build such wonders. It was humbling to consider the hardships endured by past generations, from wars to epidemics, and I felt gratitude for the opportunity to exist. Traveling had significantly shifted my perspective and enriched my life in ways I never imagined, inspiring me to encourage others:

I am absolutely loving my life. I urge anyone who is putting things off or simply daydreaming about what you could be doing, to get out there and do it. This life is for the living, so get out there and live your lives exactly as you want to. Fulfill your desires, your destinies. There isn't a moment to lose. Live like today is the last day of your life, and you will have no regrets. I miss those of you the most that have taught me the greatest life lessons; you are irreplaceable and priceless.

As we headed further north through increasingly difficult terrain, the days grew shorter and colder, slowing our progress even more. We deviated west past Derby, Wyaston, Mayfield, Alsop en le Dale, and Newhaven as precipitation became a constant threat, causing us to stop and put on rain gear. The dampness still seeped into our belongings, though, adding to our weight and diminishing our pace further. Amidst the challenges, we discovered Arbor Low, a Druidic henge, and learned the value of simply asking homeowners to camp in their yard. Our first attempt at an elderly couple's home was successful, and upon further attempts, the residents graciously accepted us more than half of the time, sometimes offering us food as well. I was beyond thankful to have a good night's sleep without needing to keep one ear open for someone approaching our tent, and a home-cooked meal without having to dig through a trash can. It was a major life upgrade and began a new bold habit.

Through practicing varied responses, we discovered that whenever someone offered something, our response shouldn't be, "Yes," but instead, "I couldn't say no," meaning that they could propose anything they felt comfortable giving us and we guaranteed acceptance. Tea? Sure! Breakfast? Of Course! Food to take with us? Why not! Twenty dollars? I couldn't say no! A night with my daughter? Show me to the bedroom! I never did get lucky enough for that last one, but this stroke of genius continued to put us in a position where people would donate whatever they were comfortable with, without overextending their hospitality, as well as made it so we simply didn't ask, preventing us from appearing like beggars. The generosity of people was sometimes short and sweet, but other times, flowed like the Nile River. As we continued to trust in humanity and made braver requests, residents rewarded us with increasingly charitable responses. My faith in mankind slowly built up again after the incident in London until the cycle of kindness became our way of life.

Chapter 11
The Peak District

The following afternoon, we cycled beyond Hurdlow, Buxton, Dove Holes, and Chapel-en-le-Frith, and made it to a region of unparalleled natural beauty, even beyond where we'd already been. It felt like we'd ridden onto a movie set with free-flowing streams uninterrupted by dams in a majestically serene place hardly scarred by roads or cottages. This was my kind of place, nature's pure splendor, unspoiled by the hands of man, attempting to capitalize on the resources on the land's surface or buried underneath. No corporation was attempting to commercialize, package, and sell it. There were no billboards or advertisements, no shops slinging their wares, no electric lines to ruin photos, no economists trying to turn a profit, no drilling, mining, cutting, burning, or destroying for the sake of the almighty dollar. I wondered if this was heaven.

As we rode along in blissful serenity, Dan found a bunch of blackberry brambles with perfectly ripe berries. It was so idyllic we could imagine notable historical figures sitting on this very wall, eating equally perfectly ripe fruit. In fact, many famous people have visited or lived there. The list of literary artists that have written within the enchanting region is lengthy, but includes Jane Austen, Charlotte Bronte, Dan Defoe, Jean-Jacques Rousseau, and Roald Dahl, the last of whom had a great influence on me as a child. While I hardly took much time to write in my journal, as the days of the international Rainbow Gathering were dwindling, I did record:

So, this peak district should actually be called the hill district. It's got some beautiful scenery, ancient stone walls, nice hills with green fields, sheep and whatnot, and a lot of clouds. The rain has been fairly consistent, as has the fatigue in my legs from constant ups and downs. Junior and I do not get along well. I can hardly manage on that bike while ghosting Fear. Dan chalks it up to the bike being too big, but I just think she doesn't like me, and it pisses me off, so I won't ride her because she likes Dan more. I've honestly come close to physically abusing the bike on more than once occasion. For some reason, I have been highly irritable lately. So many of the smallest things are bothering me. Like Dan not keeping up on hills when I know he can, or the gears catching on the bike, or excess wind resistance—just little stuff like that. I know the weather is getting to me pretty badly. Most of my clothes are wet or damp and stink miserably. If we can't get them cleaned soon, good grief, am I going to smell horrible. And it's not even my smell but a wet-stinking cloth smell. I desperately want to be in good weather again.

While my companions seemed less affected by the weather, seemingly due to having each other for the boost in morale, I felt increasingly isolated and longed for companionship. I missed Red, and began to doubt if my ex-girlfriend would actually join us, as she suddenly stopped emailing weeks ago, raising surprise and concern in me. Despite our past struggles, I still had strong feelings for her and wanted her to join more than ever.

As we pedaled toward Leeds, we detoured into a village in search of food. Seeing a castle in the distance, we continued past it and found a field to sleep in. That night, the smell of Dan's socks and shoes filled the air, prompting jokes from Hanna and laughter out of me. We had ridden for eleven straight days, only covering three hundred miles because of the slow pace from the rain and hills. This was one of the most difficult legs to our journey, which had been ongoing for five months now. Dan and I covered over four thousand miles and counting.

We went to bed hungry that night, which turned into a determined morning of laundry and busking. After trekking into town, we found a frigidly icy stream in the village center. Hanna and I stripped down to our underwear and scrubbed all our clothes with a bar of soap against rocks. Meanwhile, Dan busked barefoot at a busy intersection. He was likely the best juggler the town had ever seen, and as they were unfamiliar with traveling performers, every passerby tipped him. We needed the income badly and split up our tasks that day accordingly. Because of the constant surprises he revealed, I wondered if Dan secretly had more of a nest egg than he told me about. When he returned after nearly two hours of laborious laundry, he surprised us with lavish purchases like a bottle of Scotch, much to our delight. While drinking on empty stomachs, we used the thin sliver of soap that remained on our bodies, shrieking at how cold the stream was after fully submerging ourselves. This event seemed to spread like wildfire through gossip, as onlookers gathered, peering at the sight of us from any vantage point they could gain. We had become the laughingstock of the village. We walked back to our encampment in our underwear, carrying our damp but clean laundry through town, lacking self-consciousness amidst pleasant inebriation.

While my companions returned to our tent and hung our clean clothes on the nearby fence, I put on freshly laundered and still wet clothes and drunkenly stumbled back to town on foot, searching for food and dumpsters at lunchtime. I must have been a sight, as I recall, in my stupor, being jeered at and otherwise responded to negatively more than once as I fished through trash cans, ravenously consuming whatever I could find and saving anything that would last for the group. Unabashed and unashamed, I continued my foraging until one townsfolk handed me money.

Back at camp, our gaze repeatedly transfixed on the castle up the hill, and with determination to sneak into yet another forbidden place, we trekked up the hillside together before sunset. Once we arrived at a closed gate, the three of us hopped a nearby fence and found a path up. The builders constructed Peveril Castle in the eleventh century to defend the region and the nearby village of Castleton, more than a millennium prior to our visit. The steepness of the hillside amazed me, and I could hardly imagine anyone carrying the supplies to construct such a stronghold up the embankment, let alone anyone daring to besiege the seemingly impenetrable position. Any charging army would be out of breath far before they could attack the fortress.

As we were the lone visitors, we climbed a low wall, found a charming watchtower with a far-seeing view, and drank with hedonistic pleasure while witnessing the most glorious sunset we had seen in weeks. Motion cameras spotted us on the way down, but we avoided the guards, tumbling and falling while exiting the premises. We laughed at the absurd thought of people trying to keep us out of places; we felt so free and liberated. The hangover I had the next morning was head splitting, but it felt better than the nauseating feeling from the stench of moldy wet clothes. We had earned the much-deserved respite from our ceaseless cycling. Sheffield was our next destination, a mere sixteen-mile ride, as we needed to busk and fill up our supplies since I'd only acquired enough provisions for a day or two at most, and there was less than a week left of the Rainbow Gathering we'd hoped to attend.

    I continued to struggle with our group dynamic as the relationship between Dan and me dissipated. We no longer shared deep conversations as we had, and I felt less fulfilled. After much thinking, I decided I would part ways with them when Red arrived, still holding onto the hope she would, aiming to reunite with Dan and Hanna further south. They wanted to see Scotland, but I yearned for warmer climates. Going our separate ways just seemed to make sense. My birthday was less than two months away, and I craved a momentous, epic, and memorable celebration; yet I wasn't quite sure what that would entail. I just knew I wanted it to be in nice weather. It felt like the first birthday where I was truly alive, and I wanted to honor my life shift.

    After three weeks of cycling, ascending tens of thousands of feet of total elevation, we finally made it out of the most difficult terrain we had encountered yet, reaching the highest elevation thus far on the trip. After the long stretch of wind and rain, two sunny days in a row were a highlight—things were looking up. We had met some cool street kids in Sheffield, acquired our supplies, and had fun day-drinking and doing poppers with them under a bridge. They proudly divulged they were filming their own orgies, all of them aged fifteen to seventeen, and sure enough, the more they drank, the more they all made out with each other, everyone kissing everyone else at some point or another, with the three of us traveling mates being the only exclusion. These kids, like us, were liberated, but they experienced it much earlier in life. Their reciprocity and depth of connection was something to learn from, and their loving kindness to one another further reinforced my faith in mankind.

    They also told us about a collective bookstore and communal space in Leeds called the Common Place, where we could get free internet and coffee, as well as have a place to hang out. Inside, a cafe created funds for the place, while a free shop and library disseminated plenty of activist and political information. I wrote the address down in my journal. After two days of replenishing reserves, resting at the communal space, and catching up on emails, we continued north. At long last, we made it to Leeds mere days before the end of the Rainbow Gathering. Despite my constant yearning for companionship, I wasn't a complete groveling slob for any sexual encounter:

The weather has stayed lovely, and I am overjoyed. We biked out of Ecclesfield to Wakefield and met some punks while I was out rummaging in the bins and bummed a cigarette. Apparently, my sexual aura shot out yesterday, as I took my shirt off to enjoy the weather, a car full of girls whistled at me, and then when we got to Leeds, a fourteen-year-old girl was outwardly saying she wanted to shag me, which was a bit scary. She was so young, and yet she didn't care at all that I am eight years older than she. Then, later that night, a drunk girl walked up and asked for a fag, a.k.a. cigarette, and since I had one behind my ear, she instantly walked up to me and took it. I started talking and before I realized it, she was trying to stick her tongue down my throat. Dan took pictures and giggled like a hyena the entire time. I probably could have had a night of fun; I wonder what would've happened had I just gone with it.

After escaping the clutches of the horny drunken lass, we hid in a cemetery as the young woman searched for us. The next day, we found refuge in another collective space, where we met a group of seasoned cyclists called Bicycology. They inspired us with their purpose of promoting cycling and environmental responsibility. We shared stories and admired their diverse array of bikes, including solar and bike-generated sound systems. We were close enough to the international Rainbow Gathering that we could have attended the final two days. But because of our delays, causing us to arrive much later than expected, we gave up our long-held dream of attending, as we'd discovered something that felt more important than our own enjoyment. While this decision pained us, we shifted our goals and mindset toward direct action and making a positive difference in the world. Our experiences had taught us the responsibility of acting on our beliefs and creating the world that we envisioned as possible. No longer were we solely motivated by our own interests, as our desires to pay forward the generosity we continued to receive overtook our own mindless self-indulgence. The cycle of kindness inspired us to do something for the greater good of humanity.

The change from riding as a group of two or three people to thirty is unimaginable, akin to the difference between charging into battle alone or with thirty allies on horseback. We felt empowered; I surged in my desire to make a positive impact on the world. We sang in jubilation, taking up the road two bicycles wide. Cars slowed and piled up behind us until they could pass. That afternoon, we arrived at camp *exultant*, where England's finest officers met us, who were ready to meticulously search all of our possessions. They took every item out of Hangar, dumped it all on the muddy ground, and left it there for us to repack. Stationed to cause discomfort for anyone entering or leaving the camp, I resented these policemen. We kept our spirits high, though, while pitching our tent in the dark amidst rainfall in a cow pasture filled with tents, vehicles, bicycles, people, and giant canopies. Over the next three days, we met other impassioned activists, discussed potential tactics, and planned our upcoming direct action.

The Camp for Climate Action was a series of non-violent protests across England and Europe, targeting major polluters. Through our actions, we highlighted the importance of civil disobedience in fighting for climate justice, showing that ordinary people can challenge powerful corporate interests, demanding and facilitating change. Our goal was to shut down the Drax Power Plant in Megawatt Valley, which produced eight percent of England's power while emitting the equivalent of one-quarter of the country's vehicle emissions. Four thousand police outnumbered the six hundred of us with armored vehicles, helicopters, dogs, the equivalent of SWAT teams, and a massive budget to ensure the plant operated as usual, maintaining profits for the wealthy owners. Every time we left and returned, they searched us again. Dan collected sharp plants and seeds so the cops would hurt themselves when they reached into his pocket; it hurt him too, but he said it was a small price to pay.

The camp had a headquarters for organizers to disseminate information, a tech station for posting updates and broadcasting non-mainstream news, as well as various workshops, presentations, and discussion groups. In a camp-wide meeting, to determine how we would take part in the largest day of protesting, the leader of the workshop asked us to move around a large tent based on our willingness to break the law and get arrested. Hanna and Dan separated, went to different areas, and joined their own groups. I met nine others in the extreme corner, all folks

The Peak District

who showed commitment, willingness, ability, and dedication to the cause. We were a diverse mix of ages, ethnicities, backgrounds, and personalities, making decisions on our strategy by consensus.

The night before the major protest, we gave ourselves the nickname of 'the Curry Crew' as we discreetly departed camp one by one and gathered for a clandestine meeting at the nearby village's Indian restaurant for a hearty meal. Someone generously covered my dinner, and we shared a variety of vegetarian dishes with naan and beer. The atmosphere grew lively as dusk became night, with laughter drawing the attention of other patrons. With a well-formed plan and newfound courage brought on by drinking, we departed separately to avoid the entire group possibly getting detained all together. At two in the morning, we regrouped at an abandoned building near the train tracks. Once we were all there, we paired up and traversed different paths as we snuck through the darkness in fields and on embankments, evading police, each with a clear mission once inside: drop banners, lock ourselves to machinery, or block emergency exits. We planned to breach a weak spot in the power plant's fence I had discovered during a scouting mission. It was as if fate was telling us this was what we were meant to do.

Before heading out, I taught the group 'skylining' or how to avoid being silhouetted against the sky, just as Dan had taught me all those months ago. We each took different routes, agreeing to meet up at a prearranged spot, guided by moonlight. Once back together, nearing the plant, a helicopter circled, forcing us to sprint and hide amongst harvested corn stalks. Despite the fear, we pressed on, finally reaching the fence. An hour before dawn, we made it to the exterior barbed wire fence, which we threw an old rug over before eight members climbed over it, entering the facility grounds. At the last moment, before trespassing into the facility, I decided to remain outside as a witness, choosing to avoid the likelihood of getting arrested and potentially facing harsher legal consequences as a non-UK citizen. I didn't want to risk being deported or denied entry in the future.

Instead, I gathered everyone's possessions into a backpack and trekked back to camp. The police detained me briefly, suspicious of the items I carried, but I got through the blockade by threatening them I needed to defecate so badly I was about to do it right there. Once inside, I went straight to the media tent to announce our success. They were thrilled to broadcast our actions to the camp, inspiring, energizing, and motivating the others who were preparing for the march. Victorious, I visited a bathroom before I collapsed in my tent, satisfied with our contribution to the cause.

The primary group of protestors, led by the Clandestine Insurgent Rebel Clown Army (C.I.R.C.A.), spearheaded the march on the gates of the Drax Power Plant. These clowns were the frontline, most likely to face police brutality, armed with days or weeks of training on how to de-escalate conflict with a variety of mood-lightening and non-confrontation tactics. Behind them were about five hundred civil activists, protesting with a purpose, knowing that some of us were already inside the plant. Dan, one of the clowns, had trained for days, ready with squirting flowers, rubber chickens, and conflict de-escalation tools. But as they approached the gates, a local farmer's truck plowed through the crowd, injuring several activists. The police stood by, doing little to prevent this, seemingly relishing the spectacle with schadenfreude, but arrested the driver afterward. Media coverage of this entire event was minimal, with most reports coming from our HQ. The plant had been burning 'clean coal' that week, so the smoke was white instead of its usual dark, ashy color. Many members of the camp faced arrest on false charges afterward, but volunteer lawyers secured the release of most of them.

After a night of helping friends achieve our goals, I awoke exhausted but triumphant. As I slept through the main protest, I learned everything that took place at the tech booth that afternoon. It was there that I also received a heartbreaking email from Red, explaining she was now engaged to another man and could no longer join me on this trip. Her disappearance over these last few weeks suddenly made sense. This news brought a mix of sorrow and freedom, as I realized I was no longer tied down by past commitments. I felt both rage and jubilation, pondering my next steps with a sense of limitless possibilities. Staying with Dan and Hanna wasn't an enjoyable option, as the distance between us was too large to ignore, especially after the protest march.

Each of us participated in our own ways, choosing unique methods to counter the extreme pollution of our Earth, but while they were thankful that I decided against entering Drax Power Plant, they believed my crew's mentality and actions were too contrary to the purpose of the protests. I thought Dan placed himself in harm's way, with too much physical and

The Peak District

legal risk, being one of the most likely to get arrested, which put the rest of our journey in jeopardy. Between this disagreement and being sick of being a third wheel, I stuck with my decision to travel alone. It took me a full day after receiving Red's email before I informed them of my choice. I recalled our initial agreement to stick together until Greece, and I didn't want to abandon the group. I felt sad and guilty about my decision, and I was concerned about how they would react, and what the consequences would be. Nonetheless, I could feel in my heart that I needed to take care of myself and go my own way. When I finally told them, we decided to save our goodbyes and rode together one last time, until our paths deviated, each of us determined to persuade the other to our preference, either sticking together or separating, along the way.

At the end of the day, no matter what side of the protest we were on, this experience underscored the power of civil disobedience, showing how ordinary people could challenge powerful entities and demand change, while also highlighting the personal transformations and decisions that came with such activism. I had gone from apathetic about life and the state of the world to, "I'm mad as hell and not going to take it anymore!" For the first time in my adult life, I felt a camaraderie, being a part of something bigger than myself that mattered immensely. The kindness fellow demonstrators continued to show me within the camp further motivated me to be the change I wanted to see in the world.

That evening, the camp celebrated with a big party, feeling accomplished despite not shutting down the plant or making significant news. Amidst the festivities, I met a lovely New Zealander, and we spent the night together in her tent—a welcome break from the tension with Dan and Hanna. I felt a mix of melancholic woe and freedom:

I am in a strange place, always traveling. I look forward to seeing what adventures lie ahead. Last night, I got a bit drunk when Dan brought back some beer that I consumed quickly and got silly tipsy. I wandered around, looking for more, but couldn't find any. Got some good, but cold, food and then some music started. I went over and saw people were dancing badly to so-so music. I sat down alone on a hay bale. People had been praising me all day for the action I took, like my parents had raised me as a hero. I heard some techno playing and went to check out the pretty good music and where the movie Waking Life was being projected on a large screen as eye candy. I ended up dancing and having fun and got pulled aside by this cute little kiwi named Elena. We sat and talked for a while, with some other friends of hers, and went back to her tent. I didn't know vegan condoms existed. Now, I do... She was a reward for being awesome, for doing what others couldn't find the courage or dedication for. Everyone in the Curry Crew made it out with only a caution, no fines or pressed charges. It was a great step for me toward being who I want to become. I learned a great deal about Dan, myself, and our convictions. We packed up and biked out in the most ridiculous rain. I've already started making plans to be off on my own.

You don't have to follow the conventional path of high school, college, and decades of nine-to-five work just to collect a paycheck. While that path has its benefits, many brilliant thinkers have encouraged taking the road less traveled, inspiring the rest of us to live examined and fulfilling lives. I implore everyone to pursue their dreams, overcome obstacles, and live fully. Many compromise their ideals for safety and security, but true freedom and happiness come from following our passions. I pursued my happiness and found it in countless ways. We can fail at things we hate, so why not risk doing what we love?

Chapter 12
Following My Heart onto My Own Path

As we cycled away from the Camp for Climate Action, I worried whether we would reunite later, and how splitting up the group for the first time could permanently tear us apart. It was one of the most painful moments of my time in Europe. We rode quietly together until our paths deviated, and I said goodbye to Hanna and Dan amidst tears and sorrowful faces. The heartache of parting from them surpassed even the physical pain of crashing into blackberry bushes or carrying Red's bike for thousands of miles. The betrayal of Red's word also hurt me deeply. These feelings lingered longer than any of my physical wounds.

Dan kept Junior and continued ghosting Fear, Hanna kept her bike. A few days later, they found a man who was willing to trade the spare bicycle for juggling torches and some woodworking improvements to our juggling clubs. The man who traded with them promised to travel with the group but quit after half a day, complaining of aches and pains. I took Lord Pancake and the cart, my sleeping bag, clothes, and personal effects. I gave up our tent to my companions, making my need for indoor accommodations crucial. As the days shortened and the weather worsened, I faced the uncertainty of traveling alone. My immediate plan was clear, but my long-term goal was simply to go south:

What an eventful day, splitting up temporarily as a clan, and being within one hundred feet of the UK prime minister, Tony Blair. I have never been more on my own in my entire life. I love my independence; I am tied to no one, free to go anywhere and do anything. Where will the wind take me? It was devastatingly hard to leave Dan. Hanna, I'm not so connected to, but Dan is my brother. We've done this whole trip together so far. I'll admit, being a third wheel was a bit tough, always seeing their affection and games. On my own, I get quite a bit of flirting, another 'social drug' that I love. It's a turn on that people are attracted to me! I got into Leeds. Had a fun night at the Common Place, met up with a few members of the Curry Crew, and crashed at one of their houses.

I spent a week in Leeds, hanging out at the Common Place and partying with locals I met there. The fourth night grew so ridiculous that I stayed up until six in the morning, taking part in hilarious antics which culminated in my chin hair being shaved off. "A marked improvement," they said. They offered me a place to stay, a job at a nearby pub, and some cash, but I felt trapped, yearning for Paris and other romanticized places. I discovered Couchsurfing, a hospitality club online, created a profile, and found willing hosts. This was a game changer, as it felt so much easier than any of the methods we were using thus far. I frantically emailed potential hosts, searching for places to stay through the variety of online communities that I was now connected to, mostly thanks to Dan.

While planning a route down England's West Coast to avoid London, I received an email about a Camp for Climate Action decompression event. I attended, ran into some Curry Crew members, and they invited me to Manchester. I rode there the next morning, feeling a growing frustration and a desire to make a real impact on the world. August turned into September, and fall set in. Over the next week, I realized how much I missed Dan and Hanna, especially when I tried fixing my bike and did other tasks alone, such as busking one day, juggling for hours without earning any tips, constantly looking over my shoulder to keep an eye on my possessions. Each day, the distance between me and my companions grew as they continued north into Scotland.

Late into the night, I wrote with creative, measured hostility. From childhood, I questioned the world's unfairness. My college politics program deepened my disillusionment with corrupt political systems, leaving me depressed and directionless. But now, immoral and greedy corporations, politicians, and their disgusting alliances angered me as they captured more wealth and power. I intensified my determination to do something meaningful with my life. I wanted to be part of actual change, more than just reducing my carbon footprint or protesting. I wanted to inspire others to feel the urgency I felt and join me in making a positive impact on the world. I hope this book helps accomplish those goals. So, I wrote this in-your-face post online titled, "The World That Will Not Be Your Children's":

How can you live the way you do?

How can you purchase products from companies that exploit slave labor in impoverished countries, commit corporate crimes costing the public billions, purchase the ability to pollute, and otherwise lie, cheat, and steal purely to make a profit?

How can you drive so endlessly in such inefficient vehicles that are the worst polluters on the planet and are also the top killer of humankind?

How can you vote to not save the Earth, to support corporate and governmental irresponsibility, to allow the continuation of global horrors and atrocities, and for the constant promotion of new ones?

How can you not act in direct opposition to the people, governments, organizations, partnerships, agreements, and systems that are committing social and global injustices now and will be the destruction of our planet and the downfall of mankind?

How can you excessively consume what you should know to be killing you or causing you harm?

How can you not know the harm you are causing, and the harm that is being caused to you?

How can you allow these global atrocities that are being forced upon all humans, including you?

How 'close to home' does this pain and suffering have to come before you will act?

By not acting, you are directly contributing to water pollution that mutates and kills animals, leaks chemicals into drinking water supplies that kill, deform, and cause disease and suffering in humans; all the while, making these precious, limited resources non-renewable. These changes in increasing pollution will soon have irreversible effects on our planet and humanity if we do not act.

By not acting, you are directly contributing to air pollution that is thinning our atmosphere and increasing carbon dioxide levels, which is a proven cause of global warming; an effect that results in rising temperatures, worldwide ocean levels, cancer rates, and many other climate changes that have adverse effects on humans and the environment. If we do not act, these changes will also become irreversible, leading to the imminent destruction of the world as we know it.

By not acting, you are condemning animals to develop diseases just like we are, causing them pain and suffering that they took no part in bringing upon themselves. You are taking away their environments, destroying their ecosystems, and driving them to extinction. You allow them to be caged in severely cramped, unnatural cages that their bodies then must deform to conform to. You allow them to be pumped full of chemicals that do severe damage to them, the food that they produce, and in turn, you, after you consume them. You allow them to be treated as a product instead of a living animal; this only paves the way for us humans to be treated the same.

By not acting, you are destroying the world. You are making it uninhabitable. You are killing your own children, grandchildren, and great-grandchildren; if we even make it that long. In fact, most ways of living now are directly contributing to the destruction of the planet.

I hope you enjoy being force-fed information to keep you complacent and apathetic so others can make money off of you, or forces you to turn a blind eye and be afraid of the horrors of the world and hide in your little security bubble.

Future generations won't have the luxuries of your ignorance or timidity, hesitation, and passiveness. They won't have an SUV to drive or be able to fly in a plane to once-beautiful areas of wilderness or cities filled with ancient architecture. They won't have a TV to tell them how to think and newspapers that tell them to live in fear. They won't have clean air to breathe, clean water to drink, or chemical-filled food to eat.

The time for positive change is now, or there will be no tomorrow. The time for action is now before changes become irreversible. It's time to save the world, while we still have a world to save.

I awoke the next morning driven, motivated, and slightly less upset. The blog entry was one of the most powerful and moving pieces of writing I'd ever created, and I was more enthusiastically inspired than ever to radically shift how I was contributing to the future of our species and the planet. Riding alone still felt odd and the pang of solitude was sharp, but I reminded myself of the absolute freedom I now had: no group decisions, no compromises—just me. However, this also meant no one to talk to, help with repairs, share meals, or engage in philosophical debates. As I pedaled alone, my mind demanded attention, throwing thoughts and songs at me to keep me engaged. Entering a meditative state was a struggle, as my brain ran in circles, refusing to quiet down. Climbing hills alone felt disheartening without companions to keep morale high.

During the climb up the Pennine hills, I stopped a few times, had a good cry, and rolled and smoked a cigarette, feeling foolish and ashamed of that habit, which had become a familiar crutch, a reminder of good times past. It reminded me of DJ and how long ago he departed, how Dan and I initially joined in for camaraderie, and because we were taking a break anyway, and the habit that previously unified the group reminded me how painfully alone I was. Despite feeling phlegmy and borderline sick, biking cleared me out. Ascending a long climb to a hilltop was a victory, affirming that I could do this on my own. Seeing the metropolis in the distance, I relied on my scout skills to find my destination, determined not to fail. The isolation forced me to confront my internal quarrels. I wanted to live a meaningful life and make a positive impact on the world. Alone, this desire burned brighter, pushing me to seek real, impactful actions. After arriving and getting settled at my host's home, I wrote a blog that outlined the day's events:

In Manchester now, quite a large city. A series of unfortunate events happened today. First, the flags for peace fell off, and I didn't notice it. Then, I flipped the cart in Huddersfield and broke one of the lights, and then lost money trying to make a phone call. I was climbing a hill for more than an hour. There was some great scenery, but I wasn't inclined to take pictures. I'm hyper aware of getting my stuff nicked, a.k.a. stolen here... I've jumped into political life, spending all my time with Adel and Arty, working on an independent publication, talking, and learning. I'm thinking about staying here for a while, even though the weather will turn bad. Adel has so many documents and books, I could read for the next month straight. There is an 'Intelli-network' I want to be a part of which includes informed, active people across the world making a difference.

Life shifted from our rallying cry, "Bike! Bike! BIKE!" to a deeper mission: Make the world a better place. Settling into a home again, I relished the comforts of consistent sleep, access to a kitchen, and the abundance of dumpsters for reclaimed food. I began teaching others how to find wasted food, leading to a community of willing students eager for my insights. As I settled into Manchester, I delved into the squatting scene, discovering a network of individuals living freely in unoccupied spaces. I became part of the Basement, a social and political hub where I connected with like-minded individuals and immersed myself in radical literature.

During the day, I worked selling books for a friend of Arty's, setting up tables as makeshift bookstores at various locations around town, arranging the novels and textbooks before honing my haggling skills until cleaning everything up around nightfall. Although I earned a meager wage of ten dollars per hour, I saved every penny I could. In the evenings, I joined meetings and got involved in projects like Openmedia.org, whose mission is to work toward an open, affordable, and surveillance-free internet. I also explored Manchester's cultural offerings, including the Curry Mile, a street famous for its Indian restaurants, all condensed within one mile. I met new circles of people and this dynamic restructuring of how I used my time shifted my focus to activism, challenging mainstream media narratives and advocating for free press. Despite facing criticism and alienation, I was steadfast in my mission to effect change. I realized the urgency of the environmental crisis and sought to educate others through film screenings, discussions, and writing. Amongst setbacks and challenges, I remained committed to living sustainably and inspiring others to do the same, driven by a desire to leave a meaningful legacy for future generations.

In many of her connective emails throughout my journey, my mother gave me quotes that helped me in these times of struggle against a socioeconomic system that appeared to be dooming the ecosystem that we live in to destruction. She said, "Show me how to show up in the world in a way that will cause the world itself to change. What can I do to preserve the beauty and the wonder of our world and to eliminate the anger and hatred and disparity (inequality) that inevitably causes it—in that part of the world which I touch?" She also pointed out that my high school motto was, "You belong where you feel free."

When a massive protest against England's participation in the G8 Summit came to the city, I felt a strong desire to be involved. I participated by juggling in the parade, joining over fifty-five thousand other concerned citizens. Although the local newspapers attempted to marginalize us, accusing us of property destruction and disrupting commerce, we were on the right path, surrounded by like-minded individuals.

The rally featured speakers who denounced political decisions, but I felt disillusioned by the lack of tangible impact. Determined to make a difference, I spontaneously led a dumpster diving workshop afterward, teaching others how to gain free food and goods while reducing waste. This experience prompted a shift in my approach to activism. Instead of focusing on anti-war rallies, I resolved to participate only in positive actions, such as peace rallies and initiatives aimed at constructive change. The only entry in my journal over a six-week period summarized:

Manchester: big downtown, over a million Mancs. They love their football. Over eighty thousand students at a few universities—parties run rampant. The people are mostly stuck in the system, though. I want to get out of it, away from the Western culture. Get more off the grid. Selling books is simple. It's good to be working out and wisening up. Occasionally, people want to buy the book I'm reading, and they are the interesting ones to talk to. We humans can learn so much from each other. The biking is unchallenging; I beat cars. Dumpster diving is uncomplicated; I give food away. This life lacks challenges, so I create them for myself. I've stayed solely because I'm learning the type of information I want to know. To 'turn green' so to speak, to care more about sustainable living, the environment, the planet, the future. I know the problems of the world. Now, I need to go forth, look for and create solutions. How to change people's minds, their mindsets. I know Dan considers all things equal, but I want to help people so they don't have to live in pain, disease, and malnutrition. I want to end the class war. To break down the systems of oppression and fascism. To make it so people can live freely.

I became deeply involved in activism, spending my nights showing people the best dumpster locations, taking part in programs like Food Not Bombs, and organizing soup kitchens for the homeless. As my dissenting behavior increased, I attended parties where political discussions were the norm, occasionally stumbling upon outdoor raves. One night, someone told me about 'Bicycle Day,' a counter-culture gathering where people tripped on acid while riding bikes to celebrate the day someone invented Lysergic acid diethylamide, commonly known as LSD. The wild ride ended at a renegade outdoor rave, complete with lights, a fire, and a musical artist on turntables playing drum and bass music I'd never heard before. I danced until dawn with the majority of the other trippers, and then we biked back into the city and to our respective domiciles.

I had a few occasional romantic interests that didn't last, and I felt like an outsider until I stumbled upon a meeting of Manchester Bisexuals. I found the two-hour formal meeting with voting and deliberation to be boring and drab, which shocked me. During the meeting, I didn't gain any insight into their personal beliefs, what being a bisexual meant to them, or how they coped with the overwhelming marginalization they experienced from heterocentric culture on one side and from homocentric gays and lesbians on the other.

Everyone went out to a bar afterward, where they loosened up and public displays of affection became rampant. I immersed myself in conversations about polyamory and witnessed loving relationships, free from jealousy and possessiveness. It was a profound experience that opened my mind to new possibilities beyond the traditional nuclear family model. We discussed relationship agreements, such as how to treat one another, how to treat other potential new partners, and sexual health. We continued to discuss the variety of relationship dynamics, including hierarchical versus egalitarian polyamory, how to deal with jealousy in a healthy manner, and the complications of being attracted to more than one gender. The warmth, kindness, openness, and unconditional acceptance were unlike anything I had ever consciously experienced before.

At one point, six people who were all in a pod, or group relationship dynamic, were loving on each other with massages and kisses without quibbles, jealousy, possession, or ownership of one another; it was one of the most ravishing scenes I had ever seen, even though I wasn't attracted to any of these individuals. What I witnessed growing up was a failing model that didn't work. I had been looking for better, more functional, effective models ever since. A different paradigm was visible in that bar in Manchester, where communication was key. Being open and honest was paramount, with transparency and a willingness to be forthcoming about one's emotions, experiences, reactions, and desires being the key inside and outside of romantic partnerships.

After my profound experience with Manchester Bisexuals, I made a commitment to myself to live honestly and authentically. I apologized to my father, relatives, and a few remaining friends from Oregon who I'd destroyed trust with, because of my past lies, especially around my reasoning for coming to Europe and my intentional homelessness. I also vowed to never cheat again, as I'd had a problem with infidelity in the past, which led to broken hearts and emotionally chaotic conflicts. I used to joke that I simply failed at monogamy and wasn't aware of polyamory or ethical non-monogamy at the time. This newfound honesty strengthened my everyday relationships and became the cornerstone of my interactions. I missed Dan and Hanna, who hadn't emailed me back in weeks. I wondered why and became fearful around us not reuniting. I prayed they were doing well. I continued with my routines, including taking part in events like Critical Mass, a gigantic congregation of bicyclists illuminating the vulnerability of individuals, by coming together as one unified mass, clogging urban streets to create visibility.

Amidst a variety of online projects, a rare piece of poetry emerged:

The more I know, the more I want to know.
Dan was right. I am a mental masochist.
The things that I find the most painful,
are the ones I feel I need to know the most.

What once drove me to depression,
I now read in fervor;
A so-called mental self-defense.
What I seek is the truth.

Why do others also not seek this out?
Why are they content to be told lies?
Content to be used? Content to have their freedoms removed?
What kind of life is that? Not mine.

Where is your passion?
Where is your zeal?
I have already asked,
how can you live the way you do?

I can't play their game. I live by my own rules.
I've confided in close friends before:
The Ultimate test of a person is to have ultimate power,
and to use it for benevolent ends to be an altruistic monarch the people
love, because you act for the betterment of humanity.

I truly believe this is a test I am capable of passing.
I'd like to think I wouldn't merely pass—I'd excel.
Who will give me the test I so desire?
When will the culmination of my life come about?

When it does, I will be ready.
I condition my body and my mind,
learn with great fervidness,
and train always.

One night, I found and enjoyed street art by the likes of Banksy and other conscientious objector artists around town, without even knowing of their fame. I loved the concept of direct action through graffiti and shining light on sensitive subjects by creating alternative art forms. Another night, one of the aforementioned squatters invited me to an exclusive meeting, where they shared that they were planning something big, and I had enough street cred that they wanted me in. There was a vacant building in the old downtown, which used to be a big disco, with light-up floors, a giant disco ball, massive speakers, and some of the hippest, swingiest, cool, jive, funky folks in town; we were going to turn it into something magical. I was getting tuned in about how art makes a positive impact and sheds light on social issues. We intended to use those principles to full effect.

In the United Kingdom, under legal squatting rights, any unused building that isn't broken into when occupied is the legal right of the dwelling party, with owners suffering through a long legislative process in order to evict them. We transformed a vacant and decrepit nineteen-seventies dance hall into a vibrant art and counterculture gathering space, complete with revolutionary graffiti and collaborative artwork, bestowing upon it the name Lost'N'Found. With custom locks and a cage on the door, we kept out unwanted visitors, especially the police. Over the weeks I lived there, we held non-violence workshops, direct-action seminars, art classes, dumpster diving tutorials, squatting techniques, and similar educational endeavors. Our efforts culminated in a massive renegade art show, drawing hundreds of attendees.

Droves showed up for the event. Hundreds of people waited in a relatively orderly line that stretched around two city blocks. This building must have been over twelve-thousand square feet, and I could hardly get through the hallway to take a piss. Punks were using our tea kettle to make a mushroom concoction that they gave me a little of upon questioning their nonconsensual use of the space. I met one man who had a studded belt, each stud concealing a little hidden compartment with single hits of acid, ecstasy, or ketamine inside. He told me he was making the equivalent of ten thousand dollars a night of profit. Despite some challenges, including discovering an undercover cop via a standard pat-down procedure before allowing admittance inside our entryway cage, the event was a success, showcasing the power of art as a form of protest.

The Cycle of Kindness

By the third night without sleep, I retreated to Adel and Arty's pad to rest. They hadn't seen me for a couple of weeks, hadn't heard from me in several days, and wondered if I'd left town. I admitted the cold and wet were getting to me, but the current endeavor was too enlivening to pass up. On October fifteenth, upon checking my email at their place, I excitedly found I'd received one from Dan, who said:

Hanna and I proceeded to bike up to Edinburgh, Scotland, and then went in a large circle first west, then north, then east, then south, back to the capitol, along the way, seeing the lowlands and midlands and some of the highlands. It has rained on us sixteen out of seventeen days in a row. Imagine this: wearing your best rain gear, and despite it, being drenched to the bone, fingers turned to prunes from gripping the wet handlebars, socks, shoes, underwear, everything wet, erecting a wet tent then sitting in a swamp of a bog inside its bag, exposed to the elements all day, carrying all of your possessions, and at the end of the day, getting into a wet sleeping bag and falling asleep, only to wake up in still wet clothes, and doing it all over again—for more than two weeks. It tore Hanna and me apart, and I want to go home. I bought a plane ticket for October twenty-third, from Edinburgh back to Portland. I won't see you again on this trip. I'm sorry. Hanna has also developed a backup itinerary of places she wants to go and will continue on alone. Safe travels and train always. Your brother, Dan.

His email devastated and disarmed me simultaneously. My surprise got the better of me, and I began bawling. When my hosts, who met my best friend at the camp for climate action, entered to see what was wrong, I told them about the email I had just received. I replied to Dan that I would be on the next train to Edinburgh, that I would not let him leave without saying goodbye. My fears about the consequences of my separation from the group had come to fruition in the worst way imaginable. We had unfulfilled dreams of adventures together, like kicking the Pyramids at Giza or sneaking into other UNESCO world heritage sites together, but soon, I would face the road alone.

Packing up, I left Hangar behind and took a train to Edinburgh, feeling a mix of sadness and uncertainty. Despite the fear of traveling solo, I couldn't bring myself to give up just yet. Edinburgh welcomed me with its iconic beauty, and though I missed my companions, I felt a strange sense of belonging in this Scottish city. Spending the night at the train station, waiting for them to arrive, I wondered how I would find Hanna and Dan without a method of direct communication.

This single event shook my faith in humanity all over again, feeling betrayed and deserted by my brother, left to continue alone. I wondered, if on a long enough timeline, that all people would do this to me, and I questioned whether the cycle of kindness would continue to aid me when I was all alone.

Chapter 13
A Birthday Reunion

As I waited for Hanna and Dan in Edinburgh, I couldn't shake the melancholy of our impending separation. When they finally arrived several hours later, our reunion was bittersweet, as within the first day of being together again, a taxi struck Hanna, flinging her over the handlebars of her bicycle, and totally destroying her rear wheel. She felt shaken, but thankfully remained unharmed, and the apologetic driver directed us to a free healthcare clinic where she could get examined and handed over cash to cover the cost of a new wheel, wanting to avoid involving his insurance company. We opted to explore the city on foot after storing our bikes inside the main train station and embraced the newfound carefree wandering. Despite the foggy atmosphere, we filled our eight days in Edinburgh with laughter and nostalgia, yet we all felt the weight of Dan's looming departure. He had brought us all together; it didn't feel right that he would leave us, and it triggered my fear of abandonment.

Because of my recently earned funds working at the bookshop, I spontaneously made my first frivolous purchase of the entire trip—a bottle of Speyside Scotch, one of Baileys, and a Cuban cigar to share with the group. The night before my birthday, we hiked up the crag that overlooks the city and set up our tent with one of the most enjoyable viewpoints of my life. Our wide-reaching perspective stretched far inland in all directions and contained a picturesquely illuminated Edinburgh castle, the parliament building, central train station, and town center brightened by the city lights, as well as the Southern Coast down into England. With rain coming down, and some fireworks going off, the beauty felt uncapturable with a photograph. Dan's midnight alarm caught me by surprise as he jumped on me, still in my sleeping bag, joyously yelling, "Happy birthday!" The three of us went outside and sipped on a bottle of Scotch, took turns enjoying some of the cigar, and cherished our remaining moments of quality time together. It was a glorious beginning to an incredible day.

We awoke the next morning, packed up camp, and trekked down the crag to buy Hanna a return plane ticket back home. She told me she planned on traveling to Ireland and Wales. In the end, I persuaded her to change her itinerary and make arrangements so we could travel together, to Paris by way of Manchester, then London. Family friends of hers offered us hospitality, and I yearned to return to sustainable living communities, which had been absent from our travels for months. Dan and I had seriously deviated from our plan, and there was so much I still wanted to do. I wasn't ready to go on alone and didn't want Hanna to leave. She was a trustworthy and reliable companion. Yet, my birthday celebration had already begun, and my head was spinning off into future planning when I wanted to stay present and have a great time.

For lunch, at an all you can eat Chinese buffet called Jimmy Chung's, we created an eating competition amongst ourselves. We engorged for two hours until our bloated stomachs ached, belts were loosened, and pants unbuttoned. Hanna came in third place, consuming six plates. Dan and I tied for first with nine plates each. We were all so stuffed that we could hardly eat a slice of birthday cake with ice cream that the wait staff brought when they came to sing my happy birthday, and the three of us sat there picking at it for a while. We departed, walking lethargically to the central train station, where we sat or laid down to digest. My breathing was shallow to not put pressure on my stomach.

We sat practically panting, hardly chatting for a couple of hours until we mustered the motivation to continue celebrating. We sought a hole in the wall Scottish pub, and walked away from the town center until we found ourselves in suburban neighborhoods, at which point we turned around. As we walked back toward the city center on a new road, we found just what we were looking for: the perfect dive bar, with less than a dozen patrons inside and a few flags flying out front—the only one we paid any attention to was the Scottish national flag.

A Birthday Reunion

We each ordered a Guinness and a milkshake, which disappointed us as they turned out to be flavored drinks without ice cream. We ordered a few rounds of the iconic stout until we asked the skinny, disheveled male bartender for permission to take drinks outside to enjoy our cigar. He obliged, and we felt safe leaving our bags inside at the table, a real rarity for us. Dan snuck out our bottle of Scotch, concealed within a jacket, and we sat at a table outside, slowly finishing it, our beers, and cigar off. By the time we returned inside, significantly more inebriated, the scene of the bar had wildly transformed. Behind the bar stood a gowned, wigged, slapdash, and makeup wearing crossdresser! We found a hole in the wall alright, and perhaps the only crossdresser-friendly pub in all of Scotland. We felt sheepish as we slid back over to our table, surrounded by a much lewder and more sordid clientele than before. With a level of uneasiness, we paid our tab and got the hell out of there! We walked wobbly down the cobblestones back toward the center of town, laughing the whole way.

Back in the city center, we encountered a couple of local blokes that we had drank with in the park just days before. Upon recalling my birthday, they insisted on buying us all a pint. We squeezed through the tightly packed pub, our backpacks bumping strangers as we apologetically followed our hosts to the back of the bar, where an entire gaggle of drunken Scotsmen and women were eager for an excuse to finish another round, which our hosts proudly gave them, as they declared it was my birthday upon arrival.

We graciously drank whatever they brought us with vigor, cheer, and merriment. A few of the women openly kissed me, receiving uproars from the crowd every time. Inebriation turned to stupor. Strangers were cordial, and the atmosphere smelled of rambunctiousness and revelry. I noticed a shift in the energy within the bar as a drunken, claustrophobic urge to leave suddenly hit me, so we said thank you and goodbye, and struggled to exit through the thickening crowd. Fortunately, the fresh air outside was crisp and slightly sobering, and I recalled an entire bottle of Bailey's remaining in my pack. We discovered a late-night eatery that specialized in fried food, including candy bars, and I ordered two—the perfect combination for our sweet liquor. We laughed while engorging ourselves with such rarely purchased pleasures. Feeling lavish in our celebration was a true treat we had only afforded ourselves a few times throughout the entire journey.

The morning hours emptied and quieted the streets, being less full of gaiety and rabble-rousing, instead turning to angry shouting, desperate attempts at getting laid, and vomiting. The time had come for us to find our resting place for the night and our inebriation led us to the conclusion that there was only one location fitting for the celebration; so, to the pinnacle of the crag, we went. Arm in arm in arm, the three of us formed a human chain, with me in the middle, and ascended slowly. Fraught with slips and stumbles, near falls, and steep inclines, we held together and triumphed, reaching the highest point in the end. I hope to never forget the blurry, delightful view, covered in serene and soppy clouds, drenching the streets and houses with their precipitation. This success atop the mountain after the glorious debauchery of our celebration made this the second favorite birthday of my life. My absolute favorite was a very private experience on my thirty-sixth birthday, as I discovered that my wife-to-be was pregnant for the first time.

I awoke to a massive, brain-splitting headache, and a lonely desire for a female companion. Dan and Hanna had each other, despite their conflict prompting my best friend's departure, alongside his desire to be with family for the holidays. To relieve my ailments of head and heart, I masturbated to the sight of the beautiful Scottish landscape. Years later, I discovered the term 'ecosexual' which describes that momentary feeling. I sat alone after, spent, and consumed what water we had, enjoying the view, trying to stave off thoughts of saying goodbye to my best friend.

My companions awoke in a solemn mood, packing quietly before exiting our best campsite yet. My attempts to distract myself from the upcoming saddest of departures failed. Dan cried silently, and I much more loudly, while Hanna made her best pleas for him not to leave, and leave her, amongst tears, anger and frustration for the decisions that led to the end of their relationship. Dan had changed my life, creating this cathartic opportunity that forged the deep bond of connection between us. In my life since, I haven't known a better friend. He felt more akin to a brother, regardless of his being so vastly different from my blood brother. If it weren't for him, I struggle to imagine what my life would have become.

As I watched my comrade board the train, take his seat, look at us, and wave through the window, tears streaming down our faces, a deep heaviness settled in my heart, my stomach sank, and a longing void

A Birthday Reunion

enveloped me, which I knew would take a long time to fade away. I left Dan with a parting gift, the half-full paper journal he had bestowed upon me, to ensure its safe return. On the final page, I declared:

There is nothing we can't do, nowhere we can't go, no feat too small, or mountain too tall; we can take on the world. There's no one I'd rather do it with. Even before I came to Edinburgh to say goodbye to you, I already missed the hell out of you. We had only been apart for a month, and I wanted to see your smiling face again. I know it's going to hurt badly to see you go, but I know there is stuff you want to do. I've never found anyone better to share my life with. It's an honor and a privilege. You've taught me so much in such a short amount of time. You've helped me to take my life in the right direction. I'm so much better off now than I was in the States. I'm glad Red didn't come, I'm glad Hanna did, I'm even glad DJ left so it could be just the two of us for a while. I feel like everything is happening for the right reasons. It's such an amazing sensation to believe only positive things are happening.

I'm sure your departure will teach me many things, as well. It will have many benefits. I can't wait to sail, hike, bike, or anything around the world with you. Traveling has felt more fulfilling than anything else I've done. I'm learning more about myself, my world, my abilities, and my talents, strengths, and weaknesses. I have more knowledge now. I've learned more than I ever did in high school or college. I'm becoming more me. I'm getting better at being who I am, and that feels like the best way of thinking about it. When the revolution comes, I'll be ready. I'll be exactly what I need to be when that day rolls around. I'll have learned all the information I need to know and trained all the skills I'll need to use. I know you will have as well. I know I've told you before, but I think you are an amazing person. The stories of our lives will continue to be awesome. I doubt they will ever be any other way. I have a hopeful idea of the role I will play in this world. I swear fealty to you. I will always be on your side, no matter the fight, no matter the foe. You can count on me anytime, anyplace—all you have to do is ask. You will be missed.

With love, Nathaniel

As Dan got on a train to the airport, carrying Junior, as well as Hanna's crippled bicycle, which a professional mechanic pointed out multiple fractures and stress points in the frame and components that could break easily, Hanna and I consoled each other. It felt like mourning the loss of a dear friend at a funeral, an unexpected intimacy amidst the ache of separation. With Dan gone, Hanna joined me on further travels, drawn by the promise of warmth and shelter amidst Manchester's exciting squat scene. Life on the road shifted again, with trains replacing long bike rides to take us south to warmer climates. Regardless of the freedom that solo travel had offered, I felt daunted by the prospect of journeying alone, missing the security of having a companion and elements of teamwork. Reuniting with friends in Manchester brought both comfort and challenges, as we navigated changes in the squatter's community together. Among the chaos, we found solace in shared meals and camaraderie, breathing new life into Lost'N'Found. Despite the uncertainty ahead, our bond grew stronger as we faced the road ahead together.

Hanna, excited at an opportunity to party, bought LSD and ketamine, having never experienced either. She offered to share it with me, thanking me for providing her a safe and friendly space to experiment within. After an early preset musical playlist, a DJ began by eight, playing the stereotypical crowd-favorite combo: house music and drum and bass. I dosed myself on acid, squirreling the other away for later. We snuck off to a private area, where Hanna created and promptly inhaled four little lines of ketamine. The previous analogy I'd heard was that this substance could turn people into little baby lambs, and sure enough, within five minutes, she grasped my arm to maintain balance, becoming like a toddler, hardly able to speak and struggling to move. She vomited quietly behind me, which I was only made aware of when she stopped and pulled on my arm. When my eyes met hers, she looked down at the floor, pointing out the puddle, declaring, "Something needed to come out of me."

After cleaning up after her, and finding a plastic bag in case it happened again, we kept wandering around the party. Her physical difficulties amused me, yet she nearly always had a smile on her face or an awestruck look of wonder and bewilderment that was equally charming. Fortunately, the initial phase of Hanna's trip was short-lived, and after she recovered, dumbfounded at her experience, the foul post-vomit taste needed immediate remedying. A speedy return to our private

A Birthday Reunion

room followed, so she could brush her teeth, which prompted me to divulge a confession that I had consumed the second dose, after not yet perceiving any effect of the first, in an act of confident carelessness. I questioned whether it was a sugar pill, a placebo, bunk, fake, no good, and a waste of money.

As the night progressed, the squat filled with people and pulsated with energy. My first experience of LSD began when I finally felt a tingling sensation that spread through my body, heightening my senses and perception. Colors became more vibrant, sounds clearer, and conversations more distinct. I experienced a state of euphoria and heightened awareness, as I danced with abandon and attracted the attention of others. The world seemed to transform around me, with psychedelic patterns overlaying everything and a sense of interconnectedness suffusing the air. Despite a few unsettling encounters, like one man's head appearing as a reptile's and another man taking shape as a mechanoid masquerading as a human, both of which reminded me of *Fear and Loathing in Las Vegas*. Nonetheless, I remained immersed in the moment, awash in a newfound love and appreciation for the world around me.

Hanna and I had separated briefly, feeling pulled in different directions, and within an hour, we found each other again. She offered me some ketamine, which piqued my curiosity. She had plenty more of the substance and was no longer interested in consuming more that night, so we retreated to our private space, where I inhaled a single line. I was already back out on the dance floor by the time the dissociative tranquilizer kicked in, which helped me relax from the intensity of the acid, causing my body to feel light, akin to a floating ghost. I felt connected to the ethereal realm and the physical one simultaneously. The sensation didn't last an hour, and I felt content with the experience.

The party raged on through the morning, with many of us still partying. Hanna had passed out before dawn. I continued until the music shut off, at which point the remaining psychedelic adventurers and upper-infused partiers shared alcohol and tobacco, with the goal of being able to fall asleep. I eventually slept on the mattress next to Hanna, with many daytime events disrupting my attempt at sleep. I roused myself by late afternoon, with dusk quickly approaching. I didn't feel as though I could handle another night of such substance-indulgent debauchery, so we packed up our things and walked a few miles to Adel and Arty's place, where we relaxed over a few drinks and epic stories of the night before, finally retreating to much-needed slumber. They remembered Hanna from the Camp for Climate Action and were thrilled to have a female brought into their home, let alone a familiar one.

The morning after the party was a mix of astonishment and physical weariness. My mind was sharp, but my body felt sore and sluggish. I needed rest and recovery while cherishing the journey I had embarked on the night before, reveling in the feelings of unconditional love I had experienced. Two days later, Hanna and I returned to the squat for an open-mic night. Hanna and I planned to leave town soon, with a few weeks remaining together; her flight from Paris back to Washington was non-refundable and looming. We bid farewell to our squatter friends and Adel and Arty, exchanging contact information and heartfelt hugs. I begrudgingly parted with my beloved bicycle, Lord Pancake, selling it and the cart for as much as I could get for them, but less than they were worth. I felt a pang of sadness from yet another separation. It made no sense to carry the cart alone, and the locals would use it well to dumpster dive; Arty emailed me several months later, letting me know someone had stolen it while it was locked up outside one night.

The plan was to walk back to the train station and buy a ticket to London, and another from there to Paris. I intended to use my bookstore job savings to buy a streamlined, more efficient bicycle, similar to the one Hanna had ridden on. She had inspired me to change how I traveled, and I felt uncomfortable continuing on alone with the bicycle and cart that belonged to our group, not just me. For a few days before we temporarily separated, I traveled on foot, just the same as during the very beginning of this wild escapade. Saying goodbye to my Curry Crew friends was bittersweet, as we were all appreciative for our deepening friendship and the plethora of ways we had benefited from and learned from one another. At this point, I had ridden over five thousand miles and had been traveling for seven months.

As Hanna and I took a train together to London on November first, seven months into the adventure, I reflected on this unconventional lifestyle, recognizing the personal growth and unique experiences that set me apart from the person I used to be. Solidly connecting with the Manchester counter-culture community further affirmed my belief in mankind and the renewed faith in the cycle of kindness left me less afraid of traveling solo.

In London, the absence of our bicycles felt strange, but Hanna and I had a brief, joy-filled jaunt to the Eye of London and the waterfront spectacle between it and Big Ben. With gratitude for the companionship and shared experiences, we parted ways at the train station amidst hesitation and concern around reconnecting in an unfamiliar city, as we each headed toward Paris via different modes of transportation. She was flying there while I boarded another train, affording me an opportunity to create the first entry in a new journal I acquired in Manchester:

I'm still afraid of going alone. I sold Lord Pancake and Hangar. I need to buy a bike with racks and panniers. It was difficult to leave Manchester. I developed a sense of belonging there, unlike any other community in my travels. I had my own small niche. I had developed so many connections and friendships. Traveling to Spain will be amazing, but I'm a little worried I'll take the easy way. I wanted to go to Stonehenge, but I'm sick of England. This journal starts a whole new chapter of the trip... I will see Paris, Barcelona, and the Mediterranean. Hanna thought that if the clan stuck together, Dan would still be with us. That's tough for me to cope with, but things will work themselves out in the end. I just go with the flow and use the force of nature as my ally. The Lost'N'Found social squat was an amazing place to set up and hold. I benefited so much from the experiences there.

Chapter 14
The City of Love—Paris Je T'aime

As the two-and-a-half-hour train journey passed through the English Channel Tunnel, I marveled at the feat of human engineering as I settled into a corner seat, eventually drifting off to sleep. I awoke to the sun rising over the picturesque Northern French countryside, greeted by an attendant offering warm croissants and tea. It was a luxurious treat compared to my recent makeshift meals. Arriving at Le Gare Du Nord in Paris, its architectural beauty captivated me, and I felt a sense of historical grandeur.

Unbelievably, I beat Hanna to the Central Train Station, as she took a train to the airport, and spent a couple hours in the check-in process, boarding and deboarding, as well as navigating to a train from the French Airport to the Central Station. With a few hours to spare, I explored the surrounding area, immersing myself in the sights and sounds of the city, before heading back to the station in time to greet Hanna. Once reunited with my companion, we set off to explore Paris together, relishing in the new experiences and the sense of adventure that filled the air. I heralded the marvelous city in my blog:

Paris is the most voluptuous, beautiful city I have ever seen. Statues, cathedrals, and art are ubiquitous throughout the city and an awesome sight to behold. There are many pictures that will come, eventually. Hanna and I are traveling together, and have been since Dan left. I am buying a new bike here in Paris. Hopefully, more friends will join us and travel together soon. The bike and I will head to Spain, through which parts of France I do not know. I have a friend in Nantes that I would love to visit, however, the weather is getting much colder than expected; I am inclined to proceed further south, sooner than planned.

Paris enveloped us in its decadent magnificence, intoxicating us with its beauty and charm. Every corner we turned revealed an unfamiliar sight to behold, a novel experience to savor. We began by ninja camping in a park outside of the center, and because of the cold November air and the quantity of early-morning exercisers, Hanna decided after that first night she was tired of it, and with money to burn, she splurged on a cheap hostel and some groceries. We enjoyed these indulgences, and the ability to roam liberated us from the weight of our possessions, making the entire experience significantly more enjoyable.

The city seemed to pulse with creativity, its streets filled with artists, lovers, and dreamers. The Parisians exuded a sense of pride and sophistication, adding to the allure of the city. We meandered amidst the monuments and landmarks, from the Sacre Coeur, the Pompidou, the Museum of Modern Art, the National Library, the Louvre, the Arc D'Triumph, Palais Garnier, Place De La Concorde, the Moulin Rouge, the Avenue of Champions, the Jardin de Tuileries, the Jardin de Luxembourg, the Pantheon, the Cathedral of Notre Dame, and the pinnacle of French architecture: the Eiffel Tower. We marveled at the architecture and soaked up the culture that surrounded us, splurged on street food, and stared in awe at the talented street performers. These buskers knew what they were doing and had perfected the art of drawing a crowd, and tourists consistently donated large sums.

Each day brought new adventures, as we roamed the streets, stumbling upon hidden gems. The lively hum of early morning activity engulfed me, and I couldn't help but feel a sense of joy and contentment. As we packed up each morning from the hostel Hanna kept renting, we enjoyed the absurdity of our situation, the simplicity of our journey, and the city's magic. Amidst it all, I searched for a new bicycle, eager to continue my journey, but I felt apprehensive about finding the perfect bicycle to purchase, especially with my miniscule funds. I did my best to not let it spoil our indulgent and giddy moments, but winter was most certainly coming, and I was running out of time. I commented about the frigid weather in my journal:

The City of Love—Paris Je T'aime

It feels the coldest it has been in a while, and it will help prepare me for days ahead on the road alone. I know I will miss the companionship of the others, especially Dan. We could always push each other to be better, to do more as a team... I have a general route planned to head straight south along the Rhone River toward the Mediterranean and warmer climates. Get into Spain and figure out where to go from there. I look forward to improving my Spanish.

Paris cast its spell upon us, weaving us into its tapestry of beauty and romance. Hanna's sudden generosity in pampering luxuries transformed our days, leading us from the cold streets to a cozy hostel room where we cherished the newfound comfort and closeness. We wandered the city streets, intoxicated by wine and each other's company, our laughter echoing through the night. As we embraced the city's charm, our bond grew amidst planning museum visits and appreciating a higher quality of life. Her generosity created a further attraction for me, and I wanted to reciprocate her kindness.

After arriving on Thursday, November second, the hostel receptionist informed us that museums citywide offered free entry on the first Sunday of each month, which we intended to take advantage of and planned out an entire day to explore the best art museums, starting with Picasso. We decided to avoid the Louvre, anticipating it would be far too crowded to enjoy. On Friday, we excitedly bounced around our hostel room like kids. The next morning, unburdened by heavy backpacks, we strolled to a nearby store and purchased high-quality mango-flavored tobacco. I found a bottle of white wine for less than a euro, and Hanna bought pricier ones. Laden with goodies, we returned to the hostel, feasting in the decadence of wine and cheese. As we savored the flavors, I noticed a new depth in Hanna's gaze, feeling a growing connection between us. But eager to seize the day, we quickly went out for another exploratory day, carrying our hedonistic supplies.

Suddenly, the majestic Eiffel Tower emerged, igniting our excitement. We rushed toward the iconic landmark as if it was a beacon of hope, ignoring any jaywalking laws. Hurrying past tourists, we bought tickets for the second deck and, upon seeing the lengthy line for the elevator, we took the stairs. We were racing against the setting sun, climbing with adrenaline surging through us, fueled by wine and anticipation. With each moment, the sunset dipped further out of view, urging us up each staircase with haste, apprehensive of missing the magnificent sight. Panting, we reached the first deck just in time to witness the sun's final moments as it descended below the city skyline. As we turned toward each other, a warm orange hue upon our faces, an unseen force drew our mouths together like magnets. We embraced and kissed, momentarily pulled back, and then reunited with a sort of ferocity and frenzy of activity, unleashing the floodgates of our passion and desire. We made out like teenagers, pausing every now and then to share a cigarette. In one of those brief moments when our lips weren't locked, we noticed the full moon rising behind us. At that moment, time seemed to stand still, making it one of the most magical experiences of our trip.

Lost in our connection, our union was beyond words, a bond strengthened by months of collective experiences. Drunk on passion and wine, we forgot the world around us, enveloped in each other's presence. From the main deck, the line for the elevator to the very top was significantly shorter, which we rode up after the intense passion cooled down. Once at the top of the Eiffel Tower, we imagined ourselves as two adventurers in a glittering, frozen wilderness, our smiles reflecting the joy in our hearts. Suddenly, the tower erupted in a dazzling display of lights, a nightly spectacle we hadn't witnessed previously. This unexpected gift further reinforced our alliance and intertwined our energies.

As we wandered back to our hostel, hand in hand, a desire we couldn't express in public filled us. Lost in the labyrinthine streets of Paris, we finally found our way back to the hostel, where our passion ignited like wildfire as we stumbled through the door. In a night full of steamy affection, words failed to capture the depth of our desire, each moment seething with lust and longing. It was a culmination of weeks of pent-up emotion, a testament to our need for each other's companionship. The night passed fitfully, cigarette smoke mingling with the chill air through the open window, as we savored stolen moments of intimacy. Hanna ventured out for more wine while I drifted in and out of sleep until she returned.

Showering together in the morning was a tender ritual, discovering each other's bodies further in daylight with a gentle touch. Breakfast greeted us with a feast of flavors, our love and endorphin overdoses filling the room with contagious joy. It was like falling in love anew. The rest of the day unfolded lazily, with aimless strolls and giddy smiles. Meanwhile,

The City of Love—Paris Je T'aime

the back of my mind stressed the importance of the looming task of finding a new bike, while I did my best to stay present and connected. After a nap in the late afternoon, we emerged to witness a serene dusk, capturing the beauty of the illuminated Eiffel Tower against the full moon. It was a synergistic moment of triumph and elation, held in silent understanding. As night fell, we basked in each other's presence, savoring the slow dance of the moon across the sky, our bond growing stronger with each carnal act of coitus, draining our body fluids and leaving us smoking significantly more rolled cigarettes than we were accustomed to.

We knew Hanna's departure was imminent; her plane ticket out of Paris in a mere ten days was a reminder of our fleeting time together. This connection was a unique reflection of the cycle of kindness, as it brought a significantly more profound bond than the passing strangers who delivered brief aid in our adventures. Amidst the uncertainty in the last few months, I had found solace in the acquaintances who had become friends along our journey. Each encounter brought a fresh perspective, a new connection waiting to be explored with lessons to gain.

Hanna's kindness and warmth surpassed anything I had experienced since my brotherhood with Dan. He and I had mutual lovers in the past, with each of us dating the other's ex-girlfriends at various times. One of the most drama-filled and conflictory of these occurred when one woman simultaneously dated both of us, weaving a web of lies as she did so, wounding each of us deeply. Over time, this experience helped us trust one another more and have clearer communication. Nonetheless, I was concerned about how he would feel about Hanna and me, due to how close we all were as travel companions, as well as how their relationship ended. Regardless, I proceeded with minor trepidation. I planned to tell him, but did my best to avoid such thoughts while in the throes of love. As I relaxed in her company, I couldn't help but dread the inevitable loneliness that awaited me once she left. I reflected on the logistics of our travels more than the romance:

I again went bike hunting and more sight-seeing, found a used bike on Craigslist, but still not quite right. We went through the Latin Quarter, one of the many tourist sections, with little winding streets filled with restaurants. Also got our train tickets down to the farm of Hanna's friends. I reserved space for a bike and didn't get a return ticket. I have yet another date set to say goodbye to a travel companion. In relationships, I've always been the one to leave. Strange how traveling is just the opposite.

I'm looking forward to being out in nature again. Dumpster diving has been fairly unsuccessful, and I'll likely have to use the Magic Note more often now. I must reiterate that Paris, while a genuine money-pit for the most part, has a thriving riot scene, squat scene, and dumpster-diving scene that I know exists and would love to take part in. It's a huge city, and there are always people fighting for their rights. Nonetheless, Paris is the most pleasing city I have visited yet. I understand why so many people get married and have honeymoons here, as couples were everywhere I looked. Each little street had its own charm and beauty, with plants growing on the sunny side of buildings. I'm surrounded by cute statues, quiet tucked-away corners, empty cafe tables for sipping tiny but strong espressos while enjoying people-watching, and clear garbage cans with visible contents!

Sunday arrived, and we woke early, eager to beat the crowds at the Picasso Museum. Arriving before opening time, we found ourselves second in line, greeted by a friendly couple ahead of us. Inside, we marveled at the masterpieces, holding hands as we admired the art and each other. The chronological presentation of the progression of uniquely styled masterpieces fascinated us. The second museum held everything from classics to modern pieces. We paused at the site of Princess Diana's accident, then continued our exploration, enthralled by the diverse artistic expressions. Around dusk, exhausted but content, we savored a meal before returning to our hostel for one last night of wine and cigarettes, cherishing each other's company under the Parisian sky.

The following day, Hanna and I tried Couchsurfing, the online hospitality exchange we learned about from the street kids in Leeds, where hosts accommodated travelers on their couches free of charge. Funds were depleting rapidly, and we wanted to slow down the hemorrhaging of our reserves. We were curious and intrigued about how the website worked, and what quality of people we might encounter—I couldn't fathom so many members opening their homes to complete strangers without wanting anything in return. Our first experience, though nerve-wracking at first, opened a door to years of incredible adventures. With a six-pack of beer in hand, we met our gracious host, who had a full

The City of Love—Paris Je T'aime

hosting schedule, which only allowed us to stay for a single evening. Our host made us feel welcome and showed great generosity, making our stay a lovely experience. We hoped we had made a good impression, and before leaving, I asked if he could leave me my first testimonial, which he agreed to, and made good on his word, paving the way for later successes.

On Tuesday, we were down to our final two days in Paris, and again, we had to haul all our possessions along with us everywhere we went. Once back in the city center, we headed straight to the Louvre and paid entry. They kept our oversized backpacks at the coat check. The vastness of the museum overwhelmed us as we marveled at ancient artifacts and world-renowned artwork. From statues to paintings, every piece exuded unparalleled craftsmanship. Hanna's company made the experience even more enchanting, with little gestures of affection that added to the magic, such as gentle strokes on my neck, holding my hand, coming in close for a kiss, and being arm in arm while observing one of the most magnificent collections of art in the world. Finally, we reached the Mona Lisa, surrounded by a crowd of admirers. After bidding the lady possessing one of the most mysterious smiles of all time farewell, we savored a meal at a nearby cafe before reluctantly leaving, grateful for another day filled with awe-inspiring beauty. I described our mobility and experiences exploring:

Paris has been amazing, with five to twenty miles of walking every day. Packs on or off, we have always been pretty hardcore about training hard and keeping strong. Throughout this week, we've been to nearly every part of central Paris. I don't know of anything that this city is famous for that we haven't seen. I'd come back after the revolution, but big cities aren't for me. Back to bike hunting, we had a few places to check out all over town, so we got a rail pass one day, but none of them worked out. We then went to the Moulin Rouge and Sacre Coeur, which had a great view of Paris. One bike shop had a single cycle that had been all over the world. They wrote the name of each country on the bike, since the nineteen-sixties, which was quite inspiring to the both of us.

The sun was nearly setting by the time we departed the magnificent museum. As we walked back to the hostel, a glimmer caught my eye from a bicycle shop we hadn't noticed before. Inside, the display was a cyclist's paradise, showcasing an array of finely crafted bicycles. Amidst the collection, one bike stood out: a brand-new Pegasus Premio SL. Its distinctive C-shaped handlebars curved elegantly, promising comfort and control. The frame, flawless in its powder coating, boasted solid welds and sturdy wheels. Equipped with a rear rack and dynamo hub lights, it was a testament to meticulous design. I approached cautiously, admiring its beauty, and asked to take her out for a test ride. Permission granted, I mounted the metal steed, feeling an instant connection. She rode like a dream, gliding effortlessly beneath me.

Negotiations ensued, and with a stroke of luck, I purchased the bike, along with a front rack and high-quality, waterproof panniers, for a bargain—the price was twenty-eight Euros less than everything I owned, nearly all of which I'd saved from selling books in Manchester, along with Lord Pancake and Hangar. I could tell how my new lover was happy for me but noticed a tinge of sadness around missing her own bicycle. With my prized possession in hand, Hanna took a picture of my new treasure, named Pearl, and I. Basking in the glow of my perfect find, a prize discovered in the Parisian twilight, my blog post that night reflected my joy:

There she was. I had picked a Pearl in Paris! Gleaming white with everything I needed. The shop also had panniers that were a perfect fit. I talked them down about one hundred and sixty-eight Euros and bought everything together. It was so exhilarating. Hanna and I went out for Japanese food and got some wine and good smokes to celebrate. It was such an amazing day. I'm so excited. I was very worried that I wouldn't find a bicycle. She found me, just like in Amsterdam, when the bikes found Dan, DJ, and me, not the other way around. One of my few concerns is Hanna spending money on us, but I can't help but enjoy myself when she insists.

With the beautiful bicycle, which appears on the back cover of this book, in my possession, and our bags hastily packed, we celebrated our last night in Paris with a final private hostel room. Wine flowed freely as we celebrated our adventures and newfound love. The morning brought a groggy awakening, but we hurriedly prepared to catch our train. As we left the hostel, reminiscences of our time together flooded our minds. Pearl waited patiently in the lobby, as the receptionist wouldn't allow me to take it upstairs with us and insisted my new aluminum companion would be safe. With mixed emotions and heavy hearts, we bid farewell to Paris, ready to embark on our next adventure, grateful for the memories and experiences that would forever linger in our hearts. I contemplated the depth of change I was preparing for:

There will be fairly drastic changes in the near future. I want to let all of you know that it will be difficult to get a hold of me. I'm starting a new life, on my own, off the grid. I can vanish any time I choose. I can completely disappear if I need. I may decide to do so. I will use technology less, but will continue to maintain email correspondence as regularly as possible. I will be living more organically, naturally, and less excessively. I have reaffirmed my vows to myself, my life, and my planet. I have renewed the energy with which I will continue to live and strive for a better world. This is difficult to say to many of you, for you know not the changes that have already taken place. I choose to debunk previous myths, controls of society, and break free from the chains that have bound me. I am, was, and will be a product of my environment, but now have more control. I do not plan on coming back to the U.S.

I call any plan, Plan B. Stick to Plan B. It's the backup because you never know what will come your way. Now, I am free as the wind, and go into the unknown. I plan to explore the world, and hopefully find a place where I belong. But I'm sure I will explore long and hard, and travel far away. I have never been happier or felt better, and yet it is so hard to be away from the people that I love... Our ways of life are different, yet if you wish to make them the same, ANY OF YOU are more than welcome to come and share my lifestyle for an indefinite period. Lastly, I ask you all to educate yourselves on ways of alternative living. Do not be content with the status quo because the world is changing, and if you cannot see it coming, it may sweep you away. I care for you all dearly, hence sharing this information. Know your past to understand your present and future. To all of you: take care. I love you. I miss you. I hope to see you again.

Chapter 15
Preparing for Loneliness—Isolation Awaits

Leaving Paris behind, we headed toward the homestead of Hanna's family friends: Pine's farm, where a rustic charm awaited us. The countryside unfolded before our eyes as we embraced the warmth of rural hospitality. Pearl, my newfound mount, was eager to hit the open road, a symbol of freedom and adventure. Upon arrival, the farm greeted us with its timeless allure of ancient stone walls, rustic sunken roofs, and a few modern tools, evoking a sense of nostalgia for simpler times. It could've existed as a medieval peasants' farm in a historical television show. As our hosts toured us around the aged buildings and lush surroundings, I felt humbled by the enduring spirit of the place. Every corner told a story, from the weathered wood to the ancient hand pump drawing water from the well. The place stood as a stark contrast to the disposable culture I was accustomed to, showcasing resilience and timeless craftsmanship.

The Pine family welcomed us with open arms, offering us a glimpse into their self-sustaining lifestyle. Despite the modest accommodations, we felt appreciative of the warmth of their hospitality. Amidst the daily rhythm of farm life, we found ourselves immersed in a world where time seemed to stand still. The matriarch, a tireless figure, tended to her duties with unwavering dedication, while the patriarch enjoyed quiet moments by the fireplace. Their children, a reflection of their upbringing, embraced the simplicity of country living with grace and humility. As we settled into our new surroundings, we couldn't help but marvel at the sense of connection and community that permeated the farm. It was a reminder of the long-lasting bond between humanity and the land, evidence of the longevity and unchanging allure of rural life:

This is truly a farm with chickens, pigs, cows, a run-down old house, five kids, bowing walls, all sorts of junk under an awning, and more. It's refreshing to hear of common people struggling against global issues like we are. I rode Pearl from the station to here; she is a dream. I could nearly keep up with a car. I look forward to months ahead on the road. We bonded immensely, instantly. I'm as prepared as I can be. I'll be more ready when I actually leave this farm. Leaving Hanna will be somewhat tough, but more so for her—even she says she gets attached easily. I'm looking forward to helping out in this place. Getting back into biking-shape will be fun also. Time to bring out the sweatband!

Life on the farm was a whirlwind of activity, from dawn until dusk. We joined in the daily chore of tending to the garden and helping with milking, herding, feeding, corralling, as well as raking and shoveling the feces of the livestock. It reminded me of my childhood, and I found a peaceful harmony in the rhythm of farm life, grateful for the opportunity to connect with nature. They treated us like part of the family; we shared stories and smoked marijuana with the older children, filling the nights with laughter and camaraderie. Yet amidst the daily routine, there was an undercurrent of sadness with each passing day of our last week together, our impending departure mere days away. We snuck away to cherish intimate moments alone together as frequently as our duties allowed.

On the fourth day, we faced the harsh reality of farm life as we helped slaughter the mama sow, and I had no choice but to confront the stark truth of where our food comes from. My experience at five years old, watching an unintelligent cow shot through the head without fear or awareness, had significantly less impact upon me than this event. This much smarter animal expressed fear, anxiety, worry, and squealed as if it knew what was coming. As I reflected on the cost of the animal's life, I made a solemn vow to change my eating habits, desiring to live more compassionately in the future. I cried a little, feeling empathy for the animal, a conscientious sadness sweeping over me, contemplating that this is what it takes for humans to eat meat.

The Pine family made sure not to waste any part of the slaughtered pig. They carefully removed the internal organs and used them for various dishes, including blood sausage made with the intestines as casing. They quartered the remaining parts of the pig and used a flamethrower to remove the hair and skin. They then hung the meat on hooks in the butchery room to dry and cure. It was a laborious process, requiring several men to hoist the heavy carcass. We all took part in this challenging task, ensuring we accomplished the process smoothly. After all, many hands make light work.

The experience of witnessing the slaughtering process left me in a state of shock and overwhelming emotion. It helped me realize how disconnected we are from the reality of consuming meat and where that meat comes from. We sanitize the process by using terms like 'beef' instead of 'cow' and 'pork' instead of 'pig.' However, documentaries like *Cowspiracy* and *Food Inc.* have shed light on these issues. While I appreciated my newfound awareness, the reality was that I didn't believe I could switch to a vegetarian diet because of my impoverished circumstances while traveling. How Dan accomplished this feat still dumfounded me. It was a sobering reminder of the choices we make and their impact on animals and the environment. I had grown in my empathy and consideration for others. What started with regaining my faith in humanity had also transformed into my empathy for all living creatures, plants, and animals alike.

Feeling raw and vulnerable after witnessing the slaughtering process, I withdrew from my usual self. Even the comfort of Hanna's embrace couldn't fully ease my distress. Her upcoming flight only added to my inner turmoil. As I prepped Pearl for the solo journey ahead, I felt calmed and grounded in the task of painstakingly organizing my panniers. I carefully arranged each item, depending on my need for easy access while pedaling. With a few days left on the farm, a sense of change settled in the air; my journal accurately depicted this:

Hanna is right. I'm nervous about what's coming up. Everything I have learned about survival has told me to stick with another person. My brain has been going crazy, having massive amounts of dreams; possibly preparing me for what's to come. I can't imagine getting into a situation I couldn't handle, but I can't see the future and have no idea what will happen. I'm facing a great fear of mine: the unknown. I recall a dream from the beginning of this trip where I was riding along a road surrounded on both sides by water, going off endlessly into such a beautiful, pristine, calm, and flat horizon that it reflected the sky, and I couldn't see through it. Going along the road with the sun beating down on me, getting hotter and hotter, sweating, yet I dare not jump into the water for fear of hurting myself, due to not knowing what's beneath the surface.

I've been spending the last few days preparing myself and my stuff. From overeating at nearly all meals to sewing clothes, minor bike wiring adjustments, doing the last bits of laundry, and packing my panniers. The partnership and companionship that Hanna and I have had over the last few weeks has probably been the healthiest relationship with any woman so far in my life. We are very open, supportive, and communicative. In many ways, it will probably be more difficult to be alone. I like to share my life with other awesome people.

In the final days on the farm, I was going through the motions, my mind clouded with knowing I would soon have to say goodbye to Hanna. With two days left prior to her departure, the Pine mother noticed my distant demeanor and asked me if I was alright. I confided in her about my fear of traveling alone. She came and sat close to me, offering wise reassurance in her soothing way. While I cannot recall exactly what she said, I remember the calming, comforting, and encouraging effect it had on me.

The eldest son gave me contact information for a man named Arny, north of Lyon, where I could stay while he worked on restoring a seventeenth-century chapel. Having a destination provided a sense of security. Although I felt apprehensive, I received an acceptance of my Couchsurfing request for hospitality from an older gentleman in Lyon who offered me floor space during the famous Fete de Lumiere festival, which celebrated the Winter Solstice for weeks in advance, three hundred miles away. With a rough itinerary in place and a decent map, I prepared for the mysterious roads ahead, planning to document my experiences to ease my fear of being alone. With introspection and trepidation, I wrote:

Dan said, "The road has never made anyone anything. It just lets them be who they truly are. I'm not ready to be who I am yet. Unlike Nathaniel, he shines like the sun... The road was the best thing that could have happened to him, a chance to be who he always has been. He's saying he changed so much. I think he finally stopped changing for this or that, and started just being who he is." I know that many of you don't profoundly know me because you knew who I was pretending to be, the visage and facade that I put on while in the U.S. to fit in, be accepted, and get along. Now, I'm not willing to put up with the bullshit, falsity, and fakeness. I will not conform. A brief detail of what I'm affirming lately: love, understanding, generosity, joy, bicycles, freedom, as well as different cultures, mindsets, and ways of living. Traveling alone, facing truly one of my greatest fears: the unknown.

Now, I step knee-deep into it with happiness to go where I please, do what I please, and enjoy every minute of it. Sometimes I eat too much because I find so much free food. It's amazing what people are willing to throw away, mere meters from where they recently purchased it. I laugh to myself at their silliness and then exploit their excess! Cities especially are too easy where everything is by the minute and everyone has something important to do or somewhere to go. The fast-paced work lifestyle that I am outside. People have had theoretical discussions with me to the effect of, "Don't you feel bad being a parasite of an over excessive and wasteful society?" and I simply reply that I wish our society was not so wasteful nor excessive, so that I would have to find a different way of living. I look forward to the day when I can't find enough food to feed ten people in several dumpsters within the same mile!

 The night before my and Hanna's departure was bittersweet, as we stayed awake chatting and smoking with the Pine family late into the night. They had become dear friends after only a week. As our love-making lasted until morning broke, sadness hung heavy in the air, the dewy dawn feeling somber, like a funeral. After the sleepless night, I finished packing sluggishly, tested Pearl, and faced tearful goodbyes with the Pine family, as well as Hanna. Embracing my travel companion openly, we felt the weight of parting. Just like before DJ's flight, I biked away before allowing her to leave me, feeling a bit better about having control of the decision, as their cheers faded into the distance. I longed to stay, yet the urge to explore and face the unknown propelled me forward. With gratitude for the support of others, especially my most recent hosts, I embarked on my journey alone, eager to discover my true character amidst the challenges ahead. I believed that the cycle of kindness would see me through any challenges within the next phase of my journey.

Chapter 16
A Lone Warrior Treks On

As I ventured out of sight, totally alone in a foreign country where I didn't speak the language, emotion overcame me minutes into pedaling away from anything familiar to the point where seeing through the tears was nearly impossible. As I got onto the main road, heading south, my vision blurred from weeping, and I had to pull over to compose myself. Turning back to comfort wasn't an option; I was driven to go on. My motivation was hard to explain, but despite countless chances to quit, I persisted. The determination came from somewhere inside of me. I was ready to be tested in ways I could hardly imagine.

For over seven months, I had been preparing. I optimized my clothes and gear, learned how to find food, juggle for tips, fix my bike, and stealthily set up camp. Yet, being alone in a foreign land, relying solely on myself, was a new challenge. I had the Magic Note translated for emergencies, provisions of preserved food, and full water jugs. The weather was chilly, but pedaling kept me warm. Several hundred miles to the Mediterranean lay ahead. My legs, hardened by hills, were strong; muscles like tree trunks. My Boy Scout training, culminating in becoming an Eagle Scout, had been invaluable and would prove even more so on this journey. Belief in myself, honed by a lifetime of overcoming adversity and besting challenges, was my greatest asset. I was strong, capable, and ready to face whatever came my way.

As both an adult and as a child, I felt alienated and as if I was an outcast on the fringes of society. Having learned my own power fueled and strengthened my fortitude, willpower, and resiliency. Regardless of my sleep deprivation, I steadied myself with self-affirmations, and I gathered my willingness to be uncomfortable and conquer my shadow, vices, or demons, gained through a lifetime of ostracization, believing that if I could get through the horrors of my past, then I could get through this. With my compass guiding me south, I started on a paved road leading away from the farm, which transitioned to gravel as it passed quaint cottages, and then followed a footpath along a tributary toward the Rhone. The picturesque countryside slowly eased my immense angst. The quiet roads and sparse encounters intensified my solitude, contrasting with the bustling farm life and constant companionship I was used to.

As I pedaled in silence, my first major challenge arose: my untrained mind became a torrent of negative thoughts full of self-doubt, unworthiness, and disbelief in my own abilities, as well as annoying songs playing endlessly in my brain. Without meditation skills, I struggled with this mental chaos; the songs replaying incessantly. Later, as I studied Freude, Jung, and other psychologists, I understood this as my ego demanding attention. I learned I am not my thoughts, but back then, I had to endure them, sometimes humming or singing to break the cycle. This vocal expression, a step in reclaiming my voice after childhood trauma, made me worry that I would seem crazy.

By midday, I stopped at a small, charming town for lunch. The minimal French I had picked up included important phrases such as, "I don't speak French," and, "Where is the _____?" and "Which way is _____?" Since reading French was significantly easier than speaking or listening to it, I vaguely understood street signs, but struggled while someone vocalized directions. The spoken language is a game of how many vowels and consonants a person can leave out of a written word when pronouncing it. As I learned more, the slang and colloquialisms grew on me. Using the Magic Note at a tiny cafe, grocery store, butcher shop, and restaurant all in one, the proprietor met me with kindness and generosity. This small success was a morale booster, reminding me of the strength and resourcefulness that had brought me this far. After my more than modest lunch, I checked my compass and continued on.

Pedaling quietly, I could hear everything around me—from the wind in the trees to approaching vehicles. I often used the canal paths, enjoying their meandering route through the French countryside. This indirect journey gave me an experiential appreciation for why the French valued bicycles enough to create the Tour de France. Infrequently, locals would approach, chuckling, and ask, "Ah, le Tour de France?" I'd respond with a grin, "Non, non, monsieur. Le Tour du Monde!" Their laughter and well-wishes buoyed my spirits, as did their evident respect for my bicycle journey. Traveling alone, I met significantly more people than when I had companions. Alone, I felt bolder and more approachable, as strangers either pitied me or, seeing me isolated, sought to relieve a social void.

Occasionally, cyclists in racing gear would zip past me without warning, their speed startling. But on this first day alone, I saw only a few people. The remote area, with its small villages and agricultural focus, was quiet and serene. Despite the peaceful surroundings, I struggled to enjoy myself, feeling like a lone soldier who has lost all of his brothers in arms, with a heavy heart, yet driven by a fathomless sense of purpose. It took me three days to cover over two hundred miles of unfamiliar territory, bringing my total to more than fifty-five hundred. I passed Vincelles, Chatel-Censoir, Avallon, Saulieu, Chagny, Chalon Sur-Saone, and more during this period.

By late November, I knew nights would be cold, so as darkness enveloped me before six o'clock, I searched for a place to settle. Lyon, where I had a Couchsurfing host named Terry, was still at least two days of cycling away, and I was eager for the festival and meeting more foreigners. I couldn't see the sun set behind the clouds, but the darkening sky signaled nightfall. I pulled off into a forest on the inside of a road curve, hidden from headlights.

Dismounting my new, trusty chariot, I felt a growing bond with this mechanical companion. She was sleek, smooth, and versatile, perfect for the long journey ahead. Her quirks made her seem almost alive, and I felt her displeasure when she fell against me or caused a gash with her sharp cogs. I removed and discarded the heavy kickstand for weight efficiency and led Pearl quietly into the woods.

Feeling secure, I left my panniers on the bike, unlike in civilization where theft was more of a worry, and locked up my bicycle, unwilling to take any risks of losing her, especially so early on. After setting up my tent, I settled into my sleeping bag, feeling tired and ready for sound sleep. One of Hanna's parting gifts was a profound blessing: she exchanged my lightweight forty-degree sleeping bag for her heavier, twenty-below bag. This thoughtful gift provided much-needed warmth on the cold nights in isolation. Her generosity filled me with gratitude, reminding me of the kindness and support I had received on my journey. Then, I discovered Hanna's last parting gift tucked away in my sleeping bag: an envelope with a letter and two hundred Euros. As I read it, my heart ached for her and tears fell silently. With less than thirty Euros, I had been worried about traveling with no margin for error, but now I had a safety net. I vowed to repay her kindness and return the sleeping bag someday. The love I felt for her propelled me to keep going. The silence of the forest contrasted with the noise of the day, so I turned on my headlamp and wrote until my mind was clear, then read until sleep overtook me. My first night alone, surrounded by nature, marked a new chapter in my journey.

I awoke in the middle of the night, a noise in the forest startling me. My heart raced as I sat up and peered through the tent's small eyelet window into the pitch-black forest, searching for the source of the ruckus. I heard *crunch, crunch, crunch*, then silence, repeating as the sounds drew nearer. Fear gripped me, and I reached for my pocket knife, preparing for the worst. With the largest blade ready, I turned on my headlamp.

To my surprise, there was no giant beast. Instead, my light caught the eye of a tiny cottontail rabbit, its red reflection glinting before it hopped away. I laughed at myself, realizing I had built up a dramatic story in my mind, only to discover the intruder was a harmless bunny drawn by the scent of my food. As I lay back down, a sense of calm washed over me. It took a while for my heart rate to slow enough for sleep, but eventually, I drifted off, dreaming of warmer days ahead. This first solo night highlighted the comedy of fear, especially when the loud, ominous sounds came from a creature so small. This event created awareness that my mind could blow something wildly out of proportion, and that I was safer than my fear let me dare to believe.

Throughout my life, and especially on this adventure, I never owned an alarm clock; the first hint of light would rouse me. Every time I have set an alarm, my body wakes me up several minutes to an hour prior to it sounding off. My morning routine was hasty: stuffing my sleeping bag into its small sack, repacking my panniers, and rolling up my tent to strap onto the rear rack before cycling away, hoping to avoid detection. I'd brush my teeth but usually skip breakfast, riding fifteen to twenty miles before hunger drove me to stop. I became a model of efficiency, maximizing the short daylight hours of winter, and often spent twelve hours in the tent each night. I read voraciously, consuming books and struggling to find new material in English in the towns I rode through to satiate my appetite for stories. Setting up and breaking down camp became second nature. With Dan, we could pitch the tent in under two and a half minutes; alone, I got it down to just three.

Continuing my journey, I passed through towns with lyrical names like Saint Marcet, Saint Germain du Plain, and Tournus. I networked along the way, jotting down contact info from acquaintances. Friends of friends were more likely to help me than strangers. I followed the Rhone River, a delightful companion, often crossing beautiful bridges and stopping to take in the breathtaking views. Majestic castles and churches perched on hillsides amazed me, and I marveled at the labor and resources that went into building them.

On the third day, I frustratingly found myself on a concrete bike path that turned to gravel, then dirt, and finally ended at a fence marking 'Private Property.' Forced to backtrack for over ten miles, I crossed a bridge I had already traversed and resumed my journey on the other side. These little frustrations festered in my mind, especially since Dan had encouraged me to never go backward. Whenever we had gotten lost, we would choose a new direction and rarely returned the way we came. Yet, each day I paced myself, averaging eleven miles per hour, except on hills, knowing winter limited the hours of daylight.

I carried a few items that were keepsake mementos, unnecessary to my survival, adhering to the philosophy that every ounce counts. However, I kept sentimental items like the Bicycology group tour dates and newspaper clippings from the Camp for Climate Action tucked neatly in my journal, reflecting on them fondly. Hanna's gift and my memories kept me motivated as I navigated the challenges and majesty of the road. At night, as I lay alone, I would record my thoughts and experiences:

Leaving Hanna was difficult. I miss her. I spent the first day on a quiet ride along the canal where I could hear few cars, see fewer people, and felt isolated from mankind. At night, I slept in a forest so quiet I could hear leaves dropping and a four-legged small animal nearby. The next day was tough, climbing hills all day on sore legs. My back feels the weakest, even though the pack is down to about twenty pounds. I'm also getting my 'biker's crotch' back, the leather chode. The French hills are

The Cycle of Kindness

as numerous as they are pleasant, with the colors of the changing season. Pearl is my warrior woman, elegant and sleek, refined and well-built, powerful and sturdy.

The wind has also been steadily blowing, catching my backpack like a sail. The weather was cloudy the first day, sunny all day yesterday, and right in between today. Last night, I asked a few people where is a good place to sleep and an older woman let me stay on her lawn. I could hear the trucks go by, which was good compared to the silence; she also fed me dinner and breakfast. I tried the Magic Note, first two bakery failures and then two successes! One at a mom-and-pop owned mixed food shop, and then at the third bakery I tried. I wanted to try it more, but decided not to be a glutton. I even dumpster'd some bread at a little park beside the road where I sat down to eat.

Sometimes, as I lay in my sleeping bag, I'd wonder whether it was the middle of the night or early morning, peering through the small porthole-like window of my tent for the first hints of dawn. Fourteen hours of solitude with little to do and an inability to sleep all night was challenging. I could understand how mountaineers trapped in a storm for days get stir-crazy, longing to climb but forced to wait out the weather in a small tent. In those long, dark hours, my mind uncontrollably raced through a myriad of thoughts: wondering where Dan and Hanna were and what they were doing, devising new juggling patterns, contemplating socio-political theories, imagining ideal models for intentional communities, reminiscing about high school friends, and what the day ahead would be like.

Now, as I traveled alone, so many past life lessons served me well, kept my mind engaged, and helped me navigate the challenges of the road. For better or worse, my thoughts were a constant companion, filling the long nights and sustaining my journey forward. Finally, dawn would break, and with eagerness, I would pack up, break down the tent, shove everything into the panniers, brush my teeth, drink some water, and get on the road before the sun rose. Each morning, I'd check my compass and map, plotting my route and noting the towns I might encounter. Though my days began and ended with a routine, the hours in between were unpredictable. I never knew where I'd end up, who I'd meet, or what events would shape my journey.

Riding through the picturesque central French countryside, I marveled at the hills, farms, villages, and charming cottages. Unlike the utilitarian German buildings, these houses were unique and artistically designed, reflecting the personality of their creators. They stood in stark contrast to the cookie-cutter neighborhoods back in America, built cheaply and devoid of individuality.

Strategically placed castles perched on hillsides or ridges captivated me, their walls overlooking vast territories with rivers flowing nearby. Aside from providing drinking water and waste removal, I appreciated how these waterways served as trade routes, vantage points, and natural defenses. The sense of history was palpable, with structures that had stood barely altered for over a thousand years. I would often stop to place my hand on ancient walls, imagining the stories they would tell if they could speak.

As I pedaled through the serene and majestic region, it filled me with a sense of wonder and gratitude for the journey I was on. Each day was a blend of routine and discovery, with the beauty of the French countryside offering endless inspiration. The air was often brisk, and sometimes damp as I rode through fog or low-lying clouds atop ridges on my trusty steed, Pearl.

In the chilly mornings, she would creak, as if complaining about not being warmed up yet. If her handlebars leaned to one side, it was her way of telling me I hadn't balanced the panniers, often making me correct our path suddenly to avoid toppling over. Riding upright without hands, she'd occasionally fling her front wheel to one side, demanding my attention and reminding me to hold her firmly. These moments, though startling, were her way of ensuring I was present and attentive. Pearl made the journey easier than carrying the cart or riding the red mountain bike, Fear, without weight, but I struggled with the backpack. Initially weighing around twenty pounds, it pained my back, so I emptied it into the panniers. Still, wearing the empty backpack was similar to wearing a five-pound wind sail, pulling me back with each gust and adding drag.

During the middle of each day, with no specific stops planned, I began listening to my intuition more. Quieting my mind, I sought stillness, where I could ask questions and receive immediate, decisive answers. Whether to stop somewhere or which direction to turn became instinctual, leading me to breathtaking views and remote scenery. This intuitive traveling freed me from overthinking and allowed me to appreciate going with the flow. Unbeknownst to me, I entered a wine-producing region of France during one of these intuitive excursions through a village, leading to yet another brilliant experience.

Entering a small town in Burgundy, I cycled into a lively wine festival with streets so full I dismounted Pearl and walked. Everyone seemed to have a glass in hand, and I joined in, pilfering a spare glass and partaking in the complimentary libation. Despite language barriers, I connected with locals, cherishing every broken conversation. Amidst the isolation of solo travel, human interaction became a precious commodity. After a few glasses of wine, I encountered someone who spoke English. A brief conversation ensued, within which they answered my questions about the festive occasion before embracing me in a spontaneous hug. I held on, feeling a surge of dopamine with my first human contact since leaving Hanna. Eventually, I biked off into the night, finding a spot to pitch my tent, careless but grateful for the warmth of affectionate connection in an otherwise solitary journey. I was amazingly grateful for the smallest acts of kindness, and the cycle of kindness continued to prove itself consistent and perpetual in its motion. I posted my excitement online at my first opportunity with great zeal:

All right, all you Winos, pop-quiz... What area of France is one of the most famous areas of the world for its high-quality wine??? Bourgogne! And let me tell you from firsthand experience, they keep the best wine for themselves; they don't export it! My God! I've never tasted such pleasures, a twelve-year-old white from one of the top vineyards in the region, a seven-year-old red from a friendly neighbor's personal stash, valued at some two hundred and twenty dollars! He helped make the wine himself. In my opinion, the reason much of this wine tastes so much better than so many other places in the world is the passion and energy that goes into making it. I've never met people who cared so much about wine. It's essentially the love that you put into something that makes it so great, yet another reason that most corporate production is absolute crap when no one gives a damn and only cares about making a buck! I got to go to a festival celebrating the best wine of the region. I carried around a wine glass and restaurants and bars would have samples of some of their best wine... too easy to take advantage of this. I, like most of the Bourgeois present, was getting drunk, and I wasn't paying for it!

A Lone Warrior Treks On

The morning after a wine-filled night, I awoke with a splitting headache, having overslept my normal routine. Despite the hangover, I made my way to La Chapelle. There, I stayed with Arny, the Pine's friend, who had previously confirmed his willingness to host me. He was a quirky man, restoring an ancient church, and we quickly bonded amidst hard labor and hash spliffs, exchanging stories and philosophical ideals while toiling away at the primitive stone walls. Arny taught me about mortar and pestle, and on breaks, I explored the area, discovering a breathtaking valley and a death-defying rope swing. Several days quickly passed prior to my departure, and I bid farewell to Arny before heading to Lyon for the Festival of Light with my Couchsurfing host, Terry. I recalled my time fondly:

Yesterday was full of enlightening experiences, fulfilling conversations, beautiful sights, and chipping away at a wall. Arny and I talked for hours while working, about traveling experiences and the like; he's eager to share helpful tips. He told me about the Roman chapel we are restoring, rebuilt in seventeen twenty-one. While chipping away at nearly three-hundred-year-old plaster, he told me stories of India and other places he's been. We would break to make food, and I even cooked dinner. Always with a variety of cheese, so much diversity, depth, and flavor. It's quite a pleasure being here, all the while listening to music I've never heard before; complete with some traditional French folk music like in the movie Amelie.

The sunset was gorgeous as well, so I ran up the road for a better view and photos. I also awoke in the middle of the night to see the stars in the clear night sky. It's a bit heart wrenching how it reminds me of growing up on a farm. I miss the peace and tranquility. Somewhere I will find my project, the community of my own. My final night, we had an amazing French feast. We carpooled to Ivry where we went to an old hotel that's now lived in by a small group of families. The wine just keeps on getting better and better. Besides the wine, we ate a six-course meal with an almond crème meringue dessert that was to die for with a raspberry sauce. What a night. We ate and drank for hours, and had about ten different kinds of cheese.

I rode through more towns with pretty flowing names like Saint Marcet, Saint Germain du Plain, Cuisery, Tournus, Macon, Thoissey,

Villefranche-Saone, and Trevoux on my way toward Lyon, and as I neared the city, the signs of urbanization became evident: wider roads, more frequent street signs, and the resurgence of sidewalks. Despite the increase in clutter, the city offered unexpected treasures, like leftovers from restaurant tables and discarded day-old bread. Replenishing my supplies, I marveled at the majestic cathedral across the river, a testament to the enduring influence of the Christian faith in Europe. As I pondered its history, I couldn't help but wonder about the sacred spaces it may have replaced and the conflicts it may have witnessed over the ages.

Amidst the juxtaposition of modern and ancient buildings, the city buzzed with preparations for the Winter Solstice celebration. Festive lights illuminated a holiday village in the park, where vendors offered a variety of delights, including frogs' legs, a temptation I resisted because of my frugality. Though the word 'Christmas' was absent, the atmosphere exuded its spirit, seamlessly blending into the season. Fortunately, when I checked my email at a local library, another Couchsurfing host, Lindsay, had accepted my request. Excited at the prospect of staying alone with her, which persuaded me to accept her invitation immediately and alter my arrangements with Terry. As I poorly navigated the city, I relied on the kindness of strangers to guide me. Eventually, I arrived at her cozy flat, where she poured us glasses of wine, and we exchanged stories until midnight. To my surprise, she invited me to her bedroom, and I gratefully accepted, feeling blessed to find warmth and comfort in her embrace. I wasn't going to let the opportunity to partake in one of my most favorite activities go to waste. This helped relieve the heartache and longing I'd felt for Hanna since our separation, and the twenty-three-year-old me was grateful for the distraction. Finally, somewhere in the early morning hours, we finished our third bottle of wine, ran out of condoms, and went to sleep.

The morning after a night of wine and music, I nursed a sulfite hangover while enjoying a long-distance call with an old friend using Lindsay's phone. Unfortunately, the call resulted in unexpected charges for my host, leading to a tense situation in which she confronted me about it, and I apologized profusely, not knowing what the consequences of my actions would be. After asking for reimbursement, prompting me to confess how little money I owned, she forgave me, thankfully, as that evening, the wine flowed again as we sang, and she played guitar, immersing ourselves completely in the music.

Even with the fun and comfort, our passionate encounter felt shallow, leaving me with a sense of emptiness as I departed the next day. Though I had hoped to cross paths with her again during the festival, our connection remained temporary. As I resumed my journey, I reflected on the transient nature of relationships, finding solace in the adventure ahead. Since then, I've heard and appreciated the term 'expirationship,' which is a relationship that one knows is going to end before it even begins. Our fling was fast and fleeting and left me drained and exhausted, sleep deprived, and in dire need of replenishing bodily fluids.

The next day, I poorly navigated the city again, felt lost for hours, and stopped to ask for directions several times before finding the correct building. Upon reaching Terry's apartment, a tall, slender man with a warm smile greeted me. Over the next few days, the apartment became a hub for Couchsurfers from various countries, including Italy, France, the Netherlands, Belgium, and Switzerland. I had no idea Terry planned to have another guest, let alone six others, who all trickled in one by one, with the exception of one triad. Our host introduced us to Pastis, a licorice liquor that fostered lively conversation among us and that I immediately took a liking to. Our first night together, we filled a restaurant with our diverse group, representing dozens of languages and cultures. Amidst the camaraderie, I received advice from a Canadian Couchsurfer about the preferential treatment of claiming Canadian nationality, instead of the highly discriminated against American, while traveling, a gesture I appreciated despite not choosing to use it. I preferred to be authentic and genuine, allowing how I am as a person to allow whoever I was interacting with to have a different experience of what someone from the United States can be. Two individuals, nicknamed One-ninety-nine and Nakimo, were particularly curious about my life and plans. We spent nights engrossed in philosophical discussions and captured the group gatherings on a variety of cameras.

Throughout the festival nights, our diverse group formed little cliques with varying agendas. Some sought romantic encounters, others were photographers or experience collectors. We roamed the streets, enjoying mulled wine from vendors, with a few new friends generously treating

The Cycle of Kindness

me to a glass. I felt self-conscious about my financial situation and how I stood out in my bright red rain jacket.

Back at our host's apartment, I provided services in exchange for his hospitality, including doing everyone's laundry to combat the cycling-induced odor. For a short while, I felt just like an everyday tourist, there to watch the festival. The viewing experience was one of the most magnificently dazzling displays of illuminated buildings, three-dimensional projection mapping, and live performances, leaving a lasting impression. Each night, we returned to our crowded accommodations, with someone inevitably passing out drunk in one of the spaces, with every available space occupied, leaving a few of us to sleep on the floor.

Every year, Lyon's Festival of Light attracts thousands of visitors to its picturesque streets along the Rhone River. Stunning light displays adorn buildings, old and new, from modern light-emitting-diode decorations to intricate projections. Everywhere I looked, the city twinkled and glowed with vibrant colors, and I'm sure it's only improved in the last eighteen years since I visited. The main gathering areas host performances, with live dancers, fire performers, troupes of artists, and musicians, captivating the crowds. I stumbled upon carolers singing in French and groups of travelers, seemingly from every corner of the globe, mingling under the brilliant lights. Although the festival was unknown to me, prior to my visit, it left an unforgettable impression on me. I collected memories and pamphlets, cherishing the experience forever:

The Festival of Lights has been, well, enlightening! Many great things have happened here in Lyon to further propel me on my travels. It has become increasingly difficult to write as life moves too fast. Every week presents something better than the last. I read the Celestine Prophecy and Siddhartha. I started the Hitchhiker's Guide to the Galaxy series. I gave up smoking. Terry opened my eyes and heart to Couchsurfing, Lyon, and the Fete de Lumiere. My French is steadily increasing, much faster now that I'm on my own.

On the final night, my host made a sexual advance toward me, catching me off guard and raising awareness of a possible pattern. He hadn't seemed homosexual, and the nonconsensual experience taught me to be mindful of potential advances from hosts in the future. Luckily, by the end of the festival, I had forged two new friendships with One-ninety-nine and Nakimo, who had visited Lyon purely for the festival. They both graciously invited me to stay with them in the South of France, a several day's ride away, where I already intended to go.

Their generosity and openness gave me a clearer sense of direction and purpose. Feeling safe amongst these newfound friends, I accepted the invitation of another Couchsurfing host, a male couple living in an old castle on my route to Marseille. Their hospitality and kindness reaffirmed my faith in humanity, making my journey southward feel guided and supported. My host, Terry, expressed his gratitude for my help, marking my departure with warmth and appreciation, even given our last encounter. I received several more positive testimonials, as well as my first vouch, further creating ease in receiving hospitality invitations from future hosts. As I left Lyon, I felt grateful for the kindness of strangers, especially within the Couchsurfing community and the friendships that helped shape my path forward.

Chapter 17
The French Riviera

As I rode all day through Villefontaine, Vienne, Beaurepaire, Le Grand Serre, and Le Cabaret Neuf, the warmth of new connections inspired me forward faster, which assisted me in generating the body heat I needed to contend with the chilly December air. I embraced the countryside's beauty while pushing myself to pedal more quickly, eager to make the most of my time. I adapted to the cold by layering up with makeshift headbands and constantly wearing my thermals, ensuring I could keep riding without pause. I turned the clothes inside out at night so they could dry and air out, as they became quite odorous after repeated sweaty uses. By this point, I learned to multitask so efficiently on Pearl that it became second nature. I ate and drank water while riding to save time, although I had a few close calls where I almost went off the road or swerved into the other lane, when there were no incoming cars, thank goodness, which reminded me to stay focused. Nonetheless, Lyon and Arny's company left me invigorated and ready to tackle the road ahead, each pedal stroke bringing me closer to my next destination.

The first night out of Lyon, I awoke to a frozen tent and struggled to disassemble it, my hands nearly going numb in the process. Seeking refuge in a church one night brought some relief, but the journey remained arduous. My biggest test yet came on the third day, as I climbed three separate grueling hills, each one nearly two thousand feet of vertical ascent to the pass. I begrudgingly climbed, sometimes cursing aloud. The only thoughts that gave me much respite were that every hill strengthened me and that they afforded great views. The second one paid off more than nearly any other throughout the entire voyage. As I crested the summit and caught my breath, I glanced around, and to my left were the French Alps, whose beauty was so spectacularly awe-inspiring and breathtaking that I nearly choked, cried, and fell over simultaneously. I don't know how I didn't crash, as I couldn't keep my eyes on the road ahead of me and nearly deviated down a gravel road to look for the clearest vista to stop and enjoy the beautiful splendor of the distant snow-covered peaks. An entire range, one mountain after the other, all heavily covered by this time of year.

I twisted and turned down unknown roads until one dead-ended in a stranger's yard, tears of joy streaming down my face. Regardless of my broken French, the elderly couple welcomed me with warmth and hospitality, sharing a meal and stories of their lifelong connection to the land. Grateful, I continued my journey, humbled by their generosity and the superb scenery, feeling the warmth of the spontaneous human connection amidst the cold.

As I pedaled onward, I marveled at the warm welcomes and amiability I encountered from strangers as I ventured further south. Despite childhood warnings to be cautious and avoid people I didn't know, nearly every time I was vulnerable and opened up to the acquaintances I met, this brought their guard down, letting out their inherent goodness. Regardless of age, gender, or appearance, almost everyone I met treated me with loving openness. Reflecting on the countless acts of kindness I received, I felt compelled to give back in some way. I contemplated how I could achieve this by hosting travelers through Couchsurfing in the future or doing nonprofit work, such as volunteering to care for others, supporting refugees or illegal immigrants or similar humanitarian relief. I noticed how important it became to me to pay forward the acts of service I had experienced on my journey. Simply taking from others was no longer an acceptable way of being. Instead, I wanted to at least be reciprocal, or better yet, find ways to give more than I took.

As I descended, enjoying the sight of the distant Alps, I remained vigilant on the narrow road, mindful of passing vehicles. Approaching a small town, I spotted a grocery store by a bridge over a river. My intuition urged me to stop at the dumpsters, a feeling too strong to ignore. And it proved to be the right decision. Not one, but three dumpsters, greeted me, and as I slowed down and parked Pearl, I detected no foul odor. I worried they were empty and questioned my intuition for a moment. To my joyous surprise, they were full of every kind of food sold in the store, as if each dumpster mirrored the aisles inside. I thought the first one was a fluke, finding frozen and refrigerated goods with meats, fishes, cheeses, dairy products, eggs, and more. So, I opened the second, brimming with dried goods, nuts, chips, candy bars, crackers, and chips. Lastly, the third, was full of fruits, vegetables, and fresh produce.

I immediately opened the lighter airy bags and engorged on fistfuls of chips and snacks, meanwhile carefully packing the heavier and denser, high caloric items neatly into my food pannier. Once it was full, I stuffed more into my water pannier, next, my clothes pannier, and then my final pannier. Everything was teeming to the point of nearly bursting at the seams, and there was so much more food I didn't want to waste, yet I couldn't fit it inside my panniers. Typically, I left my one-hundred-and-twenty-eight-liter backpack completely empty, but by the time I was finished cramming all sorts of foods into every nook and cranny, zippers barely able to be closed, it weighed at least eighty pounds.

After engorging on a hearty meal from the dumpsters, I struggled to pedal with the added weight, prompting Pearl to audibly protest. Realizing I couldn't conquer the upcoming hill, I resorted to walking, with Pearl complaining at the burden, being so over encumbered. When I saw a local walking to their mailbox, an idea came to me. I practically blurted out, "Joyeux Noel, aliments gratuit!" I grabbed a fistful of candy bars and thrusted them in their direction. My statement meant, "Merry Christmas, free food!" The man looked at me with utter perplexed vexation, confused by my statement to no end, as I appeared to be the one in need of food, not in a position to give it away; yet, after an unusually lengthy, awkward pause while he weighed his options, unsure what to do, he closed his slack-jawed mouth and extended his hand while saying, "Thank you," and proceeded to quickly retreat to his domicile. Afterwards, to every person I saw and at each house I passed by, until I got to the top of the hill, I made the same offer, a couple rejecting me, one offering me money, which I actually declined. Here was something I could do to give back to others, and it felt rewarding:

Making good time amidst amazing sights and hilly roads, I even spent a while in the fog. As low as minus two degrees Celsius, but I found a warm spot for lunch and a joint. Then came the Alps! I almost crashed Pearl and then went off-road to a small country house with very nice people. What a view. I had started the day determined to bike sixty miles, but in the end, it was more like one hundred and twenty. It felt hardcore, and my legs burned, lots of up and down hills. I found a set of dumpsters behind a supermarket and filled my bags with candy bars, chips, croissants, bread, energy drinks, tomato sauce, and a little juice. It was so heavy I had to walk up the next hill. Then I started to give away the food at houses I passed. I felt like Santa Claus.

Finally, I'd relieved enough weight and hiked up to a less steep part of the hill so I could actually pedal the beast of a powerhouse with pedals between my legs once more. With a second round of creaks and groans from Pearl, away we went. It must've taken a couple hours to get up that hill because at the bottom, there was full daylight, and by the top, it was the beginning of dusk. At the top, I stumbled upon a closed market where I ate another full meal before continuing my journey. After stuffing myself silly to unburden some of the excess weight, I headed downhill toward Romans, eager to reach my Couchsurfing host before nightfall. The descent into the village was smooth and effortless, carrying me into the town with perfect momentum.

An hour after the darkness of night settled in, I arrived in town, greeted by a mechanical bugler atop the clock tower. Layering up against the biting cold, I navigated the winding streets in search of my hosts' castle, the Hotel de Cleriu. Even though the building was close, the convoluted streets made it feel like I was going in circles. After I struggled to get someone's attention to ask for directions, I finally found my hosts' home. However, getting my bike inside proved to be a comedic challenge, and when they attempted to help me, the surprisingly heavy weight of my bags puzzled them. Eventually, I detached each pannier, hauled everything up two flights of stairs and settled in, grateful for the warmth and shelter but sweaty and out of breath from carrying everything up to their section of the castle.

My hosts gathered together with another Couchsurfer for the night, curious to see what I brought. I pulled out and tossed them chips, cookies, candy bars, cheeses, and all variety of foods I had obtained earlier that day. Their eyes widened in amazement, and our conversation quickly switched to English, which they spoke well and expressed their wonder and awe, questioning where I had acquired this cornucopia and how difficult it must have been to travel with it all. I responded honestly, amongst bewildered and jaw-dropping expressions. The other guest was a Canadian, and he immediately tore into a candy bar before our hosts scolded him, letting us both know that dinner was ready and not to spoil our appetites.

They had prepared a four-course meal for us, complete with appetizer, dessert, a roasted duck, and some kind of rolled meatloaf, with pairings of wine for each course, of course. I devoured all of it, to their somewhat ghastly amazement. They looked at me as if they had never seen someone eat in that manner before, and I ate as if I hadn't eaten a meal in days, regardless of having already stuffed myself silly twice that afternoon. I told stories between shoveling forkfuls of food into my mouth and got louder and more animated with the wine. They were beside themselves with disbelief, and one of them informed me he worked for the local newspaper and asked politely if I would allow him to write an article about me to go into the next publication; I gladly consented and felt triumphant, hearing he'd highlight me in the newspaper. After dinner, I asked to get on their computer so I could email my friends with the story of my best dumpster score ever. I wrote an honest and unembellished version of what happened:

I rode through Avignon, Valence, Romans-Sur-Isere, and St. Remy-de-Provence. I went to a church to seek refuge from the cold the night after my tent froze! Hanna, Dan, did the tent ever freeze in Scotland? Some of the towns are at least seventeen-hundred years old, dominated by the church for over a millennium, one of which was a place where the Pope lived before Rome. It had the first bridge over the Rhone River and was a place where they had sent crusades from. The history is overwhelming, understanding the geography makes the past chronicles all make sense so much more. I'm also going to be in a French newspaper! Oh, joy is me, learning the language while biking toward the Mediterranean, sun on my face—in December! It's upwards of sixty degrees Fahrenheit in the warmest part of the day. It's been so long since I felt warm rain. It reminds me of a cross between the coast of Oregon, Northern California, and heaven! I've started to listen to nature more. It laughs at me just when I need it; it has taught me to laugh as well. There is no wrong road. I've learned to enjoy the uphill challenge. It's one of the few difficulties left that truly feels like an empowering sense of accomplishment once I get to the top, although it takes some work. My legs are stronger than ever. I wonder how much weight I could dead-lift with these tree-trunks of mine. On this trip, I've been called a saint, a hero, and now, a champion.

The cycle of kindness reflected its gold in a new way, with me finally being reciprocal with my host couple that bewildered the imagination with generosity and abundance. As I sank into the comfort of my bed in the castle, a sense of drunken exuberance washed over me. It seemed like the universe was rewarding me for something, showering me with blessings since I embarked on this solo journey. From elaborate meals to lavish hospitality, life felt richer than ever before. With each positive Couchsurfing review, getting hosted became easier, and I had two more stops before reaching the Mediterranean. Yet, the direction of my journey remained uncertain—Italy to the east or Spain to the west? Despite the whirlwind of thoughts, the plush bedding lulled me into a catatonic and contented sleep.

The next morning, I woke up in my room as the castle's grandeur struck me anew. The stone work, wrought-iron lamps, and heavy wooden doors whispered tales of centuries past. Learning that French kings had once lived here only added to its mystique. Descending to the aroma of French coffee and a spread of breads and cheeses, I joined my host, who invited me to accompany him to his classroom for a unique presentation to his students.

Walking through the small village, I felt a sense of nostalgia as I entered the school, reminiscent of my high school days. Standing before the class, I explained the story of my incredible journey, sparking gasps of amazement and curiosity from the students. My unconventional lifestyle and the lack of a set plan for the future intrigued them. Despite their initial surprise, they thanked me for broadening their horizons. After the session, my host took me to the newspaper office, where I comprehensively explained more of my story for an article. It was a moment of recognition after months on the road, a testament to the richness of my experiences. Yet, as I daydreamed of grand outcomes, I realized that sometimes recognition comes in quieter, more subtle ways.

After the interview, I roamed the town on my own while my host wrote the article, enjoying its quaint charm and crossing an ancient bridge. Back at the castle, I was greeted by the other Couchsurfer. We chatted lazily about our travels until our hosts returned, bearing wine and fresh food for a celebratory feast. The article they had written about me earlier in the day printed in the next day's paper and quickly became a hit and the talk of the town. That evening, we filled the air with merriment and engaged in borderline flirtatious banter. Over an elaborate dinner and dessert made from dumpster'd candy bars, we shared stories late into the night. They insisted I stay longer; I thanked them graciously, but declined and packed my bags. With a copy of the article safely stowed in my journal, titled "Extraordinary Adventure," I bid farewell that night, as I intended to leave before dawn and didn't want to wake them, eager to continue my journey with newfound energy and ardor in my heart:

I speedily biked ten hours into Romans, including breaks and hills. I saw the village lights in the distance under the starry night, then spent a half of an hour finding the place I was two hundred meters away from! Magnificent Hotel de Cleriu, over one thousand years old, and two kings have lived here. How unresponsive and unreceptive people can be to a total stranger surprised me; who turns down free food? What an incredible accomplishment, a hard day of biking, just as much as the ironman triathlon, but carrying full gear.

Heading out toward the Mediterranean, I rarely paused, except for essential breaks and occasional marvels along the way. Through various villages and towns, I felt the geniality of French hospitality. I occasionally faced challenges like traversing freeways. The journey tested my resilience and strengthened both my legs and willpower. In defiance of the chilly conditions, I pressed forward, knowing that warmer days and the company of friends awaited me ahead.

The first night I slept alongside the Rhone River, in a fairly open clearing with my tent nestled behind a few bushes. Hoping for a better night's sleep, I obtained a small bell from the castle and attached it to my tent's guy line. I believed that if anyone moved Pearl, it would wake me up. However, as the night became windy, the incessant jingling of the bell infuriated me. With bitter frustration, I arose and removed it, acknowledging that my idea had proved a failure. The wind quickened through the nearby bushes and howled through the distant trees. I pulled the drawstring tightly against my face until there wasn't much more than a hole to breathe out of. By the time the first light of morning came, my lips felt cold and wind-kissed, chapped and dehydrated.

The second night was one of the worst of my life, still along the Rhone River, having gone down a pretty steep hill, zig-zagging down a switchback road to the bottom of a dam. I found a gate left unlocked and open. As it was late and no lights were on, I tiptoed in and put my tent alongside a concrete building, knowing I would be gone before anyone arrived in the morning. I was noticeably damp by the time I got into my tent. So, I switched clothes into dry thermals to sleep in. Throughout the night, the slow falling mist, combined with increasing cold, and a microclimate of swirling winds around the moving water, compounded. It froze my tent into sheets of ice, and when I arose to urinate in the middle of the night, I struggled with the zipper, and in my groggy state, couldn't understand where the problem was arising from. When I finally got it to zip open, I shuddered as I exposed myself to the chilly night air, hurrying to get back into my warm sleeping bag, my feet feeling as though they had turned to icicles atop the bare ground, even though I had been out for less than a minute.

By the time I wiped my feet and retreated into the cozy bag, my body heat had departed. I didn't have a sleeping pad or anything to insulate my sleeping bag from the frozen ground; the temperatures left me shivering. I fell asleep thinking I would be fine, yet I awoke multiple times, aching in the cold, grabbing whatever clothes I could reach and stuffing them in with me, barricading the tiny entrance at the top and curling into a ball down at the bottom, hoping to stave off the frigidly biting air.

By the time I sensed the first light of day, I was shaking uncontrollably, found my water bottles frozen shut, and tent poles covered in icicles. I threw on every article of clothing I had, wrapping an extra T-shirt around my neck. After having to nearly break open the frozen zipper, I got out of the tent with a shriek at the slap-in-the-face temperature that met me. I immediately did rapid jumping jacks and ran in place while breathing into my hands. Repacking my panniers and tent usually took less than fifteen minutes, but on that morning, it agonizingly lasted for nearly an hour because of how many times I had to pause to warm up my hands. I would shove them into my armpit one at a time, under my layers, while trying to work frantically with one hand, or resume my rigorous exercise movements to create more body heat. I

The French Riviera

wanted to cry so badly but was genuinely afraid the tears would freeze my eyelids closed, as I had to remove some freezing snot dripping out of my nostrils. My gloves became crunchy doing the work and my hands trembled and shook, but thankfully, never changed colors.

When I got on Pearl and painfully pedaled out of there, I experienced an increase in wind because of being in motion. I thought it couldn't get worse before that. Several miles went by before the air warmed up and more light peered through the clouds. The sun was still nowhere in sight, though. Finally, it emerged later that morning, prompting me to lie in a sunbeam and pray to whatever God or creator, thanking them for my life and for helping me through this unbelievably challenging trial. I hoped to find a stranger willing to host me that day, but after knocking on a few doors, I had no solid leads. Defeated by the constant rejection, I feared the thought of having to go through another similarly horrific night and worry for my safety preoccupied my mind.

Over the next three days, I continued through Valence, and on the west side of the Rhone River past Le Pouzin, Rochemaure, Viviers, crossed again to the east and alongside Pierrelatte, Bollene, Orange, Sorgues, Avignon, Chateautenard, Saint Remy-de-Provence, Cavaillon, Salon-de-Provence, Istres, Marignane, and Chateauneuf-les-Martigues, where the night air stayed relatively warm. I could tell I was within a day's ride of the sea, and felt thankful that my food supply had lasted, as I was engorging on it every chance I could, trying to lighten my load so I could move faster. I must've consumed at least five meals and over ten thousand calories a day. Over those few weeks, I'd added several hundred miles, crossing most of France from north to south, bringing my total to over sixty-five hundred.

As I neared the Mediterranean, each hill promised a glimpse of the sea, but it remained elusive until I reached a viewpoint obstructed by a train bridge. Finally spotting the shimmering blue waters through a gap, I cheered with delight. Excited to reach my destination in Marseille, I descended toward the city, relishing the warmth of the coastal air. Savoring the view, I stopped to embrace the Mediterranean climate, feeling the anticipation of leaving behind the frigid days. With reinvigorated energy, I continued my journey, anxious to see a familiar face and for the adventures that lay ahead.

As I coasted into Marseille, the warm breeze and gentle downhill were a reward after enduring the challenges of the past days. I spent half of that day exploring the city's bustling streets, and eventually found Nakimo's restaurant, my destination for the last few days. As I surprised him during his shift, we enjoyed our reunion immensely. I wandered the city, mindful of Nakimo's warnings about theft, while waiting for him to finish working. After he was done, we headed straight to the beach, because of my request, where I eagerly stripped down to my underwear and then dove into the sea, feeling refreshed after days without a shower. Nakimo guided me to his dormitory afterward, where we shared stories, and he introduced me to his passion for architecture. Our conversation led to Ayn Rand's The Fountainhead, sparking Nakimo's interest in reading it. As we talked late into the night, I couldn't help but appreciate the sense of accomplishment and fellowship that came with reaching my destination and reconnecting with a friend.

Waking up the following morning, in Nakimo's tiny but warm college dorm room, was a stark contrast to the frigid nights I had endured. After a refreshing shower, Nakimo couldn't help but comment on his admiration of my lean physique, a result of months of cycling. Wishing to share his favorite beach spot, we packed up supplies, met two of his friends who had a car, and headed to the Calanques, a region famous for its natural beauty and steep cliffs. We all traversed a rocky descent to a secluded pebble beach and embraced the nudist vibe. The four of us plunged into the chilly Mediterranean waters, marveling at the underwater scenery. Even with the language barrier, I found joy in the company of Nakimo and his mates, soaking up the laughter and friendship, after feeling desperately alone since leaving Lyon.

We returned to his dorm room, where I drifted off, exhausted from the day's adventures, while Nakimo worked on his studies, grateful for the newfound friendship and the moments of closeness. I felt a strong bond with him, regardless of our diverse backgrounds. I welcomed our discussions and the insights into each other's cultures, feeling an attachment I hadn't experienced since Hanna departed. Nakimo wished he could join me on my travels. However, his ties to his family and financial obligations kept him rooted in France.

We spent the following day exploring Marseille, from its bustling center to its historic landmarks and ancient buildings. Walking through

The French Riviera

streets steeped in centuries of history, I couldn't help but marvel at the endurance of this city through countless trials and tribulations. As Nakimo returned to work, I found myself lost in contemplation on a nearby beach, pondering my place in the grand tapestry of history. Later, we indulged in a lavish feast to celebrate our friendship, enjoying good food and wine until we were both contentedly full. I felt grateful that Nakimo hadn't made unwanted sexual advances and respected my boundaries, as we shared a genuine connection. When I prepared to leave, Nakimo's wistful gaze mirrored my own feelings of reluctance to say goodbye. Promising to stay in touch, we shared a heartfelt hug before I set off on my next adventure, carrying with me memories of our time together. Even years later, our friendship endures, reminding me of the value of genuine kinship in life.

Leaving Marseille, I faced a grueling ascent through the Calanques, a landscape known for its punishing hills and breathtaking views. As professional cyclists whizzed past me, I struggled to conquer the steep switchbacks, my lungs burning with exertion. At the summit, I took a break to admire the expansive sea stretching out before me. Continuing along the cliff tops, through areas steeped in history and surrounded by rugged hills, I reflected on this region being an extended part of the cradle of civilization. Eventually, I reached Toulon, a military stronghold with a serene beauty marred by remnants of its wartime past. Navigating the steep streets, I finally arrived at my next host's house, greeted by the familiar face of my friend I met in Lyon, One-ninety-nine. Despite it being less than a full day of exhausting hill climbing, the reward of the challenging journey was my sense of joy at reconnecting with a familiar face in this new setting.

One-ninety-nine had earned his nickname because of his extraordinary height, being just shy of two meters. He was a handsome and agreeable Belgian au pair with a knack for charming the ladies. As we relaxed on his balcony, he shared his fascination with my way of life, likening me to the fictional character John Connor from the Terminator series. He saw the trait of a leader in me, one who was committed to fighting for my beliefs without relying on technology, drawing parallels between my values and those of the movie persona. After sharing this story on my blog, Dan coined the nickname 'Johnny Conny,' which stuck, and soon, it became my identity among friends and even family.

Embracing this new role, I shed my childhood name, which no longer felt like me, and embraced the role of J.C., a moniker that would define me for years to come. It was a symbol of my desire to lead humanity toward a greater destiny, a more peace-filled world, and to give back, after having received so much.

One-ninety-nine and I spent the first afternoon indulging in snacks and conversation, our spirits lifted by laughter and philosophical discourse. Surrounded by the warmth of friendship and our haze of marijuana smoke, I felt a profound sense of connection and purpose. It was as if he reflected the significance of my journey, reaffirming my path, and its impact on others. His words ignited a surge of emotions, dispelling doubts and reminding me I wasn't alone and could make friends wherever I went.

With Christmas fast approaching in a few days, I was torn between two contrasting paths. On one hand, there was the enticing prospect of meeting another Couchsurfer, named Syrun, a seasoned traveler with an array of captivating tales to share. His journey, spanning across continents, beckoned me with the promise of adventure and enlightenment. On the other hand, there was the allure of Italy, the homeland of my ancestors, calling me to explore its picturesque coastline and reconnect with my roots. The thought of spending Christmas alone filled me with dread, yet the appeal of these adventures was equally compelling. As I weighed my options, the clock ticked closer to the day of decision, and I knew I had to make the difficult choice soon.

After a full day enjoying comfortable living and exploring Toulon on foot, we ended the night by smoking another joint, drinking wine, and having more incredible conversation. Waking to a message that confirmed acceptance of Syrun's hosting me was enough to tip my decision toward Toulouse to meet him. With One-ninety-nine's help, I secured a train ticket, marking the end of our days together. The farewell was bittersweet; we spent the final afternoon in quiet reflection, cherishing our last moments. As I boarded the train early the next morning, I felt a mix of excitement and nostalgia, ready to embark on the next chapter of my journey. We promised to stay in touch before I rolled away, heading westward for the first time in months:

I have found that things find me just when I am ready for the knowledge. I've understood how much wiser Dan is than I had realized before. I feel like I am going in the right direction, while I may not be on the right road... There is no wrong road! The way of the warrior is true. I miss reading the Warrior of Light. It will find me when I'm ready for it. I love my life. I received the best compliment of my entire life, which has led me to contemplate a new nickname: J.C. Oh, and by the way, I figured out how to slow down time. Time! It's great! It took me long enough, but I finally figured it out. Ah, how the days just go on and on.

Chapter 18
Christmas and the Coldest Day of My Life

The strategy I'd devised to slow down time came from a growing ability I'd developed. When I could simultaneously hold two different perspectives, everything was more vibrant, interesting, and alive. The details popped out, and I soaked in more out of every moment of life, in a deep state of presence. I would concurrently have the perspective of a newborn, looking at everything with amazement and wonder, in awe of the incredible newness of everything I encountered, viewing everything as if I were seeing it for the first time. The second perspective is one of an elderly person, on their deathbed, cherishing everything around them, knowing they are seeing it for the last time, grateful for every moment, holding onto the beauty and majesty of life, not wanting to let it go. As I practiced these complementary perspectives on the train ride to Toulouse, I drifted in and out of sleep, relishing the Southern French countryside and enjoying a complementary glass of wine. I worried I might miss my stop, but thankfully, I arrived safely to find Syrun waiting for me at the station, true to his word. The journey had been a peaceful respite, and I was grateful to be in his calm presence and companionship in the chilly evening air.

    Syrun's demeanor was stoic and unwavering as he greeted me at the train station, leading me back to his sparsely furnished apartment with little conversation. The space reflected his minimalist lifestyle, with only the essentials and no signs of extravagance. Despite his few words, I cooked us a meal with what food I had left, and we sat together in silence, smoking cigarettes as tendrils of smoke curled toward the ceiling. Syrun retreated to his bedroom early in the evening, leaving me to ponder his enigmatic personality. I wondered about the impact of his extensive travels on his demeanor and outlook on life, eager to uncover more about him in the days to come.

Syrun's quiet morning routine, marked by the smell of coffee, contrasted with the chill of his unheated apartment. As we ventured out into town, his taciturn guidance left me to lead our exploration. As I'd noticed his bare refrigerator and pantry, I focused on searching for dumpsters to dive into, which he seemed to be comfortable with. We secured a bounty of bread behind a local bakery to ensure we had enough to eat for the holiday ahead. After our day out, I recorded my recent experiences:

I spent December twenty-third cleaning up trash strewn about the streets of Toulouse. Walking with the man who walks the Earth, for a better world, for peace. A simple man, a plain man some might say, but in him, I saw glimpses of what it was probably like to know Jesus. There is a sort of eerie calm within him I cannot explain. He taught me many lessons, especially about games— relationship games, individual games, group games, and more. Many of these games are basically the same at the core, and now that I can identify them, it becomes easier to see which games I enjoy playing, and which ones I don't. I can move on from games of old and get better at the games I choose to play now. I got to be Santa Claus, in plain clothes, and a little early. Besides picking up trash, I gave out bread to anyone who would take it. Imagine: a stranger with a bag full of bread stops you on the street and speaks brokenly in your language, "Hello Sir/Miss, free bread for Christmas. Please, for you, it's free. Merry Christmas!" Would you take that bread? Many would not, but after much persistence and many streets, I was able to give one hundred baguettes to complete strangers. Always met with mixed reactions, the facial expressions are such a pleasant thing to watch.

The next day, the chill seemed to intensify, hinting at a storm. I ventured out alone, hoping to find a better stocked dumpster, but found the city eerily quiet and devoid of people. Snowflakes fell, a reminder of Toulouse's proximity to the Pyrenees Mountains. I noticed I didn't have

Christmas and the Coldest Day of My Life

adequate winter gear compared to the locals, who bundled themselves up in layers. I reminisced about the early frigid nights in the Vondelpark in March, and how I'd come to take for granted the seemingly endless summer I had experienced on my journey until recently. Regardless of the cold, I found solace in the fact that I had a warm place to sleep indoors, unlike some previous nights. That evening, Syrun and I followed our routine of a modest dinner, a single cigarette, and an early bedtime, with no special preparations for the seemingly unimportant holiday ahead.

As the morning unfolded, it felt like any other day, with the same routine downplaying the significance of Christmas, a day I had dreaded spending alone. While I woke up with excitement, greeting my host with enthusiasm, Syrun seemed oblivious to its importance, responding with a casual, "Oh, yeah," when I mentioned it. We spent the day watching movies with the audio dubbed over in French, like, *It's a Wonderful Life*, *The Life of Brian*, and *Die Hard*. I struggled to grasp the spoken language's rapidity. Our Christmas dinner was simple: a pot of rice and plain baguettes, devoid of any traditional foods or the usual festive trimmings.

Although he told me his parents lived downstairs, Syrun showed no interest in visiting them, adding another layer to his enigmatic persona. While he remained aloof, I busied myself with sewing, cherishing every piece of clothing I had. As I packed up to leave the next day at dawn, I couldn't shake my curiosity about Syrun's solitary existence and what had shaped him into the person he was. He had traveled to nearly fifty countries, all on foot, over several years. All the while, he never asked for help, but accepted every bit of aid that was offered to him. I wondered if his path and my own paralleled each other, and whether his way of being would be my fate if I continued traveling as long as he had. I explained to him I would leave the following morning before he arose, and we exchanged a single hug, bidding farewell to a holiday experience unlike any other, leaving me pondering the mysteries of his life.

As I laid down on the dilapidated mattress on the floor of his spare room for the last time and drifted off to sleep, I felt homesick and deeply missed my family and wished to have the kind of Christmas with them I had dreamed of recreating here. Feeling hollow, I wondered if they missed me like I missed them, and what my mother and father were experiencing, not having me home for the holidays. I had sent an identical digital letter to everyone who was important to me, not having time to write individually. It updated them of my activities and whereabouts, my plans, and offered the typical season's greetings. I let them know how difficult it was being separated, but I expressed my determination to continue on my own and explore more unfamiliar places. I wasn't done yet.

The following morning, after leaving Syrun's house, was the coldest day of my life, the story told at the beginning of this book. It was the closest I came to perishing on the entire adventure, and it was scary. After unlawfully entering the desolate building with a stack of mattresses and televisions, I slept and waited out one of the longest nights of the year. I needed to get out before other people were awake to witness that I had committed a crime, trespassing without breaking in. I continued checking for any light in the sky each time I awoke, and when I finally saw dawn's aurora, I packed up quickly and got back onto the road shortly after.

It was nowhere near as cold as the day before. Within a couple short hours of pedaling, I could see the Mediterranean again. I almost always rode in the morning until I was hungry and then stopped for breakfast. After departing Perpignan, I traveled through the towns of Collioure, Port-Vendres, Banyuls-s-Mer, and Cerbere. The coastal towns had much more bustle to them, and I successfully found a dumpster to replenish my reserves. I turned to parallel the sea and continued going my favorite direction thus far: south. When finally on a computer at a library in Barcelona, more than a week later, I tailored my blog post so as not to scare my family and friends back home:

Biking in the snow... that was unexpected, and my camera batteries died. I apologize that you only get one photo of the snow, and that I get a lifetime of memories of the extraordinary things that I have seen and need no proof of. They say when it rains, it pours, and after having not spent money since Paris, I've now dwindled my funds to near emergency levels only. The road was easy. My hands were cold, but the way was majestic. Trees with snow sticking to the outstretched branches, as they had nothing else to cling to. I infrequently stopped to fully experience moments of blissful peace in which I don't hear the cars anymore. After spending so much time in serene nature, I can smell and taste cars. They are putrid. The second day brought me almost to Perpignan, my target destination. However, I fell short as I got lost too many times and spent too long biking on dirt roads leading to the back of an African wildlife preservation where I could hear animals. I was a little sad not to see any and almost tried finding a way inside or around the fence; I'm glad I didn't end up as lunch for the lions. The potential host contacts didn't work out anyway, so I slept between an airport and a freeway, neither affecting me. Even the bumpy ground didn't bother me.

Cycling into Spain marked my seventh country on this tour, a milestone in my journey of over seven thousand miles. While I felt abandoned by my best friend and my short-term romance with Hanna along the way, since then, I had grown accustomed to solitude and self-reliance. Each possession became precious, essential for survival. As I pedaled through picturesque towns along the western edge of the Mediterranean, I marveled at the vibrant colors and quaint harbors. The residents primarily travel by boat over vehicles, as the distance between the villages is short, but the hillsides separating them are surprisingly tall, with switchback roads traversing both sides adding considerable mileage to the relatively short distance as the crow flies, or as a boat sails.

Climbing thousands of feet under the scorching sun, I wiped sweat from my brow and wrung out my sweatbands, pushing onward through the agony of the belabored ascent. Crossing the border into Spain was similarly unceremonious as every other country thus far, marked only by a sign and a painted line on the street. As I ascended my first incline in Spain, I spotted an abandoned home with a breathtaking view, tempting me to linger, but my determination to reach Barcelona for an epic New Year's Eve party motivated me to carry on. With plenty of daylight left, I pedaled forward, excited about the adventures that awaited me in this new country.

Scaling the inclines brought memories of my early struggles in Germany, now dwarfed by the repetitive and lengthy hills of Spain. During each ascent, I rarely paused, fueled by determination and adrenaline. Because of depleted camera batteries, I could not capture the picturesque towns, but I etched their images in my mind and continued riding relentlessly. While the first three hills took over two hours each to climb, the final hill, whether steeper or just the cumulative toll on my legs, took over three grueling hours to conquer. Exhausted, I found refuge on a rocky cliff side, barely bothering to conceal my tent, but despite physical exhaustion, sleep eluded me.

The Cycle of Kindness

I lay there hoping to meet an alluring woman in Barcelona, for her to whisper sweet nothings in my ear in a language I barely understood. I thought about how far I had come, and how if I could do what I did that day, I could do anything; ride up any mountain, cover any quantity of distance. I had this underlying thought of what's next? I felt a sense of accomplishment, fulfillment, and completion. Not like arriving at a destination, but a more conclusive thought: it can't get any harder. I had ascended around twelve thousand feet over eighty miles with nine hours of climbing in a single day, carrying around forty to fifty pounds of gear, plus the weight of Pearl herself.

I awoke in the middle of the night with a start. I could hear something very close to me with muffled and uneven breathing, making snorting and grunting sounds. It must've heard me sit up, as before I knew it, the tusked beast was leaping up the slope above me from boulder to boulder. I could barely catch a view of the silhouette of the animal crested atop the hillside against the skyline, but illuminated ever so faintly from the nearby streetlights, was a wild boar. It had come to search for food and would've scrounged my supplies had I not awoken. I chuckled to myself as I lay back down, thankful that the hog hadn't skewered my tent, tearing holes in the fabric. I documented the day:

The third day from Toulouse brought the most difficult biking yet. But also, one of the most beautiful. The road along the coast was up and down all day long. I calculated I did over twelve thousand feet of ascent in one day! My legs were burning, but the sights just kept on coming, and I powered through. What amazing views of the Mediterranean. People pay so much just to have these every day. I wonder if they appreciate them as much as I did. I'm at the point of rationing food, with only bread, some chocolate, and apples left. I slept on a cliff outcropping overlooking a charming bay. I made it to Spain, the seventh country on the ever-growing list of places I've been. Amazing to think I'll be here for a few months. My old Spanish classes are coming back to me rapidly, and I should be conversational in no time, but all the dialects make it just a little more difficult!

Unaware of Catalonia's primary language, Catalan, I stumbled through unfamiliar linguistic terrain. Legend has it that the dialect was born to honor a king with a lisp who liberated the region. Regardless of the linguistic shift, I felt a kinship with the liberal and progressive Catalans. As I set out the next morning, the toll of endless climbing and sleeping on stone left me sore. I'd literally rode right off of the maps I'd received as a gift in Germany. I began the day with a lazy start, regardless of my drive to reach Barcelona. As I pedaled, I relied on intuition, trusting in my ability to interpret Spanish signage.

The challenge of tackling another towering hill with fatigued muscles pained me, and the downhill ride provided a welcome reprieve. Zigzagging my way south, I went beyond Portbou, Platja Grifeu, Llanca, Vilajuiga, Vilatenim, Vilamorell, Viladamat, Verges, Pals, Palamos, and into Platja d'Aro i S'Agaro. I mostly followed signs to Barcelona while keeping to the coast, only leaving the sea behind momentarily. Motivated by thoughts of my impending stay in the city, I cycled on, legs burning with lactic acid buildup. Like a scene from *Fight Club*, I persevered through cramps and stiffness, fueled by the need for hydration and salt. As the afternoon waned, I pedaled until I found the Gold Coast, a once bustling region, now an eerily deserted ghost town in the off-season.

As the sun dipped below the horizon, I found myself amid another town, unsure of how far I'd traveled or how much farther I had to go. Disappointed by an empty dumpster, I reluctantly went on, eventually reaching a large intersection. Feeling frustrated by my earlier inefficient wandering, I followed the coastal route, pushing past the agony to climb another hill, as my legs wobbled and muscles spasmed. As darkness fell, I searched for a safe spot to rest, but the steep inclines offered little refuge. Disheartened, I trudged forward, my spirits lifted briefly by the sight of a passing cyclist, only to sink again as they rode on in the direction I had just come from without acknowledgment.

Moments later, I heard a faint sound approaching behind me; the cyclist had circled back. Seemingly, his entire intention in turning around was to connect with me, as he initially spoke Italian, then French, and then Spanish before finally settling on English. We struck up a conversation, and I explained my situation, to which he introduced himself as Giuseppe and insisted I stay with him at his sister's family home for the night. He was an Italian cycle-enthusiast on holiday, who worked for a major manufacturing company. Even though I was reluctant to backtrack, his persistence won me over. We retraced our route, with each hill feeling more daunting than the last. Three hours and at least twenty miles later, we arrived at his sister's extravagant home. Overwhelmed by the luxuriousness, I wondered why he was extending such kindness to someone like me. Was it simply our mutual love for cycling? Was it the desperation of my predicament in the story I had told him earlier? Was it pity? Would he try to sleep with me?

 I expressed my ravenous appetite, and he bid me welcome to any food in the house, informing me we would also go out to dinner after his sister and her family returned. I made and ate two massive sandwiches. By nine o'clock, the sister arrived home with her husband and son. Despite the initial confusion, they warmly welcomed me into their lavish home. The sister was charming, her husband exuded an air of aristocratic opulence, and their son remained quiet throughout the evening. Around ten, we ventured to a high-end restaurant where we received celebrity treatment. As we dined, the restaurant filled up, surprising me with the late dining culture.

 After the vehicles received valet parking, we walked through the restaurant doors, being held open for us by a waitstaff in tuxedos. I felt awkward and out of place, in clothes too baggy that weren't mine. The contrast in our outfits compared to the servers further enhanced my discomfort. The wafting smells of freshly baked bread entranced my nostrils as I sat down in a chair that was pulled out and pushed gently back in for me, a perfectly crisp, pressed napkin placed carefully on my lap. I had never had treatment like this in my life. The server brought a wooden tray of still steaming breads, rolls, and baked delicacies to our table and placed them on a shared plate; I tasted one of everything, finding what I liked most.

 The second course was a light soup. The third being black rice and mixed seafood with mussels, scallops, shrimp, octopus, and the like; I devoured every bit and then asked to eat what the sister didn't. She laughed at my request, but passed her plate along, nonetheless. I must've looked like I had a shovel in my hands. The fourth course was the entire half of a whitefish. I didn't care which kind. I ate mine, half of Giuseppe's sister's food, and all the potatoes. The fifth course was filet mignon and asparagus, the sixth course I don't recall because of my inebriation, and finally, the last course: a smorgasbord of tiny desserts and coffee, with two after-dinner drinks—sweet and warm dessert alcohols.

Christmas and the Coldest Day of My Life

A bottle of finely aged white wine was gone before the third course arrived, the first red disappeared after the two seafood courses, and the third bottle drained by us four adults before dessert. My temples were buzzing, my cheeks felt flush and red, my eyesight had gone blurry, my stomach totally bloated and engorged, and my mental faculties lacking, unable to make further decisions other than to say, "Yes, please." As all of this was taking place, the restaurant was slowly filling up with a buzz of people, all dressed significantly nicer than us, none of which had children at their table. This must have been one of the nicest restaurants in town, with upscale clientele.

It was a challenge to maintain composure as I got out of the seat smoothly. A man who seemed like the owner came over and thanked my hosts before we left; I can only imagine what the bill was. I didn't get so much as a glance at it, not that I tried. I was simply thankful to receive such indulgences. We had taken two cars so we could part ways after dinner. The son needed to go to bed, as it was almost midnight. Giuseppe wanted to show me a night out on the town, so he drove to the nightlife district, and on the way there, rolled a hash spliff and lit it, all while speedily weaving through traffic with ease. It looked like he had done this before. He told me not to tell, and after smoking half of it with me, told me I could have the rest. I smoked until I could hardly see.

The road went by in a blur. He wanted to show me all of his favorite destinations, but they were all closed. It must have been Monday or just the off-season. After nearly an hour of driving around, I could tell he was disappointed, yet determined. He had one more place he knew was open. Although he said it was a nightclub, it was, in truth, a brothel. There was no actual sign, as he turned off an unmarked road onto a descending driveway into a gravel parking lot. Hidden amongst a tree grove was a large two-story building, which we entered through an unmarked door after parking. I didn't stumble out of the car, but I was wobbly and couldn't walk a straight line to save my life.

I tried to compose myself before going inside and used my host to block the view of the bartender, feeling extremely self-conscious of my inebriated state, until we sat down at the bar. He ordered two beers for us, and the heavyset, middle-aged gentleman with a beer belly and gristle for hair on his face gave me a once over and immediately questioned Giuseppe, "Hey, is your friend eighteen?" Apparently, that's the legal age for both drinking and being a patron of a prostitute. So, he turned and asked me. I laughed and said I was twenty-three, which was true, although I had no way to prove it. The restaurant hadn't said a word about my age. I don't know if it was the laughter at the question or the response I gave, but the bartender didn't push the subject. We received our beers, and I took a sip out of obligation.

Within a minute, two young, attractive, scantily clad women entered the room and approached us, both of them flirting with Giuseppe; giving me no attention whatsoever. They knew who the money was. One of them sucked on one of his fingers and glanced over at me. I felt sheepish and embarrassed. I'd never been in an establishment of this nature before. I also had some ethical opposition to paying for sex. Finally, one came and sat down next to me, but realizing I didn't speak Catalan, got right back up again. Meanwhile, my host asked if there were any other ladies of the night.

While waiting, Giuseppe told me he would buy me any woman I wanted, and although I felt desire, I couldn't bring myself to accept his offer. I felt like someone had put me inside a dryer and put it on at a fast speed—my head was spinning and my thoughts with it. *Maybe this will be the only chance I ever get, and I ought to live life to the fullest. It's not my money, and it would help the prostitute out...* On the other hand, my Roman Catholic upbringing led me to believe that this was wrong. On principle, I felt attractive enough that I would never need to pay for sex, and that I would regret it if I accepted my host's offer. In the end, he wasn't interested in the last woman, and I was ready to get out of there. He had hardly drunk his beer. I had finished mine despite my inebriated state. Admittedly, I don't remember the car ride home, but I recall getting out, being shown the guest bedroom, hardly able to remove my clothes before passing out around two in the morning.

In the dead of night, I awoke to the urgent call of nature, stumbling in the darkness to find a light switch. When I finally located the bathroom, the sudden brightness was a punch to the face. As I raced in, I got onto the toilet just in time for a barrage of foul-smelling emissions evacuating my bowels, rivaling the bathroom scene from *Dumb and Dumber*. After a tumultuous bout on the porcelain throne, I battled the noxious odor, desperately opening a window and praying for relief. My body continued to unleash a torrent of putrid smells and defecations, leaving me dizzy and disoriented. I couldn't find incense or a fragrant spray and worried I would poison my hosts on the other side of the house with the fumes. Finally, after an agonizing eternity, I collapsed back into bed, hoping I'd done enough cleaning up to conceal the aftermath from my unsuspecting hosts.

The next morning arrived, and I found myself still drunk, not hungover. Grateful for my host's generosity, I dressed in the clothes he had provided and tidied up before waiting for him to awaken. He offered me breakfast, to which I declined. Instead, I expressed my gratitude and let him know I had to get going. He gave me his business card, but my attempts to reach out over the following weeks went unanswered.

As I set out on the road, I encountered a series of misadventures, from struggling to navigate out of the housing complex to being interrogated by a suspicious guard. Once again, I found myself back at the perplexing intersection that seemed to plague my journey the day before. Pedaling through Llagostera, Vidreres, Tordera, Calella, Arenys de Mar, and Mataro that day, drunkenness morphed into a relentless hangover, my efforts to hydrate notwithstanding.

As I cycled down unfamiliar roads, I evaded entering a freeway, and followed any sign pointing toward Barcelona. My discomfort and lack of appetite from the previous night's excess caused my stomach to ache as I digested pounds of food. No matter what, with complete determination, I pressed on, sticking to the coast and edging closer to my destination. As night fell, I settled into a secluded spot by the sea, pondering the distance left to Barcelona and resolving to reach it the next day. I remained hopeful and eager, anxious with anticipation:

Ah, watching the sunrise come up over the sea on the last day of the year... what a good way to end. One road, all the way to Barcelona. I'm getting a tan in December! It's pretty damn beautiful, around sixty-five degrees, just wearing one biking shirt and loving it. Had a nice relaxing day with just a few wrong turns. I found a city named Roses where there seemed to be as many canals as roads. Gold Beach with camping spots as far as the eye can see. Coincidences no longer exist, it's like my will finds these people. No, the things find me when I'm ready for them. For now, I bike, and then will party for New Years. Who knows what's going to happen when I get there?

Chapter 19
New Year's Eve in Barcelona

With the vibrant sunrise motivating me, I broke camp early, anxious about reaching Barcelona in time. Surprisingly, the journey was quicker than expected, and by noon, I reached the outskirts of the city. I had cycled around seventy-five hundred miles in nine months, around fifteen hundred totally alone. As I rode through the evolving landscape from rural to urban, Barcelona's unique architectural style, particularly Antoni Gaudi's influence, became apparent.

    I had already reached out to several hosts from Syrun's computer in preparation to visiting the city and found a host named Jaime who agreed to accommodate me for a week. He warned me about the cramped conditions because of having custody of his four children while his ex-wife was away on vacation, but I wasn't in the position to be picky and still gratefully accepted his offer. Upon arriving in his neighborhood, I explored the city until his workday ended, immersing myself in its distinct charm and embracing the freedom of wandering without a set destination. After exploring the city, I rummaged through trash cans for food, finding success for the first time in a while. After going to a library, I received an email from Jamie instructing me to meet him at a cafe when he finished working. Over a couple of appetizers, he seemed to be confirming that I was safe to allow into his home, and once he concluded I was alright, we headed to his tiny apartment together. Once there, I lugged my belongings up five flights of stairs. As he had forewarned, the studio apartment was cramped, with two sets of bunk beds, four computers, a tiny bathroom, kitchenette, and a partition separating the living space from his bed.

During my week-long stay with Jaime and his children in Barcelona, I explored the city on foot and mostly left Pearl locked up inside the flat's landing. The kids engrossed themselves in their online game, Second Life, creating a virtual world where they could be anything they wanted. It reminded me of my past immersion in gaming and how it helped me through a tough time. Reflecting on their dedication to the virtual world, I pondered my own habits and journey since overcoming depression after college. This contemplation verified how different I'd become, with so many new behaviors becoming habits, especially focusing on how I could perpetuate the cycle of kindness to benefit others.

While searching for my destination for the New Year's Eve meetup location within Park Guell, I admired its whimsical architecture and cleverly crafted sculptures. Before arriving in the park, I searched for specific squats I had read about, people covering many of them in graffiti or political signs, such as, "If they call it tourist season, why can't we shoot them?" I knocked on a few doors, but people rejected me as I was unknown to them, and I didn't have anyone vouching for me. Despite receiving confirmation from event hosts, I failed to find the Couchsurfers gathering right away, so I enjoyed every moment exploring the park's imaginative landscape, feeling like I was in a dream, influenced by Gaudi's artistic vision.

As the official event start time approached, my excitement grew, though I felt unprepared. I lacked money for drinks and didn't have the essentials for potential romantic encounters. Despite these concerns, I steadied my resolve and found the group forming in Park Guell, where I recognized the familiar face of a local host I'd reached out to, amongst the early arrivals. Soon, our numbers swelled to over sixty people, representing countries from all over the world. We kicked off the celebration with a flurry of wine bottles being opened, plastic cups being distributed, and a collective toast to an unforgettable night ahead. It was the perfect start to the evening.

We consumed a seemingly endless supply of wine, and then our group of mostly twenty-somethings, with a smattering of older members, made our way down the hill to our first destination. Amidst the lively chatter and attempts at flirtation, I received little in reciprocal interest, my initial attempts at creating a romantic connection failing outright. A local bar, offering us a generous deal on drinks, became our first stop. I purchased a beer to blend in and ended up with more drinks thanks to the friendly atmosphere. The bar quickly increased in voluminous laughter and excited conversation from our group. My intention was to pace myself, and it seemed others were significantly more intoxicated than I, leading to vomiting, being rejected by women, and the bar asking our organizers to remove a few of them, although it was still early, especially by Barcelona standards.

Our merry band made our way to La Oveja Negra, a popular counter-culture bar in the town center. Along the walk, we passed around joints, and I expressed my gratitude for the generosity of many new acquaintances. The bar had prepared an entire room for our arrival, with ample space for pool and other games. Throughout our celebration, some couples formed, as did small social cliques, which I floated between. The American women rejected my initiations at conversation and paid me no attention. They seemed more interested in international men, so I sought connection elsewhere.

One lone Austrian woman caught my eye, and I established a connection with her, recalling a humorous article about her nation's openness to promiscuity. She and I spent hours chatting and enjoying each other's company. We discussed the risks women face when traveling alone, contrasting with my experiences of cycling solo. I didn't share my traumatic London experience, not wanting to burden her and depress our good time. She was charming, with adorable dimples when she smiled, and her English was impressively good. Her passion for travel surpassed mine, and I didn't care that she was older than me. It felt good to have someone interested in me, especially in a bar fittingly named, as I often self-identified as a black sheep within any group. She seemed to like me, but we both hesitated to make a move. When she inquired about the bulge in my jacket pocket, I pulled out my juggling balls and put on a show, impressing the crowd with my skills. Undeterred by a few jeers when I dropped the balls, the applause was encouraging, and my romantic interest expressed her admiration.

Our group lingered at the bar well past midnight, with some members leaving because of exhaustion or intoxication. I resorted to sneaking half-consumed drinks left behind by others, as I refused to waste my meager finances buying my own, but when my new romantic interest noticed my behavior and insisted on buying me a beer, I felt embarrassed.

Just before midnight, the bartender surprised our group with two cases of champagne, and we counted down the final seconds until the New Year together. Everyone toasted, cheering and raising our glasses together. Afterwards, my romantic interest and I shared a passionate kiss, feeling exhilarated by the moment. As the night progressed, our group dwindled, but the energy in the streets of Barcelona remained lively.

We strolled through the ancient stone pathways, swept up in the festive atmosphere of Barcelona's nightlife. My new companion and I shared moments of joy amidst the revelry. Unlike the usual scene in American bars at this hour, where tensions often ran high as men became more desperate in their failing attempts at getting laid, here the mood was light-hearted and celebratory. However, our group faced a dilemma when we reached the next bar, encountering a cover charge which divided our group. My romantic interest and I opted for a more intimate setting nearby, where we could enjoy each other's company in a relaxed atmosphere.

Half of our remaining group continued into a sumptuous and sultry establishment, decorated in maroon and velvet, as well as being dimly lit in a provocative way. In the cozy confines of the small venue, my date and I connected in an affectionate moment, with her sitting on my lap as we indulged in tapas plates. As the night wore on, we played drinking games and exchanged stories, reluctant to depart each other's company even as others drifted off to bed. When the venue closed at four in the morning, we braved the chill of the night air together, hands intertwined, and I seized the opportunity to walk her back to her place, which she graciously accepted.

As we walked, we clung to each other for warmth, cherishing the embrace as I placed my fleece skull cap onto her head, as a gentlemanly gesture, even though it barely fit over her hair. When she revealed she was also Couchsurfing, implying she was not alone at her place and unwilling to invite me into their domicile, this dampened my hopes for intimacy. I was grateful for any kind of connection, though. In the stairwell of her building, we made out for twenty minutes, things getting hot and heavy as we both wished for a private location to devour each other. Before I left, we discussed wanting to meet again soon.

Navigating my way, on unfamiliar streets, back to my host's home, I briskly walked, soaking in the picturesque sunrise as it transformed into another ordinary day. Emerging into the dawn's light, I was awestruck by the breathtaking sunrise, capturing its beauty in a photo that symbolized the promise of a bright future ahead. Around six in the morning, I returned to my host's apartment, where he was already up and preparing for work, his kids still glued to their computers. I secured a bed instead of the couch for some much-needed rest. Waking up groggy and dehydrated around midday, I struggled to fall back asleep amidst the tapping of keyboards. Eventually, I engaged with them and watched movies until Jaime returned home from work.

I told my host stories of the events from the previous night as he ordered pizza for us all, a gesture of generosity that never failed to astonish me. It reminded me of the old adage: if you care about someone, feed them! When the food arrived, the smell alone made me realize how hungry I was after barely eating for the past day. Jaime and I discussed the city's highlights over dinner, and I took notes, thankful for the insider information. I'd felt the cycle of kindness in full force that evening, and noticing it continue the following day had me convinced I would live in service to others for the rest of this worldly existence.

Using his computer later that evening, I found my Austrian romantic interest through the Couchsurfing site and messaged her, while also checking out local events to see if she was attending any. I found one on the following night and hoped to see her there. With no other way to contact her, I had to be patient.

Still exhausted, I slept for almost twelve hours that night. Although I missed the sunrise, I awoke to find my host already gone. Feeling refreshed, I prepared to head out myself, self-consciously wanting to contribute to the community meeting that night. Once I emerged, the crisp air outside invigorated me. With a rough idea of the city's layout, I headed toward the iconic La Sagrada Familia, marveling at its grandeur from afar. The intricate details of Gaudi's masterpiece were mesmerizing, each element a reflection of the whole. Yet, upon reaching the entrance, I found out that I couldn't explore further without a ticket, which dashed my hopes of seeing the interior. I pleaded to be allowed in, but they firmly refused me. Disappointed, I circled the building in search of a way in, but to no avail. It seemed there was only one entrance, denying me the chance to experience its ornate grandeur inside.

Downtrodden, I moved on toward Las Ramblas, the famous pedestrian street known for its street performers and living statues. The first performer I saw had dressed himself as a devil with a fire staff, making funny faces, and posing for pictures. Then came a fairy, a golden angel with massive wings and a sword, a man in chains inside a cage, and others still setting up. At the end, two undead, skeleton-like men caught my attention. They sat on bicycles with skeleton puppets attached by rods to kids' bikes on either side. Motionless until someone tipped them, they would then pedal, making the skeletons move in a Halloween or Dia de los Muertos style. They posed for pictures or tipped their hats in gratitude. The attention they received and how frequently people donated to them amazed me. Notably, about eighty percent of people who tipped one bucket also tipped the other, effectively doubling their earnings with minimal effort. Watching them, I realized they had found their niche. It made me contemplate my own future. What could I do that would work as well for me? What routine could I master that would bring me success? It was a reminder that sometimes, the key to success is finding a simple, unique angle and sticking with it.

I wondered if I could find my niche here, juggling on Las Ramblas, or if the locals would run me off for being a foreigner. I doubted whether I was good enough or could earn a living. I considered doing this back in the United States, and I felt a spark of hope. While I had previously believed I wouldn't be returning for several years, thoughts of home had been creeping into my mind since missing my family around the holidays. While I'd earned a little busking before, my skills and confidence had improved enough to show off with confidence at the New Year's party. Inspired by the street performers now, I wanted to give it another shot, as well as create something unique and not plagiarize their costumes or acts.

Leaving Las Ramblas with racing thoughts, my stomach reminded me I hadn't eaten. I shifted focus to finding free food but quickly learned that this city wasted little. Large grocery stores were scarce, and dumpsters behind small shops offered nothing worthwhile. Eateries' trash bins had some scraps, but it took two hours of roaming and scrounging to feel full. I had nothing to bring to the event that night, which worried me.

I continued toward a large military establishment atop a hill with a magnificent view of the Mediterranean. The strategic location, with old cannons and mortars behind fortified walls, was a brilliantly designed maze which would thwart invaders by putting them in a disadvantaged position below raised walls where ranged weapons would rain down on them without much risk of retaliation. I wandered through, taking pictures, careful to keep my camera secure from pickpockets, always keeping Jaime's warning in mind. I'd begun to love the city, its architecture and style, its ancient history and culture. I wanted to do something to benefit and enrich its aesthetic quality as I explored Barcelona.

Leaving the fortress, I noticed trash scattered on the ground. Despite my ambivalence to it thus far in my adventure, I began collecting it as I walked. I found a large plastic bag amidst the debris and filled it as I returned to the touristy area. By the time I returned, the thirty-gallon bag was full. A passerby asked me in Catalan why I was doing this. Struggling with the language, I asked them to switch to Spanish and explained that I wanted to help keep their lovely city clean. They mentioned they never saw locals doing this and thanked me. This small validation motivated me. I vowed to continue this act of community service whenever I could, in admiration for the city's beauty, history, and architecture.

As I continued along, I returned to the center and crossed Las Ramblas, heading closer to the ocean. I entered a large square surrounded by beautiful buildings with wrought-iron balconies, reminiscent of a movie scene where people cheer or celebrate by throwing flower petals. Moving down a smaller street, I saw laundry hanging between buildings, drying in the afternoon sun. Captivated by the simple, ancient scene, I felt completely present, almost outside of myself. Suddenly, I heard a zipper. Turning, I saw a young man with his hand in my empty top backpack pocket. Caught, he pinched my butt cheek, blew a kiss, and sauntered off gaily. Stunned and disarmed, I checked my pack. Nothing was missing. I chuckled at his clever distraction, realizing how effective it was in preventing me from raising an alarm. Continuing my wanderings, now more mindful, I avoided further incidents. Eventually, I got to a residential zone, eager to return to the intriguing landmarks I had been discovering earlier.

As I searched for a way out of the tight corridors and unusually narrow staircases, I came across an ancient wall with a plaque explaining it had stood for over two thousand years. The thought that these walls existed when Jesus walked the Earth struck me. Touching them, I felt transported back in time, imagining people in sandals, a bustling market, and animals being traded and cooked.

I realized it was getting late and nearly time for the sunset gathering on the beach. I still needed food, so I scoured the city, checking outside cafes, in alleys, and residential areas. My haul was meager: some sparkling water, little food, and wrinkled clothes. As the sun set, I rushed to the beach, where a small group had already congregated. They welcomed me cordially, passing around cheap wine that brought heat into my body and color to my cheeks.

As twilight turned to darkness, a chill set in. Someone suggested we needed a fire, and everyone agreed. We dispersed to gather burnable materials, but the city was devoid of anything we could use. My search for cardboard or wood seemed futile as the night grew colder. Suddenly, I remembered a construction site several blocks away that had pallets lying around. I quickly led an expedition with a couple of the other guys right to it, the buzz from the wine fueling my excitement. We found the site quickly, and each of the guys grabbed a pallet while I carried one awkwardly under each arm. Winded but triumphant, we hauled the lone wood supply back to the beach, greeted by cheers from the group, which had grown in our absence. As I dragged the pallets across the sand, I spotted my Austrian love interest. As she hadn't responded to my message yet, this was an exciting surprise that hastened me to her. She embraced me with a big kiss, inciting whoops and hollers from the group. Blushing, we held hands and turned toward the crowd of Couchsurfers, who continued to shower us with approval.

We faced the comical task of disassembling the pallets without tools, using a single board to pry the others apart while being mindful of rusty nails. Soon, we had a cozy fire, and we all huddled around it to keep warm. I felt like a hero, especially with my cuddle buddy by my side. The group praised my ingenuity, calling me an urban scavenger, a term I later held dear to my heart.

The pallet fire quickly burned through our minimal resources, leaving us in the cold, but my love and I kept exchanging kisses and snuggling together for warmth. More alcohol emerged, and we smoked spliffs with a mixture of marijuana and tobacco, as well as pure weed joints. When it got too cold, we all headed back to La Oveja Negra, where the same bartender from New Year's Eve welcomed us with a free round, grateful for the generous tip from before. We bought the same room, though this time we shared it with others, repeating our grand celebration, filled with more kissing and intimacy, not just between me and my love but among other reunited pairs as well. Later, I walked with my love interest back to the same stairwell, but finding it occupied this time, we snuck into a dark corner and passionately made out. She then surprised me by going down on me, making it hard to contain my pleasure. We had to pause when someone passed by, giggling quietly before she finished the act.

She then told me she had a train ticket back to Austria the next day and work thereafter. This would be our last time together. We embraced and kissed, reluctant to let go, and eventually, the cold drove us apart. I jogged the few miles back to my host's home. Jaime and his kids were asleep, so I quietly crept in and crashed on the couch, reflecting on a night of fleeting romance and a bittersweet goodbye. I wrote extensively that night before sleeping, obviously having a lot on my mind:

After a hungover day filled with movie watching, I ventured into the city. I started thinking about how so many cities seem the same. Always similar massive urban sprawl, a good viewpoint here and there, architecture, museums, churches, a harbor or river, stylish worldly shops, small local markets, tourists and trash strewn throughout, with the money grabbing hustle everywhere. I love the newness, people I meet, and experiences I have. But I feel ready for a change, perhaps taking to the sea, but it's the wrong season... Perhaps a farm, or a squat. I'd love a traveling mate.

Walking around the city and picking up trash, only one person asked me why I did it, or said anything. Lead with my actions. I want to organize people to do positive things. I want to change the world. I want the bad shit to change. Are people worth saving? Is it even possible to stop or slow global warming? Or is doom eminent for the human race? I want to be in love. I do love, but I do not feel loved, except for the unconditional love of a mother. What a beautiful thing. I've had such a plethora of fleeting feelings lately. I've had no real news from the U.S. in months. Will anyone actually join me in spring? Will they want to bike? The G8 feels so far away. Will something similar come before? Can I do a sort of Bicycology trip? I want a personal music player, especially when I'm sick of the songs playing in my mind. What would I think of if that wasn't there?

We look at progress as an end in itself, and see it as inherently good, not necessarily closely examining what we are willing to give up for progress. We also aren't critically evaluating it as a means, specifically as a means to what end? Originally, I believe progress began as a way of exploring our world and our limits. We sought to easily be able to fulfill our needs for food, shelter, and security, so we could progress to other things. We wanted to answer such questions as, why are we here? Are we alone? What is our purpose? We improved what we had, invented new technologies, tapped new resources, and made everything more efficient. We have done so many things in the name of progress, and now that we have made our lives so easy that we rarely have any challenges, what do we do with ourselves?

Progress may not necessarily be a good thing. I have begun to notice that every major city is a single blueprint. The buildings may be different, one style chosen over another, but nonetheless, it's the same functional design. The process of progress and modernization has killed culture. I am tired of walking through massive shopping areas. The same stores existing in every major city in the world is a bigger dilemma. Where is the difference, the variety? Where are the traditions, the differences in people, in culture? When was it consumed by this massive blob of commercialistic conformity?

Is it a good thing that hardly anyone dances in ancient Catalonian ceremonies anymore? Is it a good thing that pre-colonized Native Americans now live in refugee camps called reservations and hardly hunt wild animals as they used to? Is it a good thing that the Yanomami people fight with shotguns and struggle with the same mental problems as the rest of the world? Is it actually better that we can drive so fast in our automobiles that we pollute the air and don't bother to look at the things around us, let alone try to understand them? Is progress such a good thing? I care about the rest of the world. As much as I love traveling, I feel that it's restricting me from being able to help others, to help the world. I benefit greatly from it, but it's not helping me accomplish my life's purpose; and yes, I feel like I know what the purpose of my life is. Maybe my ultimate question is, can humans be saved? Or will we have to go through a period of mass crisis, death, chaos, and destruction?

New Year's Eve in Barcelona

For a long time, people have talked about a Judgment Day, but I don't think it's one day. If we listen to science, then we can look at global warming research and understand that massive changes are coming in our lifetimes... I want to organize like-minded people that agree with taking the positive actions toward constructing a better world and alternative models of living and put them in action—getting twenty people together and picking up trash, making a community garden, dumpstering food all day and then handing it out to people, offering free bicycle repair, or anything along these lines. Yet, in one city, it's not enough. The changes need to be made worldwide. How do I do what feels like so much? I feel like I'm failing. And I don't know what to do.

I woke up to Jaime preparing his kids for school. Jaime said I needed to leave as well, since he didn't have an extra key and wasn't comfortable leaving couch surfers alone in his home. He told me to meet him at a nearby restaurant after work. I quickly prepared, swapped out my camera batteries, and set off to visit Tibidabo, with its amusement park and the Temple Expiatori del Sagrat Cor de Jesus, also known as the Church of the Sacred Heart, with its iconic Jesus statue atop.

Leaving the urban area, I ascended the hill, vowing to pick up litter along the way. I found and filled another large trash bag. At one point, I noticed a small plastic bag with white powder, which I tucked away separately in my pocket. Partway up, I discovered an abandoned building adorned with decorative graffiti and paused to admire it. Cars honked at me as I walked along the narrow road, probably more due to the danger because of the lack of a shoulder, than my trash-cleaning efforts.

At the top, I disposed of the trash bag outside the amusement park and continued to the church. The view was magnificent: a sweeping panorama of Barcelona and the sea on one side, and hills and mountains fading into the distance on the other. The photos I took couldn't capture the breathtaking experience of standing there, as I took in the captivating scenery. Wherever I went on this adventure, I continued to be drawn toward and enchanted by a far-reaching vista.

I took off my shirt to soak up the sun, ate a pilfered apple, and juggled for tips, making a few euros. My motivation from the day before at Las Ramblas waned as I continued to be financially unsuccessful at busking, although it was still the most I had yet to earn while juggling alone. Tired, I strapped on my backpack and entered the ornate cathedral filled with stained glass windows and rows of pews. Reflecting on Jesus and his teachings, I wondered if someone like him could make the same impact today. I kneeled down to pray for guidance and for a figure as influential as Jesus to inspire the world.

Departing the cathedral, I took the only other road down the hill, picking up litter along the way once again. My time at Jaime's was nearing its end, having been there five nights already, and I sensed he might ask about my departure whilst at the restaurant. I was aware of how adding my extra body to an already tiny apartment caused things to feel even more cramped, and his hospitality had waned over the course of my stay. My energy levels were low and hunger pained my belly as I filled another plastic bag with trash and tossed it into a dumpster at the bottom of the hill, checking for anything edible, but with no luck. The city impressed me with how little food it wasted.

Resting on a park bench, I found a bin with discarded lunch items and a mostly full bag of fried pork rinds, my luckiest find of the day. I ate everything before heading to the restaurant. When Jaime arrived, we shared tapas, and I devoured a plate of potatoes with aioli he didn't like. Surprisingly, he didn't ask when I was leaving. Even though I sensed my welcome was wearing thin, he had accepted my initial Couchsurfing request for a week-long stay without question, leaving me just two days left.

When we returned to Jaime's house and found the kids absent, I checked my email, Couchsurfing, IC.org, and LiveJournal on one of the computers. Excitingly, I received an acceptance from a host at an intentional community squatting at an abandoned leper colony on the far north side of town, around ten miles away. They welcomed me to stay as long as I contributed. I immediately responded, highlighting my skills in growing food, cooking, and my willingness to learn and help in any way they asked. However, my inbox was nearly empty, and I felt hurt by the lack of communication from friends and family. I sent out emails to those close to me, challenging them as to why they hadn't responded to my correspondence and questioned what was so important that they neglected our relationship. It seemed like a recurring pattern in my life: giving more than I received and often being disappointed by the lack of reciprocity. Regardless that I was the one with unreliable technology, my emails and blog posts frequently went unanswered.

New Year's Eve in Barcelona

One of the few pieces of digital mail I received was from an acquaintance who had asked me, with amazement and wonder, how I could travel so long without money, so I gave them a lengthy response about how I was living, the importance of radical self-reliance, navigation skills, and connected them with the online resources I was using. I guessed how wasteful the cities are would surprise him, and how fortunate I've been to pilfer such abundant scraps. This helped me to realize how many resourcefulness skills I had gained, as well as being continually supported by the generosity of mankind. After Jaime's kids returned and reclaimed the computer, I wrote in my journal before laying down to rest, with my sleep cycle remaining erratic as my sleep schedule had been highly irregular. Suddenly awakened by a physical sensation in my gut, I rushed to the bathroom and vomited profusely, followed by diarrhea. The children, playing games with headphones on, didn't even notice the putrid noises. Flushing repeatedly, I struggled to keep control.

After cleaning up and attempting to rehydrate in the shower, a second round hit me. In pain and worried, I tried to manage alone, but eventually crawled back to the couch, praying for relief. Awakening to Jaime's reminder that it was time to leave, I explained my sickness and begged to stay inside. Reluctantly, he agreed. Alone, I scoured my supplies for rehydration options, finding a packet of rehydration salts and old Gatorade mix. After consuming both, I returned to sleep, hoping for improvement. As I battled another round of nausea, the kids returned, skipping school to play video games, which I found amusing but wouldn't snitch on them to their father.

Jaime arrived with pizza after work, their typical weekly routine. Unable to stomach it, I requested plain crackers. Jaime diagnosed it as food poisoning, a first for me after nine months of dumpster diving without issue. Unsure of the culprit, I vowed to do my best to avoid a repeat experience. After resting, I felt relief as evening approached. I informed Jaime of my intention to leave the next morning, expressing gratitude in the face of the inconvenience. When I could finally muster the energy to clean up and pack, I did so very slowly. I stayed up late that night, sleeping just before dawn, readying myself for departure. Jaime woke me within a few hours of me falling asleep, and I bid him and his kids farewell, leaving them with a departing message about living life as a video game. We hugged, and with urgency, Jaime rushed the kids off to school. Following my handwritten directions I'd receive from my next hosts, I left for the north side of town, never to see Jaime again.

I'd ridden for several miles and was significantly more fatigued than normal. Try as I might to follow their written directions as precisely as possible, I still became a bit lost and finally asked strangers to guide me, as I'd failed to find the last turn, which led me uphill to a sprawling complex. Initially sterile, it transformed into a wonderland of handmade structures and art. Cultivated gardens, inventive tools, and repurposed items adorned the space, showcasing the creativity of the collective. When I arrived, my host gave me a comprehensive tour of the expansive property, featuring over twenty-four rooms, a hand-built sauna, three terraces decorated with plants, an outdoor living area, and various workshop spaces. They operated on a simple lifestyle, free from many modern obligations. Despite owning few possessions, they found fulfillment in volunteering, creating art, and cultivating connections with nature. Their communal atmosphere, marked by affectionate greetings and shared responsibilities, left me questioning my own path. I wondered why I should continue my traveling when such a paradise existed, offering a harmonious way of life:

I find myself at the crossroads of life; the long, sometimes dusty, path that I have just come from has been challenging and great. I can see the road extending out in front of me as far as I can see. Even though I cannot see the end, I know what it will be like. Fortunately, there are many other roads branching out in other directions. Currently, I'm sitting at this intersection of life meditating, occasionally looking up and gazing down one road or another, trying to receive the wisdom of which way to go. I am at this crossroad because it feels like I won. I beat this game. I learned these lessons. I gained all the skills available to me, and I definitely leveled up. I pushed myself to find my limits, and I have. There is no hill in the world that I cannot climb, and within the realm of reason, I have pushed myself to the very limits of my capacity without endangering my life. I have overcome many great difficulties. I have now made this life an easy one. I can bike in a similar country and know that I won't have major problems. Yes, there are still places that I would like to visit, sights to see, things to learn, and people to meet, but I'm ready to move in a new direction, and things come to me when I'm ready for them, so maybe it's a question of what am I ready for? I see many distinct possibilities, but I will not share them for now. I just wanted to let everyone that reads this know I am at a crossroads. My direction will most likely be a different one.

I joined the communal dinner and enjoyed everyone's camaraderie, with residents ranging in age from twenty-five to fifty. They felt like one big family and their familiarity struck me. Conversations flowed freely, with people swapping seats to engage with different members without any hint of discord. They invited me to join a sustainable lumber collection trip in the woods, and I eagerly accepted the offer. A few days later, I'd become familiar with the gardens, community routines, and what they expected of me.

As I settled into my routine, I remembered the bag of white powder I had found earlier. Soon after inquiring about it through an email to Dan, I received his reply, telling me to rub some against my gums, and if they responded with a numbing sensation, that would confirm it was indeed cocaine. After the testing strategy confirmed my suspicion, I proceeded to inhale it for the first time during our work in the woods. We spent the day hauling logs and chopping them into firewood, amongst criticism about the noise disrupting the peace. I took breaks to indulge in cocaine, which energized me to keep working. By dinner time, we had enough wood to heat the facility for a year. Undeterred by my blistered hands, I ate heartily, ignoring my uneasy stomach. It was difficult to sleep that night; I put thoughts to paper in order to rest:

What to do? I feel constantly pulled in so many directions. Oregon, Olympia Washington, and the thought of friends and family. Barcelona, squatting, riling shit up around town with great people, and learning Spanish. Going is good—Plan B has worked so far. Only time, thought, and patience seem to be capable of helping here, and a few good mates. I've already given in to the idea of flying back. Bearing the cold and rain is worth it to see friends and family. Maybe something will happen here in the squat and anarchist scene, but I'm ready to move on. I'm tired of big cities, although they are necessary to bring people into action together. What do I want to be organizing? Autonomous projects that enact positive change and can exist without me. Can I get one founded, running smoothly, and then move on to the next one? Is that possible? Would people keep going after I'm gone? Or should I just keep traveling?

The Cycle of Kindness

My life feels so complicated all of a sudden, compared to life on the road. The question remains, what to do next?

Over the following weeks, I pitched in with various tasks around the property, including helping with gardening and gathering surplus produce from the local market, after which the community welcomed us back with enthusiasm, treating us like victorious warriors.

Days passed leisurely, as the community operated with minimal reliance on technology, reminiscent of a simpler time. I caught up on reading, journaling, and correspondence while also doing my laundry by hand. I marveled at their sustainability practices, from harvesting fresh greens for lunch to practicing community composting techniques, learned from an expert. Each member had their own passions and quirks, yet there was no sense of excess or addiction among them. I evenly spent time with everyone, enjoying their company and the relaxed atmosphere that seemed to slow down time itself. This community exemplified the cycle of kindness on so many levels, as everyone helped each other out and maintained balanced reciprocity, with no one seeming resentful of another for any reason. I loved living within this modality, as the way of life appealed to me on nearly every level. Yet, amidst this contentment, I couldn't shake the longing for love and intimacy, which remained elusive. While I had a great affinity for the community, I pondered what my next move should be, feeling a lack of attachment that left my path uncertain.

Among the tranquil days in the community, I wrestled with a whirlwind of emotions. Homesickness tugged at my heart, reminding me of the dear ones I left behind. Emails from home carried echoes of routine and monotony, which weren't in alignment with the transformative journey I was on. My worldview expanded, altered by experiences far beyond the confines of my previous life. As I contemplated my next steps, I received an email from my father offering a one-way ticket home, which added an additional layer of complexity. He had read my blog posts and emails and noticed my uncertainty about what to do, and he took advantage of the opportunity to bring me back to Portland and have me safely in his care. It was a tempting lifeline, promising familiarity and comfort, yet I hesitated, unsure of the path I truly desired to tread.

That same day, I received a very different email from Dan that had a profound impact on me—a link proving our positive impact on the world. The article read:

New Year's Eve in Barcelona

Mark Milner, Thursday, December 14, 2006. The Guardian

Europe's biggest coal-fired power station, Drax, is to spend £100m improving its efficiency in a move that should cut carbon dioxide emissions by the equivalent of taking 275,000 cars off Britain's roads. Drax Group, which owns the North Yorkshire plant, said it will spend the money on reblading the turbines used in generating electricity. The program will run between 2008 and 2011, and the improved efficiency is expected to cut carbon dioxide emissions by 1m tons a year and save 500,000 tons of coal. The plant is the biggest single industrial emitter of carbon dioxide in the UK, and this year was the target of a protest by climate change campaigners. The plant emitted some 21 tons of carbon dioxide last year. Drax said the turbine replacement program would improve efficiency by 5%. Dorothy Thompson, chief executive, said, "The decision to go ahead with the turbine reblading project demonstrates our commitment to invest in the future of the business and importantly to tackling climate change through an annual saving of carbon dioxide emissions equivalent to taking 275,000 cars off the road."

I felt elated when I read this, so I immediately posted it on my blog, ending with the sentiment: If you think you're too small to be effective, try sharing a tent with a mosquito. This slogan has later become a motivational life motto. If I ever felt too small or insignificant, it helped me feel empowered, encouraged, and uplifted.

One day, the community fired up the handmade sauna, and we all coordinated a communal massage exchange. Twelve of us gathered in the steamy rooms, taking turns giving and receiving massages in a non-sexual setting. The experience was deeply relaxing and peaceful, with thoughts arising about how such experiences could promote global harmony. After a refreshing shower, I retired to my tent, feeling content and grateful for the abundance of life's experiences. I witnessed so many examples from this single group about the power of living in community, with intention, and the positive impact on those closest to us. It reminded me of designing my ideal intentional community with Dan, many months ago, as just the two of us cycled across Germany, and caused me to miss him terribly.

I still felt torn between the tranquility of the community and my desire for movement. Unable to find a companion thus far in Barcelona, or from my friend group back home, my homesickness grew, alongside having imposter syndrome that left me lonely. I struggled to maintain motivation to continue and expressed many of these thoughts and emotions via emails and blog posts. I contemplated how my actions affected my family and friends back home. Only in hindsight did I reflect on what continual danger I had put myself in, and what the consequences of being struck by a vehicle may have been, while alone in a foreign country with little more than a passport with an expired visa to identify me by.

After days of deliberation, grappling back and forth with my father's offer of a gifted plane ride to return home, amongst feelings of alienation and loneliness, I accepted the non-refundable ticket and began preparing for the final stretch of this incredible adventure. A few days later, I informed the community of my decision to leave. The day before my flight, I packed Pearl in a bike box as I couldn't logistically figure out how to ride her to the airport and disassemble her there, as I lacked the proper tools to take her apart. I mentally and emotionally said goodbye to Barcelona and the community that had housed me for the last three weeks. It was late January, ten months after landing at Schiphol, when I cherished my last moments in the city before embarking on the next chapter of my journey. In the last weeks, my mind rambled:

James Joyce—A Portrait of the Artist. "His mind seemed older than theirs; it shone coldly on their strifes and happiness and regrets like a moon upon a younger Earth." I can truly relate to this. Oh, to have a clan again. I'm hardly even working toward cycling again. I'm searching for a way out. I definitely know I need this sort of warmer climate in the future, but where? Still struggling with my lack of money, I don't want it, but I realize it will help me get the things that I do want. My mind is already in the U.S., and I want it to be a surprise when I return. I'm thinking six months max between Oregon, Washington, and California. There are so many people to visit, but once I actually get there and see them, the time will be shorter than I think. I need to practice more of a life lacking expectation—just let things happen. Plan less and go where things take me. I have to figure out how to get back right now, on my own. So many travelers still seem like tourists, just trying to party and use drugs until they've used up their youth. I lack a strong desire to engage in casual sex with random women, as nice as it is when the option arises. There is no need to constantly go out of the way for it. When I don't use that sexual energy, it can be built up and harnessed in other ways. Why

New Year's Eve in Barcelona

not have more energy? Listen to me, how I've changed so rapidly. My catharsis here is complete.

The night before my departure, I thanked everyone in the community for their hospitality, kindness and kinship; there was a pain in leaving this all behind. I was unsuccessful in falling asleep early, my mind double-checking my preparations. I set out the clothes I would wear and loaded and tightened down my pack. I awoke prior to the borrowed alarm sounding before daybreak, donning my clothes, backpack, and bicycle box before slipping out quietly. I descended the hillside, carrying all of my possessions, and was sweating profusely before arriving at the local train station a mile later. I struggled down the escalator and almost fell down the last twenty feet. I caught the very first train at the otherwise empty stop, thankful to have had no catastrophes thus far.

At the main station, I bought a ticket and asked which train went to the airport. The directions I received were unmistakable—down the stairs right next to the ticket counter, the first train on the right. I felt confident and secure that I would make it to the station on time. I garnered unusual glances and gazes, half carrying and half dragging my bicycle box and big backpack through the station and onto the next train. There wasn't an attendant to punch my ticket or for me to ask again whether this was the correct train, so I sat down near the front and looked at my compass as the train departed. It was going in the right direction.

Unintentionally, I fell asleep and awoke suddenly to the attendant asking for my ticket; I handed it over and confirmed this train went to the airport. He informed me that this train didn't go directly there, and that I needed to transfer three stops ago. I felt a flush in my face, an immediate rush of blood, nervousness, and fear. I asked him what time it was; only six thirty-five in the morning. I still had four hours before my flight took off. I got off at the next station, crossed the tracks, and looked at the timetable. Another swell of emotions hit me as I quickly calculated how long it would take me to backtrack to the airport via trains and their schedule. There wasn't enough time, after all. I would have to do something drastic to make it there. I'd have to rely on the cycle of kindness.

I lugged my box into the station's terminal waiting room, where there was a smattering of people sitting down, drinking coffee, and reading newspapers and periodicals. I cleared my throat and loudly asked for their attention. In my best Spanish, I stated my situation and begged for help. No one did anything more than lift their head, glance at me, and go back about their business. Without luck there, I went outside to beseech the taxicab drivers for help, pleading my case, and begging for a ride. They simply shook their heads no. It was truly the only time that I didn't receive generosity when I needed it the most.

In my moment of desperation, I asked them how much it would cost for a ride to the airport; I was out of options. Plainly, they told me seventy Euros, and checking my emergency fund, I only had one hundred and twenty-five remaining. I accepted my fate and told them I would pay for the ride. Two of them strapped my bicycle into a trunk sideways, leaving the lid open but secured in place. I heaved my backpack into the back seat, hopped in, and wept.

The crying and the gentle vibration of the vehicle must've lulled me back to sleep over its hour-long duration, as I jolted upright when the taxi stopped and saw that we had arrived at the international terminal. I begrudgingly handed the money over, retrieving Pearl, and hustled to the airline counter, praying I had made it in time. I was panting from the effort and being an anxious mess. The minutes waiting in line felt like an anxiety-ridden eternity, my mind racked with worse-case-scenarios, wondering if I had missed my only way home, squandering this gift from my father. What little resources I had left created even more worry. I couldn't even afford two oversized baggage fees and prayed to not have to choose between my bicycle and all my other possessions.

The agent greeted me with a smile. I presented my passport and asked if I had made it in time. She reassured me that I had and processed the paperwork. Handing over my trusty steed was a moment of vulnerability, the vehicle of my freedom, the medium through which all of this traveling had taken place. I worried about her safety. I'd read how airlines consistently wreck guitars. The proximity during the flight didn't relieve my apprehension of giving her to a total stranger, and I struggled to my core. Relief washed over me when they didn't charge me for the oversized box. When I put the backpack on the weighing device, it read fifty-two and a half pounds, but to my amazement, the attendant lifted the strap gently, relieving some of the weight, then declared it safely under, smiling at me again while handing over my boarding passes.

New Year's Eve in Barcelona

Suddenly unburdened, I felt naked and empty. Only my remaining money, passport, and tickets left. I floated between sleep deprivation, an adrenaline dump, and fatigue from the effort of hauling everything this far. In the last ten months, this was the least encumbered I had been, causing life to gain a surreal quality. My feet, feeling numb, subconsciously carried me over to the security entrance, going through the motions, handing over documents, hardly noticing questions being asked of me, struggling through a lack of mental capacity to find my terminal empty and not knowing why—they had finished boarding already.

I hastened to the service attendant, who remarked how I barely made it. Boarding the plane and finding my seat, I noticed everyone else already had drinks, were asleep, or buried in a conversation or book. It felt as though they had waited for me and knew making this flight was my only chance at going home. As I sat down, I again burst into tears and bawled myself back to sleep.

An attendant woke me serving food and beverages, handing me a beer as well. I felt amazingly grateful for these acts of service. I devoured the surprisingly good airline food and drained my beverages. The next time she came around, I asked for more and felt delighted when she gave me a dozen bags of peanuts and pretzels, as well as another beer. I looked out the window, chasing the sun back toward the United States of America, land of the free and home of the brave. Yet, I worried I was giving up my freedom, and that cowardice had gotten the best of me. This worry caused an overwhelming sensation of defeat to come over me, as if I had given up on my dreams... and Dan's.

I had only seen one continent, yet we talked about going around the Mediterranean to Africa, seeing the pyramids of Giza and hitch-hiking on a sailboat to see Crete and the thousand islands of Greece. We dreamed of tearing down the wall dividing Israel and Palestine, and of visiting the shores of Istanbul before heading inland to see how far across the great continent of Asia we could get. I fantasized about shipping my bicycle from India to China and hiking up the Anna Purna circuit in Nepal, into Tibet, and out through the Chinese empire. None of this had happened, and the weight of the feeling of failure suddenly felt crushing. I had done so much, yet focused on all the things that I didn't do. I yearned to see familiar faces so badly, but I instantaneously felt trapped, caged in this metal apparatus soaring through the air; my capitulation brought pain and discomfort like a stone in my stomach. I had met so many people and wondered if I would ever see any of them again.

I lacked motivation to journal and had stowed everything in my backpack. My pungent body odor prompted my fellow passengers to distance themselves from me. An attempt at perusing the airplane magazines quickly left me feeling disgust and disdain for their marketing and unadulterated commercialism. Time crawled on as I stared out the window for the rest of the flight, as the sun ever so slowly changed its position relative to us. The flight back seemed to last for days, despite being only seven and a half hours long, crossing five time zones.

As the flight crew stopped bringing free drinks, my inebriation faded, leaving behind only dehydration and exhaustion as I shuffled through JFK airport, akin to an automaton zombie. I idly waited for four hours before boarding a six-hour plane ride to Seattle. Fortunately, more sleep refreshed me. When I landed, Hanna was waiting to pick me up and bring me back to Olympia. The acts of exchanging currency felt like legal extortion, getting a nearly equal sum of dollars for my euros, cursing under my breath at the person responsible for depriving me of what little I had. All of this was a blur, myself a foreigner in a foreign land. I was going back to what I called home, which felt neither comfortable nor familiar. I had gone at such a slow pace for so long. I had absorbed so much of my surroundings, whereas planes moved so fast that my head was in a foggy haze of disassociation and disconnection.

I couldn't tell if I had finished or was just taking a break, if the trip had defeated me or if I was recovering from a knock-out blow. I saw signage in English all around me for the first time in months, and yet struggled to understand and comprehend the directions. Everything was so out of the ordinary compared to what I was used to. It felt sterile and lifeless, a forgery of reality, a sham of existence, a hoax of the present, as if I was in a dream imitating reality. My journey had taken me so far, yet this phantasmagorical ending made no sense to me. Whereas I was used to being solid and grounded on the road, on that day, I felt akin to a wisp of a specter. What a long, strange trip it had been indeed.

Epilogue

There is nothing like getting picked up from an airport by the familiar face of a loved one after a long time away from home. While Hanna and I had only been apart for a few months, the first sight of her had me smiling and crying simultaneously. The drive to her home felt long and tiring, but gave us time to catch up with each other. Being in her company felt easy and was a delightful reprieve from all I had been through in the last twenty-four hours. My father bought the cheapest ticket, which didn't take me right back to Oregon, but delivered me into the arms of my former lover and travel companion, an interest that did not rekindle with our time together again. Part of me wanted it to, and another part of me saw it as an expirationship, a temporary fling of convenience that was only meant to last for the short while it did.

After a lovely evening of story sharing amidst laughter and disbelief, jet lag got the best of me, and I went to sleep early. I woke in the wee morning hours and reassembled Pearl to prepare for a bus ride down to Portland, where she would have to sit on the front bike rack throughout the journey, and couldn't do so in pieces. The time with Hanna felt melancholic in its brevity, but I owed it to my dad to get to him as quickly as possible. I worried my trusty old faithful steed had suffered damage in transit, but thankfully, the box was in near perfect condition, and Pearl didn't seem to have a scratch on her. I caressed and held her as I cleaned her off, putting the handlebars back on and then the fork, tires, and pedals, reattaching the brake lines, and giving her a test ride before placing her into the back of a college colleague of Dan's truck, as he wanted to see me and Hanna had work. After a brief chat, we exchanged sleeping bags, as I apologized that my smell might never come out of her most precious gift, and expressed immense gratitude for how it literally kept me from freezing to death. We engaged in a long embrace, said goodbyes while maintaining a long-lasting eye gaze, and I departed to the bus stop. Early that morning, I wrote:

How strange it is to be Stateside. This reverse-culture-shock is just bizarre. The people seem fake, a lack of meaningfulness in their lives. They feel like hollow, empty shells of human beings. I feel different around Hanna. There is an awkwardness in the place where our intimate connection used to be. I'm not sure how to tell her about it. I want to start speaking one hundred percent truth, not even fabrications or exaggerations in stories. I know this truthfulness will help put me on the right path. I need to break down my reasons for lying and sweep away all the bullshit. I look forward to seeing my mom. It's part of why I returned here. I'll have a little indulgent relaxing break at Dad's, a mini recuperation holiday. But I know I'll never really stop traveling. It feels so strange to be out of Europe, and already, I miss some of the differences. I definitely have a problem with the mass-consumer culture, like the three Starbucks in one airport. Honestly, who wants to drink coffee when you're going to be forced to sit still in a plane for hours? Although, the comforts are nice to return to, but I know they only make me soft.

When I arrived back in Portland two and a half hours later, covering a distance that would've taken me two days of cycling, my father was still at work, so Dan, my brother, was waiting for me, grinning widely, with arms open. We embraced as if it had been years or lifetimes that we had been apart. I had emailed him back at the community in Barcelona, divulging my decision to return and the itinerary of my journey home, and he had written an elated reply and made plans to see me as soon as possible. The last four months held so much for me, and he fell back into old habits and familiar routines, but had a few surprises to share: a small bottle of alcohol and a different bicycle than we had traveled with. We finished the former together and rode away in nostalgic joy, as he explained how Junior, that had carried him thousands of miles across Europe, needed repairs and was no longer operable.

The sadness I felt was as palpable as the worry I felt imagining Pearl someday being unrideable. It reminded me of the heartache of selling Lord Pancake and Hangar back in Manchester, as my newer metal steed had become one of my closest companions. I vowed to keep her going for as long as possible. It had grown dark by the time we cycled the fifteen miles back to our childhood homes and a chilly wind crisped our fingers. Although very little had changed about my hometown, the familiarity I usually felt turned into a foreignness. Europe had transformed me. We agreed to meet up the following morning to go snow-shoeing, and I pedaled alone toward my father's house, entering through the garage like I had in my teen years.

Just as when I was a kid, he heard the door of the house open and was expecting me. He was inside the garage before I even took my pack off. It was one of the greatest embraces of my entire life, a hug long and deep, but too short. The phrase that departed his lips, "I missed you," didn't do justice to the emotion that swelled up within him, evident by the happiness showing in his eyes that I was home. We ate dinner together, and I told him about the crazy train mix-up trying to leave, and how I had just barely made it at all.

I used this time with him to apologize for my past lies, and told him I was committed to being fully transparent, honest, straight-forward, and up-front with him and everyone I knew. If they asked a question, they got a real answer, despite how painful it may have been for them to hear. No more sugar-coating, no more white lies, just pure, raw, unfiltered truth.

Two weeks passed by in a blur of excessive sleeping, sloth, and laziness. On the first day in Europe, I weighed one hundred and eighty-seven pounds, and I returned home at one hundred and fifty-two, a whopping thirty-five pounds lighter, and I definitely had way more muscle. I felt the draw of comfortable, old familiar habits resuming; hanging out with old friends who were still playing games, and I wanted to join them to reconnect. Another month passed by quickly as I cycled less in the winter cold, got rides from friends, and was a hedonistic mooch. I didn't like what I was becoming. Even getting a girlfriend, who admired what I had done, further entrenched me in my old way of life. I confessed to Dan my feelings of entrapment back in capitalistic culture and my worry around getting stuck and never traveling again.

To get out of this rut, I stayed with my mother in central Portland, which allowed me to be more central. The downside of it was being further away from Dan in the suburbs. I spent hours every day juggling, doing calisthenics, and reading books and material online. I returned to

Olympia, visited some of Dan's friends there to share travel stories and inspire people to train for our next adventure, ensuring one was coming soon. By mid-spring, the hype had grown. Dan and I planned to cycle across America, from west to east, down the Atlantic Coast and back across the nation. We estimated it would take us at least seven months.

My desire to direct action was rekindled by a global call for a protest at the G8 Summit, and as Dan and I actively recruited people for the cross-country ride, successfully convincing six friends who all agreed to depart from Olympia on May twenty-first to ride across our nation, I would wait for my best friend to finish his job and leave a month later on Summer Solstice. We believed, because of our experiences in Europe, that we would catch up with our friends very quickly. Our hope of creating real change stayed alive as we plotted our route and emailed potential hosts and non-violent direct-action collaborators.

I was hardly living the cycle of kindness ethos, and it pained me. I had tuned in and dropped out as the phrase went. I woke up and realized how oddly messed up the world was. I resisted so much of the status quo, beguiled by the fact that to be in our natural form, naked, was illegal. I minimized my ecological footprint and refused to contribute to capitalism. Yet, I wasn't changing the world, other than being the change I wanted to see in the world—Gandhi's timeless philosophy.

As I wanted a more fruitful and effective ability to create a profoundly positive impact on the planet, I dove into reading about radical leaders, esoteric ideologies, and counter-culture successes. I was inspired by Martin Luther King Jr., his non-violent methodology, and his iconically masterful ability to speak in such a way that enrolled millions across the nation to his cause. To further ingrain and share these ideas, I posted on my blog to a dwindling and limited audience, as many friends stopped paying attention once they knew I was safely back home.

To this day, I am still searching for more ways to create highly beneficial effects, have a positive influence, and constructive outcomes in our world. If you're inspired by this book, and I hope you are, I highly encourage you to contact me to join forces on this mission. We will be stronger together, united for a healthier humankind. It is up to us, you, and me to lead by example and forge coalitions with peaceful goals of bringing together our species into harmonious mutual benefit. It is our responsibility to do something with our lives that creates ripples of social breakthroughs, humanitarian improvement, and individual transformation. I beseech you to stand with me and others who are doing our best to envision the world of our greatest dreams and the most altruistic ideals. Let us sprint toward it as if our lives and those of our descendants truly depend on it. My lone journal entry in months reflected my realigned perspective:

We are alive beings, capable of examining our lives in terms of what we have, what is working, and what isn't—only in control of ourselves. We can lead by example and encourage others to change, but we are not our brothers' keeper. My question is this: what is the purpose of our individual lives? Is it the pursuit of happiness? Learning lessons to progress our 'soul' or 'spirit' toward a Zen, enlightenment, or otherwise blissful state? Is it service to others and improving the world we live in? Is the purpose to ask questions such as these and never find an answer? Is it merely to reproduce? This life would be incredibly dull and boring if the only reason for existence is to procreate and gain power over other species to ensure the survival of our own. You can remove any semblance of God or spirituality or mysticism and look at everything from a very scientific point of view. One could even make the argument that mere survival is inherent in our DNA to the point that we are driven by it unconsciously. If we only believe in what we can prove, this restricts imagination, faith, and our capacity to think. We are already limited by vocabulary and word-based concepts, the structure of our society, and the conditioning that we have received from the day we are born. It gives our lives more spark, more liveliness to believe in things greater than ourselves. Does answering, let alone asking, these questions make mankind happier? Does the thoughts of God and other spiritual concepts increase the joy in our lives? Do they help us better overcome the difficulties we face in our lives?

We've been socially conditioned throughout our entire lives. It's difficult to think about a life without work, wanting to get married, success in all its aspects, having a family, driving a car, or owning a lot of material possessions, let alone think outside of this conditioning altogether! Are these superimposed goals in life truly what we should be living for? Are these social norms so essential to precipitate lifelong work enslavement? I don't believe that the only thing we should pursue in our lives is happiness. We gain a lot through struggle and strife, gaining great wisdom from difficult situations. And overcoming adversity leads to a happier life as we grow to avoid the pitfalls that led us to unhappiness in the past. Selflessness and service to others create self-fulfillment and happiness as we make the world a better place. Are all actions reduced to the pursuit of happiness? There must be a greater sum of existence, a more profound meaning of life.

The news that I would be leaving for at least seven months, if not longer, disappointed my girlfriend. This caused us to quickly fall out of the honeymoon phase, officially breaking up before I left. I tuned up Pearl and began training again, and Dan came across a steer skull, mounted it on his new mountain bike, attached a rear rack and panniers, and we were ready to travel lighter and more efficiently than ever. There was no lying to family or friends this time as we said goodbye and biked away from our childhood homes, ready to test our skills in our homeland. We believed the cycle of kindness would guide us wherever we traveled.

Over a total of six years, I eventually pedaled across ten countries and thirty states. The rest of the journey is the subject of another book. These adventures went across America and around Kauai, where I hiked into the Kalalau Valley and lived off the land for two months. I then cycled down California from the north end to the very south. On a separate trip, the following winter, I hitched a ride into Baja California, Mexico, and ended up living in the southern tip, at San Jose del Cabo, for ten months over two winters, traveling back to Oregon in between, where my family lived. I met fantastic friends in Mexico and integrated into a community who gave me my start as a professional circus entertainer, as I continued to improve as a juggler throughout years of practice. I still maintain close friendships with my Latino brethren there.

Departing Mexico for the second time, a lover flew to Florida and bought me a ticket there, so we could both visit Dan, who became a professional bike mechanic and took a job in Lake County. I faced one of the most difficult decisions of my life: return to Mexico, stay in Florida with Dan, or accept my brother's invitation to live with him in San Diego. Despite Dan begging me to stay, I chose to rekindle a relationship with my blood brother. Perhaps I resented him for abandoning me and breaking some of my trust. Plus, regardless, I didn't like my brief experience of Lake County. I believed that the cycle of kindness could

Epilogue

create something different from our childhood. From our home in Pacific Beach, I pursued connections with local circus performers, Burning Man attendees, and other free radicals. I learned how to stilt walk, got a job with a company called Dragon Knights, and began traveling the United States, getting paid to perform on stilts while manipulating giant puppets. I eventually bought a van I named Oyster, as it held myself and Pearl inside.

Since 2011, I have laid down roots in San Diego, starting my own circus entertainment company: Cirque Quirk. It has since become the highest rated entertainment company in the region and has continued to fill my life with all kinds of unbelievable stories. I have started a second company, Allenby Arts, to sell my artwork and international photography. I got married in 2015, hiked with my ex-wife and mother to Machu Picchu in 2017, and took Ciprofloxacin due to a four-day hellacious bacterial infection, a side effect of which was spontaneous tendon rupture, which happened to my Achilles tendon in 2016, which hastened our divorce in 2018. Under divinely serendipitous synchronicities, I met the woman who would become the mother of my children in 2019, Alexandra Lee, whom I later married. I now have two beautiful, intelligent, and loving daughters, named Aurora Lee and Ivy Rose. I began writing in 2020 during the Coronavirus pandemic quarantine, and wrote 310,000 words over three and a half years, until beginning the editing and self-publishing process in 2024, a full eighteen years after the journey began.

I have traveled throughout the United States, as well as to Peru, New Zealand, Australia, Fiji, and Zimbabwe, often to perform. I've appeared in online periodicals and on the news countless times, as well as on *Judge Judy, Let's Make a Deal, Fight to Survive, People Puzzler, Paris in Love, The Gong Show,* the movie *Crimson,* the short film *Anything But Frogs,* as well as various Music videos. In 2018, the Department of Defense photography staff approached me and created a miniature documentary about me titled *Being* and is available on YouTube.

In January 2024, I discovered Next Level Training, a personal development, transformation, emotional intelligence, and leadership course that is helping me strive toward my dreams, my vision for the world and humankind, and my desire to further perpetuate and live by the cycle of kindness. Without them, I don't know how long it would have taken me to finish this book.

My intention is to graduate from college with a master's as a Licensed Marriage and Family Therapist and get certified to become a Psychedelic Assisted Psychotherapist. Because of the incredibly eye-opening and moving experiences I have had, I want to help others heal their trauma, core wounds, and become the best versions of themselves they can be. I am also focusing on motivational speaking, to inspire, empower, and uplift audiences worldwide to live their best lives and create their life visions. Together, we can reinvent humanity, powered by the cycle of kindness.

My goal is to deliver a sequel to this story, to all of you, my fantastic readers. Hopefully, depending on when you read this, another one will be in the works or already published. I thank you for finishing this book, and am grateful for your receptivity to these wild and unbelievable stories, with more incredible ones to come.

To be continued…

Acknowledgments

I am thankful for my parents, Thomas Allenby and Rose Allen, who fostered and nurtured my love of books and reading as a child. For my high school English professor, John McCulloch, who had an enthusiasm for teaching and ability to impact my life, as well as for the gifts he gave me: a passion for writing and a list of the greatest novels ever written.

    I am also grateful for Jeanette Joy Fisher, who believed in me and this book from our first meeting, and the opportunities she has given me. For my consultant, John Perkins, whose valuable knowledge and advice have been highly helpful. For William "Uncle Bill" Matthews, whose years of mentorship and constant encouragement motivated me to complete this project. For my editor, Mozelle Jordan, and her incredible editing ability and willingness to work with me and my deadline to bring this project to reality. For Clementine Kornder, and her guidance and creation of the interior book design and formatting. I am also appreciative of Arthur Meier and his creation of the cover art.

    I am blessed to have Jennifer Gold in my life, who believed in my vision of a transformed world, for her introduction to Next Level Trainings, and for Jessica Burrell, Dean Thomasson, and all the coaches and trainers there within. Without them, this book may have never come to life. I would also like to thank the circumstance of the Covid quarantine, without which I would not have had the abundance of time to write the original manuscript.

    I have the utmost gratitude for my wife, Alexandra, who supported me throughout this entire process and has been the most amazing mother for our children, Aurora and Ivy. And last, for Dan, without whom this adventure would have never happened and for the incredible twenty-four years of friendship. May he find a cure for and relief from his unique and unknown memory condition. May he also find all the love and joy with his family that is available in this lifetime.

www.ingramcontent.com/pod-product-compliance
Lightning Source LLC
Chambersburg PA
CBHW030516080526
44586CB00011B/217